THE GREAT TRADITION

An
Interpretation of
AMERICAN
LITERATURE
since the
CIVIL WAR

BY

GRANVILLE HICKS

NEW YORK
THE MACMILLAN COMPANY
1933

THE GREAT TRADITION

THE MACMILLAN COMPANY
NEW YORK · BOSTON · CHICAGO · DALLAS
ATLANTA · SAN FRANCISCO

MACMILLAN & CO., Limited
LONDON · BOMBAY · CALCUTTA
MELBOURNE

THE MACMILLAN COMPANY
OF CANADA, Limited
TORONTO

TO

MY MOTHER AND FATHER

ACKNOWLEDGMENTS

The author wishes to record his gratitude to the authors and publishers of all works quoted in this book. In particular he thanks the following:

THE CENTURY COMPANY
   for permission to quote from
      The Book of Jack London, by Charmian London.

DOUBLEDAY, DORAN AND COMPANY
   for permission to quote from
      Life in Letters of William Dean Howells, by Mildred Howells, copyright 1926.
      The Octopus, by Frank Norris, copyright 1903.
      The Pit, by Frank Norris, copyright 1903.
      The Collected Works of Frank Norris, copyright 1901, 1902.
      Leaves of Grass, by Walt Whitman.
      Democratic Vistas, by Walt Whitman.

HARCOURT, BRACE AND COMPANY
   for permission to quote from
      Smoke and Steel, by Carl Sandburg.
      Selected Poems, by T. S. Eliot.

HARPER AND BROTHERS
   for permission to quote from
      Mark Twain: A Biography, by Albert Bigelow Paine.
      Life on the Mississippi, by Mark Twain.
      The Innocents Abroad, by Mark Twain.
      Autobiography, by Mark Twain.
      The Bread-Winners, by John Hay.
      Hawthorne, by Henry James.

The Letters of James Russell Lowell, edited by Charles Eliot Norton.

Good-Bye, Wisconsin, by Glenway Wescott.

The Grandmothers, by Glenway Wescott.

HOUGHTON MIFFLIN COMPANY
for permission to quote from
The Education of Henry Adams.
The Letters of Henry Adams, edited by Worthington C. Ford.
The Letters of Sarah Orne Jewett, edited by Annie Fields.
The Life and Letters of Lafcadio Hearn, by Elizabeth Bisland.
O Pioneers!, by Willa Cather.

ALFRED A. KNOPF
for permission to quote from
Stephen Crane, by Thomas Beer.

THE MACMILLAN COMPANY
for permission to quote from
A Son of the Middle Border, by Hamlin Garland.
A Daughter of the Middle Border, by Hamlin Garland.
Roadside Meetings, by Hamlin Garland.
Companions on the Trail, by Hamlin Garland.
Revolution and Other Essays, by Jack London.
In the Heart of a Fool, by William Allen White.
Selected Poems, by Vachel Lindsay.

CHARLES SCRIBNER'S SONS
for permission to quote from
The Letters of Henry James, edited by Percy Lubbock.

CONTENTS

THE GREAT TRADITION

Chapter I

HERITAGE

WHEN Lee surrendered at Appomattox, more was settled than the preservation of the Union or the abolition of slavery. Even while the war was going on, capitalistic industry demonstrated that it was the ruler of the nation. Congress, at the command of business enterprise, voted higher tariffs than ever before, created a national banking system, granted generous assistance to railway corporations, and encouraged immigration. At the same time a shrewd Ohio lawyer wrote into the text of the Fourteenth Amendment the notable "due process" clause that was to protect business from state interference. Once the war was over the victors hastened to enjoy the fruits of their victory. Industrialism had been advancing, but slowly; now it strode forward in its conquest of the continent. John Sherman wrote in 1865, "The truth is, the close of the war with our resources unimpaired gives an elevation, a scope to the ideas of leading capitalists, far higher than anything ever undertaken in this country before. They talk of millions as confidently as formerly of thousands." Rockefeller was just making his first independent venture in oil. Experiments were going on with the Bessemer process. Chicago had opened its union stockyards and was ready for Armour and Swift. Collis Huntington was building the Central Pacific Railroad to meet the Union Pacific, and Cornelius Vanderbilt had just got his hands on the first unit of his Great Lakes-to-ocean railway system. Within a few years the num-

ber of manufacturing establishments doubled and the amount
of capital invested in industry nearly quadrupled. The era of
the machine had begun.

The planting aristocracy, which the war had destroyed, had
been not only the chief political rival of industrial capitalism
but also the principal critic of commercialism as a way of life.
There seemed to be nothing to oppose the triumph of business
enterprise. Both the farmers of the West and the workers of
the East had made common cause with the industrialists
against the South, and they were slow to distinguish between
their interests and those of the ruling class. The revolution in
agriculture had destroyed the farmer's self-sufficiency, and the
Greenback Movement testified to the existence of unrest.
Many workers, seeing how small a share they received of the
nation's increased wealth, organized into unions. But the
promise of the frontier was always there to lure the venture-
some, and the sight of great fortunes, seemingly built so casu-
ally, by the exercise of such familiar attributes, encouraged
even the least self-confident American to hope for comfort if
not for wealth. Movements of protest received little support,
and at best they offered no fundamental criticism of the conduct of industry, for they merely expressed the eagerness of
the less fortunate to share in the prizes that were being so
lavishly distributed. Farmer and mechanic alike admired the
heroes of financial battles, dreamt of speculation, and looked
forward to riches. If many were pushed away from the table
so luxuriously laden with the fruits of mechanical ingenuity
and the gifts of nature to the nation, they knew that the table
was there, and they did not despair of finding a place at it.

So capitalistic enterprise swept ahead in the sixties, seventies, and eighties, bearing opportunity in one hand and destruction in the other, promising more than it could accomplish but accomplishing more than an earlier generation had

dared to dream. On the material level the profit and loss account of that mad advance is not easy to calculate. On the cultural level it can, alas, be more easily estimated. In a society that regarded chaos as natural, that made greed a virtue, that placed financial achievement before personal integrity, culture was not likely to flourish. When things are in the saddle, the artist, if he deserves the name, is almost certain to be trampled underfoot. Especially hazardous was the position of any artist who might venture to do what artists so commonly try to do, to mirror his own times. Where was he to stand in order to see that society of his in terms that would permit him to describe it? How was he to find a pattern in a world whose lack of order was its distinguishing quality? All about him were stirring scenes, titanic combats, harrowing defeats, and stupendous victories. In this march of the machines and their men were all the elements of an epic—except evidences of some shaping destiny, intimations of some divine or human goal towards which events could be observed to move. The maze itself was fascinating, but there was no Ariadne to guide the aspiring author through its mysteries. Not at once were artists to discover where the difficulty lay; not for many, many decades would they find a way of mastering it.

* * *

One thing might well have been apparent even before the sixties had run their course: the promise of the quarter-century before the war was not to be realized. For there had been giants in the land. Despite the storm clouds of the impending crisis our literature had for a time put forth a rich and variegated foliage. The collapse of Puritan dogmatism had released men's powers of speculation; repeated cries for a national literature had weakened the hold of colonial imitativeness; and in the West the common man was affirming his faith in his own destiny. There was a new spirit in America, and there were books that expressed that spirit. *Moby Dick, Walden, The Scarlet Letter, Representative Men*—these constituted a heritage of which succeeding generations could have no reason to be ashamed.

How well these books and the others by their authors summed up all that the American adventure to that particular point signified! Emerson had hacked away at Puritanism, slashing off this and salvaging that, tempering what remained at the forge of German idealism, until the very essence of Protestantism stood forth hard and sharp and bright in his essays. Thoreau had stripped from the pioneer spirit the husks of materialism, reducing it to an inexorable demand for independence of soul. Hawthorne, brooding over the consequences of pride and isolation, had conceived darkly beautiful allegories of sin and death. Melville had found in the harsh reality of Nantucket whalers and navy frigates a vision of the undying struggle against cosmic evil.

Now Hawthorne and Thoreau were dead, and Melville was about to sequester himself in the New York customhouse. Emerson remained, but even he, writing "Terminus" in 1866, was and knew he was at the end of his creative days. Far worse than the departure of these men was the silence of their work amid the clamor of the age. What, after all, had any of them to say to the new generation? What did self-reliance mean to Jay Gould and Commodore Vanderbilt? What could it mean to young girls in New York sweat shops? Could Thoreau's account of his life at Walden be taken as a guidebook by a generation that had committed itself, or been committed, to the frantic multiplication of the machine? Were Melville's records of lands beyond the grasp of industrialism the proper inspiration for young men whose eyes were focussed on the march of steel rails and whose ears were tuned to the hum of engines? Could one find in Hawthorne's subtle analyses of sin any clue to the demoralization of a nation? These men were the consummation of an epoch that, by 1865, was ended. Though it was in their day that industrialism was gathering its forces for the decisive conflict and the ultimate victory, their roots were in a different soil, and the fruit they bore could never grow again.

Of them all Hawthorne kept himself most remote from his own period, and it is his work that has suffered most with the passage of time. The first American artist and one of the most nobly serious novelists the world has produced, he made the opportunity to practice his art and conduct his spiritual quest by deliberately isolating himself from the occupations and preoccupations of his fellowmen. Whether he wrote of a Boston that might have existed two centuries before or of a Salem that has "a great deal more to do with the clouds overhead than with any portion of the actual soil of the County of Essex," of a Blithedale that is not the Brook Farm he knew but "an available foothold between fiction and reality" or of an Italy that afforded "a sort of poetic or fairy precinct, where actualities would not be so terribly insisted upon as they are, and needs must be, in America," he squarely turned his back on the factories and market-places, the plantations and farms, the capitols and prisons of his own United States. And yet he knew that United States, and was not unaware of soap-makers and dentists, ship-captains and war veterans, politicians and business men. He could not take a trip without recording the features of some representative man of the people; he could not go out for dinner without noting the aspect of prosperous streets and sordid alleys; could not, at any point, meet his fellowmen without listening to their stories and finding them worthy of his attention. But between his art and his deepest interests, on the one hand, and these vivid scenes and active lives, on the other, his imagination could establish no effective contact.

We need not wonder, then, that the characters of Hawthorne's books seem so remote and insubstantial. Looked at from precisely the angle that the author chooses, they have the illusion of life, and they perform their assigned tasks with an air that is momentarily convincing; but if we chance to examine them in a sharper light they vanish. With few exceptions they never suggest a capacity to step, robust and insistent, out of their books and into our lives. What is Dimmesdale without his sin, or Hollingsworth without his fanaticism, or Hilda without her purity? Are they much more than artfully contrived figures in an allegory? These sinners —who can imagine their having passion enough for sin? These lovers—what can they possibly know of love? That Hawthorne was a magician, that he can delude us even now as we read his books, who will deny? But his shadow-shapes do not long deceive us, nor can we remain oblivious to the manipulating hand of the master of the show.

Hawthorne's chief bequest to the generation after the war was, perhaps, not the moral he so repeatedly drew in his books, but the moral, not wholly dissimilar or unrelated, that might have been drawn from his life. Despite his profound knowledge of certain of the springs of human conduct, despite his sincerity of purpose, despite his gift for the selection of details and the ordering of incidents, he fell short of the first rank of greatness, and the reason for his failure lay in his inability to come to terms with his generation. In the end all his efforts to participate in the united effort of mankind came to nought: when he was a representative American, he was not an artist; when he was an artist, he was not a representative American. The artist triumphed, and at last his painful solitude could not be endured and he died of it.

Not much more successful, in this matter of participation, was Hawthorne's sometime friend, Herman Melville. Some inner necessity drove him out of the familiar paths of his fathers, but not, for the moment, into brooding isolation. More fortunate than Hawthorne, he spent his early years in hearty toil, perilous adventure, and pagan relaxation; and his first books mingle a warm and spontaneous joy in life with an acute and detailed perception of the realities of human conduct. But Melville was no mere wanderer, nor yet a complacent chronicler of entertaining novelties. Scarcely were *Typee* and *Omoo* off the press when he announced, in *Mardi,* his great preoccupation—with the nature of evil and the mysteries of life and death. Unable, as Hawthorne remarked, either to believe or to be comfortable in unbelief, he wrestled in solitude—and eventually in silence.

Melville did not state these problems to himself in terms of contemporary society. Like Hawthorne he simplified his task, but he did not have to turn away from his daily experiences as Hawthorne did, for one part of his experience lent itself admirably to his purposes. To what extent his first voyage had revealed to him the evil in the world *Redburn* shows, just as *White Jacket* suggests how inevitably a ship symbolized for him the world of men. What more natural than that, for his supreme effort, his great symphonic development of his chosen theme, he should find in the *Pequod* of Nantucket the epitome of the world, in its captain the titanic protagonist of a cosmic drama, and in a great white whale the perfect symbol of blind, unreasoning evil? What had been for him the world of reality, what would remain to the end—as *Billy Budd* shows—the most vivid setting for his allegories that his experience had revealed or his imagination could conceive, gave him in *Moby Dick* a flawless metaphor.

Melville attacked his problems in *Moby Dick* so coura-

geously and resourcefully that one marvels at the failure of
the book to impress and influence the generation after the
war. But the explanation is simple: after the war men were
wrestling with the problem of evil as it presented itself in
concrete economic phenomena. Melville's problem was real
enough, but the terms in which he stated it were irrelevant.
This explains, in part, why *Moby Dick,* with all its virtues, is
not comparable to the great metaphysical epics of the past,
which have made room for all the principal varieties of experience in their eras. It is impossible to suppose that Melville—or anyone else living in mid-nineteenth century America—could have been a Lucretius or a Dante, and the mere
fact that he could conceive of writing an epic is itself magnificent. There is every reason to be thankful that, in this era
of intellectual expansion, there was one writer who could
find terms, whatever they were, for the expression of his
vision of the universe. But Melville paid his price—part of
which was the failure to win disciples in the following generation.

Yet we have to recognize that the concerns of Melville and
Hawthorne were the concerns of the most thoughtful men of
their day. They were, according to Emerson and Thoreau,
the only proper business of mankind. Emerson could not
open his mouth without making clear his indifference to political parties and economic programs, so certain was he that
the great human issues were superior to them. For him the
only important activities of the race of man took place upon
that level whereon the individual soul merged with the Over-
Soul. Hence he believed that all considerations of social position or economic status were insignificant, since no hardships
of a material sort could prevent the exercise of what he regarded as the peculiarly human functions. His mission was
the liberation of men from chains that were self-forged and

self-imposed. He challenged the individual to achieve his own salvation, and his optimism blinded him to the obstacles placed in the individual's path, to the handicaps imposed by accidents of nature and injustices of society.

That is not to say, however, that Emerson, even at his most optimistic, was uncritical of the commercial spirit or indifferent to its results in the life of the community. On the contrary, he clearly perceived and heartily condemned the mixture of timidity and greed that called itself economic policy and even went by the name of statesmanship. He was not without his realistic side and on occasion could describe, shrewdly and accurately, the play of economic forces in the life of the country. But always the vision of realities grew dim as he came to the task of prescribing means for correcting the evils he saw, and he usually ended his discourses by abandoning himself, with rhapsodic fervor, to his faith in the beneficent laws of the universe. For all of his wisdom he was a child of his time. In his veins ran the blood of men who had made, were making, and were going to make an America of gold and steel. At the same time his generous spirit responded as did that of no other literary man in the East to the spirit of the frontier, to the faith in the average man that was fostered by the sight of apparently boundless opportunities. He was the spokesman for men who were doing things, and, though he might doubt the value of what was done, he could not question the ultimate triumph of resolute individualism.

Less given to rhapsody but no less reliant on the power of the individual was his fellow-townsman, Thoreau. He was not so optimistic as Emerson, not so wantonly inconsistent, not so preoccupied with the reconciling of opposites. Hence, starting from the same premises, he came to different and much more violent conclusions. Self-reliance was for him a doctrine to be literally observed, with no qualifications and no exceptions. When he perceived that the whole structure of society was contrary to the principles in which he believed, he did not hesitate to repudiate society. He was ready to disregard law as freely as he disregarded convention, and he had no fear of consequences. It did not occur to him to leave to the operation of divine law the elimination of evil, nor was his faith of a kind to blind him to his own duty. Even his love of the beauties of nature never befogged his vision of human injustice, and the death of John Brown killed for a time his pleasure in his native lakes and hills.

Nothing in American literature is more admirable than Henry Thoreau's devotion to his principles, but the principles are, unfortunately, less significant than the devotion. From *Walden* the men of the post-war generation could learn how to live if they wished to abandon forever the fruit of industrial progress, but they were by no means willing to make such a renunciation, nor could they have made it had they so desired. What they needed was someone to humanize their faith in the machine and make it discriminating, and with that problem Thoreau had no concern. His recognition that society was in no wise so organized as to guarantee the well-being of its members might have been made the basis for a program of reorganization, and his courage could have been the inspiration of a revolution; but, unless they could be restated in terms of the machine, his teachings had little significance for the new era.

And so they stand, these four men, the finest perhaps that our literature can boast, and their very virtues serve to make us conscious of the gulf that separates them and their age from the men and the times after the war. It is idle, of course, to reproach them for not being something other than what they were; and yet it is only by understanding what they might have been that we can realize their short-comings and appreciate their failure to inspire their successors. Obviously there was much value in their work, or we should not be reading them today; but it was not in such form that the post-war generation could utilize it. Under different conditions, one can imagine, rich fantasies and satires might have risen on the ruins of *Mardi,* profound psychological studies might have grown out of *Pierre,* a whole school of metaphysical novelists might have been fathered by *Moby Dick.* The wisdom of Emerson and the courage of Thoreau might have inspired a nation of heroes. The subtlety of Hawthorne might have guided a generation of craftsmen. But all that was impossible. The writers of the post-war period could no more have brought into their greedy, machine-dominated, expansive age the glories of the Golden Day than the first settlers could have carried across the Atlantic the glories of the Elizabethan drama. They lived in a new world, and they had to explore that world for themselves.

Melville was completely neglected, and Thoreau, so far as he was not neglected too, was regarded as a pleasant, eccentric writer on nature. Emerson and Hawthorne were honored, but honored for their least admirable qualities. It was easy for the conventional and comfortable citizens of New England to praise and for their writers to emulate the lifelessness, the moralizing, and the prudery of Hawthorne's novels, though Hawthorne's earnestness and craftsmanship were harder to achieve. It was easy to canonize Emerson the optimist and the consoler, the preacher of sturdy individualism, but Emerson the rebel was better forgotten. The post-war generation not only failed to rise to the level of the heroes of the past; it brought them down upon its own plane.

* * *

Something like a literary tradition had been developed in America, but it was a tradition that could not be perpetuated in the form in which it had grown, since it was the product of a mode of civilization that was passing and assumed the existence of conditions that each succeeding year after the war helped to destroy. The tradition had to reshape itself or be submerged, and submergence was its fate. The men who bridged the two periods and were the official guardians of the tradition—such men as Longfellow, Whittier, Holmes, and Lowell—had breathed the same air as Emerson and Hawthorne and shown themselves not insensitive to its tonic qualities, but we know all too well the story of their failures. Something of Emerson's hatred of evil had moved in Longfellow, but it had spent itself in his *Poems on Slavery*, leaving no gift of indignation to temper his sweet-souled contemplation of the world about him. Some perception of the literary potentialities of the American scene had inspired *Evangeline* and *Hiawatha,* but even in these poems he had chosen those aspects of America that, by virtue of their picturesqueness, could be most easily associated with the European traditions in which he was so absorbed. Time passed, and the professor in Longfellow, the student of other cultures, crushed such original and indigenous impulses as may once have moved him, so that, in the later decades of his life, he became important chiefly as transmitter and interpreter of other literatures, steadily increasing the distance between him and the realities of contemporary life, meeting his fellow citizens only upon the level of domestic sentimentality. Never quite at home on the mountain peaks that Emerson had frequented, he adapted himself to the comfortable pedestrianism of dwellers in flat places, refreshing his eyes at times with glances at the remote and no longer dangerous heights to be discerned on foreign shores.

Whittier had always been more truly a poet of the American soil, and despite his crudities might have been one of its more distinguished growths; but that soil in which he had his roots was as arid as any that had ever balked a New England farmer. One strong passion moved him, calling forth his most eloquent songs. But he felt only that one impulse, as he saw only one duty, and when the slaves had been emancipated he felt the impulse no longer and saw no implications of the duty. His greatest talents, aside from his power of indignation, revealed themselves in *Snow-Bound,* in the writing of which his nature responded to the harsh provincial landscape, the proud isolation, the self-righteous poverty of outlook that he described. Much of New England was in his verse, but it was the New England that literature could least afford to accept, the New England whose borders the true writers of the enlightenment had struggled to extend.

There is nothing, perhaps, to be said of Holmes, who drifted comfortably through the years after the war. But to James Russell Lowell we may pay more attention, partly because there is something in his life and work that suggests greater capacities for the task of criticism and adaptation than we have found elsewhere, partly because his failure was so typical. Here was a man who had listened respectfully to Emerson and found much to admire in Hawthorne, whose earlier work was touched by impulses not unlike theirs, who had felt within himself the courage and hope that were alive in the thirties and forties. And after the war he continued his labors, with constantly growing prestige. He, it would seem, might have interpreted to the post-war generation the spirit of the Golden Day.

Yet we have only to glance at his career to understand why, though in the seventies and eighties he achieved a more and more prominent position in American life, his leadership was so nearly fruitless for our literature. Born in the same year as Melville and Whitman, he was born to very different circumstances, son of a prominent and conservative minister, grandson of a distinguished lawyer and publicist, nephew of the founder of the industrial community that bears the family name. He was sent, of course, to Harvard, whence he was graduated with a record that his devotion to the college magazine had marred, and with a consciousness that he had rather a pretty gift for verse. Accepting the law as a career through inertia rather than choice, he found his chief satisfaction in writing lines in which the virtues of the English romantic poets were more easily discerned than any personal qualities.

To this point Lowell had almost completely identified himself with the Cambridge and Boston tradition of respectability, with the cultural and political outlook of Fisher Ames, the literary modes and ambitions of Robert Treat Paine; and in his class poem he had taken sophomoric pleasure in ridiculing both Emerson and the abolitionists. It was through his meeting with Maria White, to whom he was married, after a long engagement, in 1844, that changes came, changes that soon brought him to the side of the men at whom he had so recently scoffed. Maria White was an abolitionist, a temperance worker, an admirer if not a disciple of Margaret Fuller, and a sympathizer—though Lowell was to deny it—with the transcendentalists. He had had, despite his pervasive complacency, his own moods of dissatisfaction with the existing order, and now, with such an example before him, he was quickly won not merely to opposition to slavery but to an interest in the propositions of Fourier and other exponents of collectivism.

Once he had given up all thought of practicing law and had determined on a literary career, he began writing prolifically, both in verse and prose. His verse, the first collection of which immediately won him some reputation, was still essentially derivative and placidly acquiescent. Only occasionally did his new passion for freedom transfuse it with vitality and almost never with originality. In his prose, however, he attacked both slavery and the cowardice in state and church that condoned it. He began, regardless of his own practice, to urge authors to find subjects in "the steamboat and the rail car, the cornfield and the factory," and he argued that no poet could achieve greatness without abandoning himself to the spirit of radicalism. As the slavery struggle grew tense in the forties, he accepted the poetic inspiration of his social zeal, and finally his concern with the Mexican situation found expression in the admirable dialect verse of the *Biglow Papers*. At the same time, however, and despite all he had said about the poetic value of the gospel of reform, he recorded in *A Fable for Critics* his conviction that his chief handicap was his "bale of isms," and in *Sir Launfal* he buried the humanitarian moral under a mass of verbal embroidery. In 1850, when the slavery fight was tensest, he wrote, "I have preached sermons enow. . . . I find that reform cannot take up the whole of me. . . . I am tired of controversy."

By the end of the fifties the one reform in which Lowell still believed, the abolition of slavery, had become respectable in Massachusetts' intellectual circles, and there was nothing to prevent either his appointment to a Harvard professorship or his choice as editor of the newly-founded *Atlantic Monthly*. In the former position, though he was irked by the academic routine, he pleasantly nourished his growing interest in European cultures; and in the latter he found outlet for his undiminished preoccupation with the slavery question. After the beginning of hostilities he urged, both in his

essays and in the second series of *Biglow Papers,* the relent-
less prosecution of the war. Toward the close of the war,
when his editorial chair was transferred from the office of
the *Atlantic* to that of the *North American,* he continued his
demands for a drastic suppression of the rebellion, and in his
essays on reconstruction called for the enfranchisement of
the Negro. When, in 1866, he prepared to take leave for the
time of political subjects, he made his valedictory an attack
on the conciliatory policies of President Johnson.

At the close of the war Lowell stood in the first rank of
American poets, was highly esteemed as a critic, and was regarded as an authoritative student of political issues. His opportunity to guide the progress of American culture was
threefold, and twenty-five years of life remained to him. Yet
his failure was almost complete. As a poet he never conquered the diffuse romanticism that had marred his juve-
nilia; rather, he became increasingly derivative, and his major
efforts, the various commemorative odes, are, despite the nobility of mood and the dignity of expression, palpably without either depth of thought or freshness of language. As a
critic he was erudite, perhaps beyond all other American
critics, and thoroughly familiar with the greatest writers of
western culture. Nor was the range of his criticism narrow:
he could speak as historian or philologist; he could write
with the gusto of an epicure or assume the manner of a
judge. But the incoherence of his critical studies, his prefer-
ence for a casual attack in the manner of the informal essay,
points straight to the deep-seated indolence of mind that prevented him from molding out of his insight and information
a solid and consistent theory of literature. Principles he had in
abundance, but, like all borrowed principles, they were a
poor substitute for that organic body of fundamental ideas

that the great critic cultivates, with the aid of his imagination, out of the soil of study and experience.

To the development of American literature he contributed almost nothing, except insofar as he may have furthered a thoughtful reading of the European masters. In addition to two brief and not particularly valuable papers on the national literature, one written at the beginning and the other at the end of his life, he left, if we exclude casual reviews and the trenchant but largely personal comments in *A Fable for Critics,* few discussions of American writers. He did write on Emerson and Thoreau, praising the former for his spirit without analyzing his work, and attacking the latter in such a way as to betray a complete lack of understanding. The younger writers he welcomed were the perpetuators of the genteel tradition he came more and more to embody— Howells the essayist, Stedman, Aldrich, and Gilder—whereas to Whitman he was utterly indifferent, taking the trouble only to say, on the strength of what Norton had told him about *Leaves of Grass,* that such things wouldn't do. In short he made not the slightest effort to understand the peculiar conditions under which American writers were working, and did nothing, either by example or counsel, to help the men who were trying to understand them. Even to Howells, whose work he praised, he made it clear that he liked the novels because he liked the man, and that ordinarily he preferred romance to realism.

But it is in his treatment of politics, to which he finally returned, that he shows most clearly his remoteness from the actualities of American life. Poor man, like many of his contemporaries he had thought that once the South was defeated he would never have to concern himself again with the state of the nation, but gradually he found the increasing corruption in all branches of government too noisome to be ignored, even from the top of an ivory tower. "The degradation of the moral tone" alarmed him, making him wonder if our government were not a "Kakistocracy, for the benefit of knaves at the expense of fools." Though he confessed that he was not so hopeful as he had been thirty years before, he was conscious enough of his duties as a citizen to share in the efforts to reform the Republican Party, and he served as a delegate to the convention in Cincinnati. The only result of this renewed interest in politics was his appointment to Spain, followed by his assignment to the Court of St. James's. But even these honors did not reconcile him to the existing order, and his temperamental tranquillity succumbed to an unrest like that he had felt nearly fifty years before. Finally, with the invitation to speak at Birmingham in 1884, came the opportunity for him to deliver his mature judgment on the progress of democracy. He chose, as he later said, "to dwell on the good points and favorable aspects," and certainly he voiced few of the doubts that are revealed in his correspondence of the period. He pointed out that the United States had prospered under democracy, that the democratic movement was growing in Europe, and that even such extensions of democracy as the founders of the Constitution had not for a moment considered had proven to be beneficial. Even farther than that he went: "The right of individual property is no doubt the very corner-stone of civilization as hitherto understood, but I am a little impatient of being told that property is entitled to exceptional consideration because it bears all the burdens of the State." Indeed, he paid his respects to Henry George, though rejecting his theories, and endorsed socialism as a "practical application of Christianity to life," though rejecting the methods of Marxian socialism. With all his reservations he had gone what was, for him, a surprising distance. But there were reservations of temperament as well as those of intellect. He could refer to "that piratical craft of the eight-hour men" and describe the Chicago anarchists as "ruffians well hanged." He was afraid of the effects of immigration, and often spoke apprehensively of mobs and the dangers of mob violence. Though he sometimes played with the idea that socialism might offer a way out of the existing chaos, he opposed all practical steps leading towards collectivism. And in his last public statement on politics, renouncing the faith in the masses that he had previously expressed, he pinned his hope on the activity and influence of a small class of independent voters.

The confusion in Lowell's political thinking gives some clue to his failure as a literary force. Emerson's virtues, as well as his faults, came from the fact that he spoke for the masses of men, who at the moment were confidently reaching out for freedom and power. Even Emerson was often shocked by the practical results of this emergence, and Lowell not only lived longer and saw more clearly its consequences but was more closely affiliated with the class whose authority was threatened. Although he was by no means fully aware how stern a struggle was going on, he felt its results in the division of his own sympathies. And there can be little doubt where the deepest of those sympathies lay. As a member of an older ruling class, he was dissatisfied with the new rulers of America, the industrialists and financiers, but he was far from willing to cast his lot with their subjects. In politics, therefore, he wavered back and forth, never clearly on one side or the other; but in literature he had a refuge— the great writers of the past.

So Lowell passes from the scene, never wholly traitor to the bright impulses that had roused him in his youth, but to the end bewildered. His followers were, inevitably, the Aldriches, the Stedmans, and the Gilders, all the men who in the eighties and nineties loomed so large upon our cultural horizon. Remote from and insensitive to the dominant tendencies and major needs of American life, they cast a fog of gentility over our literature. They came from and spoke for the least fecund class in the commonwealth, the class of the comfortably situated, governed by prejudice, incapable of realistic thought, committed to the worship of respectability in every sphere of action. Like that class they mistook prudery for refinement, timidity for self-restraint, and abstinence from the taking of bribes for civic duty. They were prepared to take Lowell's absurd dictum that no man should write what he was not willing for his daughter to read, and turn it into the even absurder one, that no man should write what they were unwilling for their daughters to read. As for the revolution that was going on in American life, they were indifferent to it except insofar as the prosperity it brought augmented their incomes and made possible their prestige. At the most they made a gesture for civil service reform, that fetich of respectable men. Since their aims were to conserve and imitate the literature of the past, they not only did nothing to help literature in its new tasks; they put obstacles in the path of those who saw the need and tried to meet it. They were, like Lowell himself, kindly men, well-informed, well-intentioned, full of eloquent professions of patriotic and literary zeal, but they were nevertheless parasites—parasites upon the past, upon foreign culture, upon an industrial order that they did not try to understand, did not think of reforming, and did not even venture to defend and advance.

* * *

It is clear that we must dismiss Lowell and all that he stands for from any just account of the forces that were making for the development of American literature, but there is another writer—one who also figures in both the pre-war and the post-war periods—of whom we shall not care to make such light disposal. This writer, this Whitman, with his rough beard and his open shirt, calling himself the poet of the people, had few of the advantages that Lowell enjoyed, but he was quite as truly a product of the enlightenment. The difference lies in the fact that Whitman saw, however vaguely, the implications of his belief for an industrial age.

It was, of course, Emerson who passed on to Whitman the fruits of the enlightenment and made him aware of the powers that, for a dozen years, had idly spent themselves in ephemeral journalism. For the acceptance of Emerson a Quaker heritage had done much to prepare him, but the doctrine of the inner light took on new meaning when he happened upon Emerson's account of it. Like Emerson, and like Emerson's other disciple Thoreau, he became the preacher of self-reliance, bard of "the beauty of independence, departure, actions that rely on themselves," poet of spontaneity and self-expression. The basis for this individualism he found in Emerson's theory of the godlike in man, in his conception of the infallible operation of those laws that guarantee the triumph of the right, and in the law of compensation. Like Emerson he accepted the consequences of individualism, praising "the American contempt for statutes and ceremonies, the boundless impatience of restraints," and repeating the summons to obey little and resist much.

This acceptance of Emerson's theories was not an affair of the moment, was no brief yielding to a magic spell; if anything Whitman grew stancher in his allegiance as age and illness brought to the fore all that was mystical in his creed. But side by side with his individualism grew the conviction that the individual could fulfill his destiny only in alliance with his fellowmen.

> *One's-self I sing, a simple separate person,*
> *Yet utter the word Democratic, the word En-Masse.*

En-masse, solidarity, ensemble, cohesion, adhesiveness—how often these words and others with the same meaning appear in Whitman's poetry. And he did not believe merely in the democratic ideal; he believed in the concrete political expression of democracy, and he knew well enough who the enemies of democracy were. If he had learned much from Emerson, he had learned something from his carpenter-father, from his reading of Leggett and Paine, and from his experiences as printer, reporter, and editor. Even while he still regarded himself as an orthodox Jacksonian, he commented with more than Jacksonian fervor on the oppression of the working class, calling attention to the horrible conditions of the unemployed and saying that there are "greater reforms needed here than in the Southern States." After the Civil War he referred to the Republican and Democratic parties as "these damned huckster parties," saw that the newspapers were "all getting into the hands of millionaires," described ministers as "everywhere the parasites, the apologists, of systems as they exist," and called the tariff "the protection of profit—the protection of the swell proprietors." And he was well aware that a program of anarchist isolation, such as Thoreau had practised and he himself really preferred, could not control the forces that were at work in America. He said to Traubel one day, "Sometimes I think, I feel almost sure, Socialism is the next thing coming: I shrink from it in some ways; yet it looks like our only hope."

That the unlimited expression of the individual will, in which he believed, might conflict with the progress of the cohered mass, in which he also believed, he was scarcely aware; but even if he had perceived such a possibility that would not have deterred him from advocating both since he found both so good. In this he was not unlike the common man he sought to represent, who also wanted a government that would advance the interests of all without restricting the desires of any. We must not forget how close to this common man Whitman was at the beginning of his career. It was not merely that he liked people, liked crowds in market-places and on ferry-boats, at theaters and at music-halls; it was not merely that democracy was with him an instinct rather than an idea, and brotherly love not a mawkish senti-ment but a spontaneous emotion; he was actually part of the common people. He displayed, for example, in his younger days, as narrow and militaristic a kind of patriotism as any Young American, and though his Quaker blood cried out for an early peace, at first he cheered for the Mexican War as lustily as any slaveholder. Even much later he could not re-frain from boasting that America could lick the world, the while he prayed that there would be no necessity for its do-ing so.

Whitman's patriotism, then, had its roots in popular emo-tion, but it was capable of idealization. What saved him from narrow chauvinism was his interest in the future. What he had read of Europe—and he had read widely—convinced him that American conditions were such as had never hith-erto existed, and that the future civilization of America must correspondingly differ from earlier civilizations. That the difference would be on the credit side of the ledger he never doubted. The doctrine of manifest destiny, in its popu-lar form so grossly imperialistic, became in his poetry a the-ory of spiritual evolution whose climax would be reached upon these shores:

And thou America,
For the scheme's culmination, its thought and its reality,
For these (not for thyself) thou hast arrived.

Yet in envisaging the details of this glorious American future Whitman took into account what he had learned from the common man as well as what he had learned from Emerson and his fellow idealists. Although he defined national greatness in terms of intellectual and spiritual qualities, and insisted that such qualities must always be regarded as of first importance, he maintained that they were not incompatible with, and sometimes even that they were contingent upon, material prosperity. However seriously he might argue, as in *Democratic Vistas,* that the wide dispersion of physical comforts could be no guarantee of a healthy society, he was careful to point out that he by no means scorned such comforts and that he regarded the expansion of American business enterprise as a significant factor in the shaping of the future. Moreover, though he was little preoccupied with concrete schemes for the more equitable distribution of wealth, it was part of his vision that there should be "a more universal ownership of property, general homesteads, general comfort." He could tolerate "exceptional wealth, splendor . . . immense capital and capitalists, the five-dollar-a-day hotels well fill'd" as evidences of a prosperity that would one day be shared by all, but it was only because they would in time be so shared, because in the future there would be "millions of comfortable city homesteads and moderate-sized farms, healthy and independent, single separate ownership, fee simple, life in them complete but cheap, within reach of all." This, he believed, would provide a basis for a true national greatness. "My theory," he said, "includes riches, and the getting of riches, and the amplest products, power, activ-

ity, inventions, movements, etc. Upon them, as upon sub-
strata, I raise the edifice designed in these Vistas."

Three articles of his faith Whitman shared with the masses
of the post-war period: belief in democracy, belief in the
American future, and belief in material prosperity as a means
to the achievement of the fore-ordained national greatness.
He was not, of course, very different from Emerson or Thoreau or any other prophet of the enlightenment in hoping
for and believing in a splendid future for America, but he
was surely closer than they to the forces that were actually
creating the future nation. He did not demand, as the transcendentalists did, some miracle of conversion. He depended upon "the crowd of the grave workingmen of our
world . . . the hope, the sole hope, the sufficient hope, of our
democracy." "America," he said, "is not for special types, for
the castes, but for the great mass of people—the vast, surging,
hopeful army of workers." "I put my faith in them—in the
crowd of everyday men." And despite his deep-seated individualism, he saw more and more clearly towards the end
that these men he admired must organize themselves for the
conquest of power.

Whatever confusion there might be in Whitman's political
thinking, he did not doubt that the common man would
create a new and better civilization on the continent of
North America. And he believed that that civilization would
demand a new literature. The rise of democracy, he held, the
emergence of the common man, the development of science,
the mingling of races, and the very physical constitution of
the land would not merely impel the poet to treat new materials but would force upon him a new point of view. It was
partly his conception of the almost religious function of literature in imparting to this civilization its shaping spirit,
and partly the mystical and prophetic elements in his own

nature, that led him to look forward to the work of "orbic bards," the "sweet democratic despots of the west." Infused with a new spirit, with a mystic sense of the unity of life, this literature would, he believed, strike deep into American society, finding not merely adequate subjects but truly heroic themes in the affairs of daily existence, repudiating the trifling arts and petty polishing devices of the poets of polite society, seeking inspiration in the tremendous sweep of the American prairies and finding guidance in the inherent good sense of the common people. The seaboard culture of the first half of the century, with its obvious dependence upon European models and upon a society that in itself was merely a colonial imitation, would have to surrender its leadership to the West, where, unspoiled by outworn customs, new bards would sing the songs that American democracy needed. In these songs the people, never truly recognized by literature, would come into their own, and the people, strengthened and led by a widely dispersed, robustly American, and thoroughly democratic culture, would be worthy of the songs.

As the forerunner and first representative of the new race of bards Whitman consciously regarded and untiringly advertised himself. His poems concern themselves with Whitman as the common man. They seek to give a complete picture of the man and his age, and since his acquaintance with American life ran much farther, both horizontally and vertically, than the experience of his contemporaries, they make a place for almost every kind of person and kind of activity to be found in the heterogeneous society of his day. He devotes himself to the farmer and the city-dweller, the mechanic and the trapper, the immigrant and the native born, the clam-digger on Cape Cod and the river pilot on the Mississippi. These catalogs of his, sometimes so dull and yet sometimes so tersely expressive, define, as almost nothing else could, the diversity of American life. Though we may criticize him for failing to synthesize the varied elements he introduced into his poems, though we may point out that he never achieved complete imaginative mastery over the materials he so recklessly amassed, we cannot charge him with timidity. Nothing deterred him from writing about America as he saw it, neither regard for poetic tradition nor concern with the moral prejudices of his readers nor even, though he was both ambitious and vain, a desire for personal success.

We can test Whitman's courage as an artist and examine the application of his theories if we observe his treatment of those industrial developments that so radically dislocated life in the period of his maturity. He was, we must remember, a mystic at heart and a nature lover, and there was more than a touch of Jeffersonian agrarianism in his political philosophy. Yet he made himself the poet of the factories as well as the farms, of the cities as much as of the country. He writes of "the factories divine," "the clean-hair'd Yankee girl . . . in the factory or mill," and "the engineer's joys," of "the human-divine inventions, the labor-saving implements," of "you engineers, you architects, machinists," of "the lessons of the concrete, wealth, order, travel, shelter, products, plenty." As a poet of contemporary America he made a place for the manifold expressions of the industrial revolution, and it never occurred to him that the millions of factory workers were less picturesque than ploughboys or red Indians, or that city streets were less expressive of the divine spirit than solitary seashores.

It is easy enough to criticize Whitman. His mind was confused, his thinking undisciplined, his assertions contradictory. His poems are chaos, built out of the most heterogeneous materials, built out of bare facts often, untouched by any imaginative effort. But what else was possible? If he had carefully excluded from his poems everything that could not be absorbed into some imaginative integration, he could scarcely have written the poetry of contemporary life. That life was chaos, chaos beyond the power of any imagination to order and control it, and Whitman chose to reflect it accurately rather than to exclude grotesque and inharmonious elements for the sake of an artificial symmetry.

All Whitman's faults, though they may bar him from the first rank of poets, seem, when one considers his situation and his task, to have been virtues. A more disciplined mind would have been rendered impotent by the mere recognition of the impossibility of reducing to a system such conflicting elements. A less buoyantly optimistic mind would have sunk under the realization of the distance to be traveled before the great vision could be achieved. A less mystical mind, a mind more preoccupied with the steps by which the goal could be reached, would have narrowed itself down to concern with a small and malleable portion of American civilization. It was precisely the broad, unformed mind of a Whitman, undiscriminatingly affirmative, unhesitatingly hospitable, sharply perceptive of concrete detail, that could plunge into the wild jungle of a national life without political, economic, racial, religious, or social homogeneity.

For the post-war generation Whitman had two gifts. In the first place, he perpetuated valuable elements in the intellectual and imaginative outlook of the authors of the enlightenment: a sound recognition that the test of any civilization is the quality of its men and women, a hearty contempt for money-grabbing, and a noble conception of the social importance of literary activity. In the second place, he suggested, as none of his predecessors had done, that the civilization of which he dreamed could be achieved by the utilization of the forces that were actually shaping American life. As the first step towards that utilization he proposed—and he illustrated in his work what he announced as theory—an attitude of acceptance, an effort of understanding. It is true that, though in time he realized the necessity for a second step, though he saw that beyond the acceptance and understanding of the new forces must come a resolute attempt to control them, he did not give a clear account of how that second step was to be taken. He could only take his generation so far; but that was farther than any other writer had taken it. He was the only poet of his day to see that the instinctive faith of the American public in its own destiny and in the part the machine was to play in that destiny might be related to the highest ideals yet promulgated on American soil.

We have already seen how Whitman's outlook on life, despite its confusions, gives to his poetry both its intrinsic interest and its historical importance. The origins of that attitude are not hard to find. Emerson's great faith in humanity was based upon a historical reality, the emergence, especially on the frontier, of the common man. But that movement was merely a preliminary skirmish, leading to a realignment of forces, to a new division of classes. After the Civil War allegiance to the common man did not mean reverence for the pioneer virtues, for the pioneer virtues, when translated into the terms of an industrial economy, were cut-throat competition and ruthless exploitation. Allegiance to the common man meant loyalty to the poor farmer, at the mercy of bankers and middlemen, and to the factory hand, held under the employer's lash in a cruel slavery to the machine. Emerson's teachings, which had seemed so clear and strong at the beginning of his life, were no longer unambiguous: they could be, and they were, so interpreted as to justify the Morgans, Rockefellers, and Carnegies, or they could be restated in terms of the aspirations of the victims rather than the victors. Needless to say, the former interpretation triumphed. Few indeed were the disciples who saw that, however equivocal the letter, the message of the spirit of Emerson was clear; and of those few only Whitman left his mark on our literature. Whitman came from the common people, liked them, kept himself close to them, and the soundness of his sympathies compensated for the inconsistencies of his thinking. As a result he was not only the truest interpreter of Emerson in the years after the Civil War; he was in a sense the founder of the new American literature, the literature of the industrial era.

Many years were to pass before Whitman's importance could be fully recognized. The common men and women for whom he wrote were little interested in his poems; for them liberation meant the privilege of amassing wealth, and each of them dreamt of the day when he would be numbered among the rulers. Decade after decade of disillusionment would fail to convince them of their individual weakness and their collective strength. In the meantime literature was left in the hands of the well-bred and the comfortably situated, who as a rule had only contempt for Whitman. Aldrich, Stedman, Curtis, and Gilder were their men. These genteel *littérateurs,* with their correct sonnets and their polite essays, served their masters well, and the masters, pleased to feel themselves the patrons of culture, liberally rewarded the service. The principal functions of well-bred literature were to entertain and flatter its readers and to protect conventional morality. It preserved its readers from sordid contacts with the facts of the fierce industrial struggle; it somehow made those facts vanish and the real world yield to a world of respectable, sentimental, lily-white ladies and gentlemen. The Civil War and the triumph of industrialism had done their work, and the Golden Day was ended. Though the years after the war were filled with literary activity, the greater and more conspicuous part of it perpetuated the traditions of colonial imitativeness and middle-class moralizing. Below the surface new cultural forces were at work, but they were not yet ready to mature. And each writer through whom these forces moved would learn, as Whitman had learned, that among the enemies of everything that was vital and hopeful in literature would be found the men who regarded themselves and were widely accepted as literature's high priests.

Chapter II

A BANJO ON MY KNEE

THE Civil War made a dramatic break where otherwise there would have been a gradual transition. In time, of course, eastern writers recovered from their shock, and busied themselves, as we have seen, with the literature of gentility; but their diligence and their erudition, their gravity and their graciousness could only serve to mask for a while the decline of literary vitality in the East; they could not restore the conditions that had created the Golden Day.

Seers like Whitman looked to the West, and by 1870 there were evidences that the West was stirring. In a way it had influenced American writers from the earliest days of national independence: the more responsive authors of the East had been touched by the spirit of the frontier as the common man rose to power in the regions beyond the Alleghanies. But the West had made few direct contributions, and on such writers as it had produced the blight of imitativeness was strong. The struggle for existence was too severe; only as the soil was conquered and community life organized could the rugged pioneering spirit create a strong indigenous literature.

As poets and novelists appeared, it became clear that the West would give birth to many regional cultures. Not only were the different regions at different stages in the pioneering process; geographical conditions and economic opportunities varied, and the settlers brought with them cultural traditions from the East or from Europe. There were New Englanders in Ohio, poor whites in Missouri, Scandinavians in Minnesota, and Mormons in Utah; there were farmers on a small scale, farmers on a large scale, cattle herders, miners of silver and miners of gold.

This situation was not necessarily a danger to literary growth. Provincial cultures, each based upon the realities of a particular situation, each expressing the resourceful independence of the frontiersman, might have greatly enriched our literature. The difficulty lay in the fact that, as a section reached the level of physical well-being and social solidarity that would permit cultural development, forces came into play to destroy both its uniqueness and its homogeneity. For the machine was reaching across the continent, not merely destroying the geographical independence of the sections, but confronting them with problems they were not prepared to solve. Before a section could find itself and give birth to men capable of expressing it, profound processes of disintegration had begun. Even before the factories themselves appeared, wheat raisers, sheep herders, and silver miners discovered how completely their welfare depended on the state of markets thousands of miles away. And the factories came quickly enough, obliterating almost every trace of sectional individuality and making the very spirit of the frontier an anachronism.

It was a kind of race between the indigenous cultural forces of the region and the destructive effects of industrial progress. And it was in the farthest removed and almost the youngest of the sections that the cultural forces scored the first victory. It was in part because California represented so complete a break with the East, in part because the prompt tapping of natural resources there encouraged expansiveness in every direction, in part because young men of talent and education had been attracted to the coast, that the state so early in its career founded newspapers and magazines around which men of literary ambition might gather. Even in California, however, many of the bright young men seemed to be living on a cultural capital accumulated in eastern centers, and their desire was less to create standards of their own than to measure up to those promulgated in Boston and New York.

California was waiting for Bret Harte, who, as editor of the newly founded *Overland Monthly,* announced in 1868 that it was the duty of the magazine to print material pertaining to its own state, and then, in illustration of his theory, published "The Luck of Roaring Camp." This young man, thirty-two years old when the story appeared, had taught school, worked in a drug store, and set type. He had also served a brief term as Wells Fargo express messenger and perhaps had done some mining. But his background was academic and his aims were literary, and the decade before the appearance of "The Luck of Roaring Camp" had been chiefly devoted to writing. He had written sketches, burlesque novels, and an occasional story for the *Golden Era* and the *Californian,* edited a collection of state verse, and published a volume of prose and one of poetry. He had been given a comfortable sinecure as secretary of the California mint, and his choice as editor of the *Overland Monthly* indicated public recognition of his talents. Already he had outstripped his friends and colleagues—Charles Warren Stoddard, Mark Twain, Charles Henry Webb, and the rest—and when the amazing popularity of "Plain Language from Truthful James" followed in 1870 the success of "The Luck of Roaring Camp," he was a national figure.

Harte had, he later said, a "very early, half-boyish but very enthusiastic belief" in the possibility of "a peculiarly characteristic Western American literature." Whatever that phrase may have meant to him, many of his sketches of Californian scenery and his adaptations of Spanish legend obviously owed more to his reading of Washington Irving than to any immersion in the life of the frontiersman. And it is clear that the same appreciation of the picturesque determined the themes of his short stories. If one examines the tales collected in the volume called *The Luck of Roaring Camp,* one notices not only the use of an amusing and perhaps inaccurate dialect, the reliance on bizarre details, and the emphasis on eccentricities of character; one notices also that the theme of each is the emergence of fine qualities in some character whose rough exterior gives no promise of such virtues. The very basis, then, of his stories is the picturesque contrast between superficial uncouthness and inner nobility, and he was far more interested in stating this contrast dramatically than he was in analyzing the true character of the pioneer.

Moreover, the California of the gold miners was being rapidly transformed, at the time he wrote his stories, into the California of the business men, and this change may have had something to do with his admiration for the miners. We know that he had once regarded these men as vulgar and unworthy of literary attention, and we know that his subsequent respect for them accompanied the growth of a bitter hatred for the money-grubbing spirit. As a boy he had worshipped the heroes of Froissart's *Chronicles,* Dumas' romances, the sea-stories of Marryat, and the *Leatherstocking Tales* of Cooper; and his own character, in its impulsiveness and even irresponsibility, was closer to the hearty good nature of the first settlers than it was to the well-mannered ruthlessness of the entrepreneurs. And this antipathy alone would have prevented him from following, in his fiction, the development of California from the pioneering to the commercial stage.

There were, then, two obstacles to the growth of the realistic elements in his stories, and when he added a third by leaving for the East he was forever committed to the romantic, sentimental tale of the mining camps. He went East both because he dreamt of living a free, idealistic life among men of literary aims and because he wanted to escape from the commercialism of his San Francisco contemporaries. He discovered that Boston had changed, just as California was changing, and the tranquil life of its men of letters did not blind him to the power of the new Boston, the city of factories and brokers' offices and struggling immigrants. Longfellow still seemed to him the embodiment of quiet nobility, and he venerated him accordingly; but the younger men of letters he distrusted. Having to make a living, he continued to write stories, tried his hand at plays, wrote one novel, and suffered on the lecture platform. Seven years passed, and at last, unhappy and poor, he accepted, from a government that he hated for its subservience to commercial interests, a minor post in Germany. Thence, in 1880, he went to Glasgow, and when he lost his post there five years later, he settled in London. America he never revisited.

Reading carefully the letters Harte wrote to his wife during those long years abroad, one detects the tragic note. Though he seems to have found life in London pleasanter than life elsewhere, and though he appreciated the prestige he enjoyed there and the larger income he was able to earn, he found much to distress him in his adopted home, and his affection for the United States grew with absence. As for his own work, it was cheap and he knew it. His writing was pure drudgery. "You," he wrote his wife, "cannot possibly hate pen and ink as I do who live in it and by it perpetually."

"Sick or not," he said, "in spirits or out of spirits, I must work, and I do not see any rest ahead." So he went on, grinding out story after story about the golden hearts of profane miners and quick-shooting gamblers. Yet sometimes, in a story such as "A Protégée of Jack Hamlin's" or "Colonel Starbottle's Client," a little of the old vigor returned, as if memory suddenly woke in him and he found himself back in frontier California. The life there, it must have seemed to him, was after all the best he had known, and he may not have been wholly sorry that popular demand forbade him to desert his one great theme.

Bret Harte's literary career ended, to all intents, when he left California in 1871, and it is possible that even his early work has been too highly esteemed. He has been called a stylist of distinction, a master of the short story, and a penetrating student of human nature. Yet it is easy to find flaws in his style, to expose the superficiality of his characterization, and to list many short story writers more dextrous than he. Even his own claim, that he founded a peculiarly western literature, will not bear scrutiny, for he owed much to picturesque writers of other regions, and he portrayed only so much of California life as happened to fit his formula. Yet it is impossible to deny that there is power in his early work, and that something of the frontier does live in these romantic tales. Harte did not found a peculiarly western literature, but he did make a beginning. And then, with the beginning scarcely made, he turned his back on the West and on the hope of literary growth. What he had written, out of a real desire to express the spirit of the region he knew, was, he discovered, merely entertainment for his readers. He accepted—harassed, one must admit, by personal difficulties and financial troubles—the rôle of entertainer, and as an entertainer survived for thirty years his death as an artist.

Harte, though he may not have been in any strict sense the founder of American regionalism, was the first writer to gain popularity after the Civil War by the exploitation of sectional peculiarities, and there is little doubt that his example directly inspired many of the writers of the seventies, eighties, and nineties. It is, therefore, striking that the pattern of his life should be the pattern, to a great extent, of the regional movement in American literature. Writer after writer began with a sincere desire not merely to portray the life of a particular section but to express its spirit; writer after writer ended as a mere entertainer, providing formularized amusement for an appreciative nation. Individual careers varied, but the fundamental pattern scarcely changed: the writer did not grow with his section. The region that appeared in his books was always the region as he had known it when he began writing, or even when he was a child. Often he left the region, and thus freed himself to live with memories of what it had been. In any case nostalgia and often sentimentality filled his tales. Again and again the tragedy of Bret Harte in London repeated itself.

*   *   *

Certainly tragedy was in store for Samuel Clemens, though neither he nor Harte could have suspected it when, in 1864, they met in California. They met almost as master and disciple, and Harte, who was by a year the younger, was master. Clemens, though enjoying a local reputation for his contributions to the *Territorial Enterprise* of Virginia City, had only recently turned to writing as a means of earning a living, and his apprenticeship had been served in printers' shops, on river boats, and in mining camps. At the age of twenty-three, as a licensed pilot on the Mississippi, he had enjoyed a position of unusual independence and importance.

Dispossessed by the beginning of the Civil War, he had set forth for Nevada, where, though he never achieved the fortune that often seemed within his grasp, he did share in the extravagances of flush times. Journalism, in which he was engaged when he met Harte, was, in his own estimation, no more than a temporary device for earning a living; it offered a breathing-spell before he launched himself upon some enterprise worthy of his talents.

There was a time when Harte and Clemens considered collaboration, and they frequently discussed their respective programs for the conquest of the East. To their California friends at the moment it must have seemed certain that the former would be the victor in that friendly rivalry, but the name of Mark Twain was known in the East as soon as that of Bret Harte, and it was Clemens who first recrossed the continent. Circumstances, whose irresistible power he was later to celebrate, took charge of his career. In 1865 a story, arriving too late for the Artemus Ward volume for which it was intended, appeared in the *Saturday Press,* and "The Celebrated Jumping Frog" took its place among the household fables of America. The next year a visit to the Hawaiian Islands provided the material for a lecture in San Francisco, and Clemens, less discomfited by public appearance than Harte, discovered a new source of income and a new means of extending his reputation. After having arranged to write letters for the *Alta Californian,* he started East, where the casual advice of friends led to the trip on the *Quaker City,* with its series of letters and eventually its book. When *The Innocents Abroad* appeared in 1869, sweeping into such popular favor as few American books had enjoyed, Samuel Clemens could scarcely ignore his destiny: however often he might try to rebel, he was committed to a literary career.

The Innocents Abroad, taken together with the stories and

sketches he had previously written, made it easy to identify the tradition with which Mark Twain was, by temperament, experience, and literary aims, identified. Unlike Harte, whose earliest impressions, whose education, whose impulse to write had come in the East, he was part of the southwestern frontier, and he naturally expressed himself in the forms that that frontier had evolved. The tall story, the expletive-studded rhetoric, and the practical joke of the Mississippi deck-hand, or the transcontinental stage-driver, or the Nevada miner were familiar to his ear and satisfying to his sense of humor. In stories and songs, handed on by word of mouth, persistently modified, often adapted to suit historical figures, the Southwest had given birth to a rich folklore. Some of this lore had found its way into print in *The Autobiography of David Crockett,* Baldwin's *Flush Times of Alabama and Mississippi,* Longstreet's *Georgia Scenes,* and similar works. Its spirit and many of its mannerisms entered into the lectures and books of Petroleum Nasby, Josh Billings, and Artemus Ward. At its worst it relied on purely verbal humor and forced exaggeration; at its best it derived from sharp observation and expressed the courage and buoyancy of self-reliant adventurers.

The honesty of *The Innocents Abroad,* its informality, its freedom from affected humility—everything, in short, that distinguishes it from the travel books of conventionally educated tourists—may be attributed to the frontier spirit. On the other hand, the book's weaknesses are the weaknesses of the tradition from which it stemmed. The frontier was, obviously, provincial, and it is provincialism that vitiates *Innocents Abroad.* Much as Mark Twain might boast of his indifference to the guide-books and his refusal to make their standards his standards, he was very much at their mercy, and his record suggests that, like the typical tourist, he was confused, a little frightened, and more than a little unhappy. For any sympathetic penetration of the spirit of other races he was quite unprepared, and his soul rendered homage most readily to the kind of spectacle that could be interpreted in statistical terms. Long before the journey was over his supply of quips ran low, for they were less the natural response of a fresh and unspoiled spectator than the stock-in-trade of the newspaper funny man; and his pathetic recourse, time after time, to remarks about dirt or relics or guide-books, betrays the inadequacy of his equipment for the experiences he was passing through. The latter part of the book, with its mixture of swaggering skepticism and senseless credulity, its pumped-up piety for home consumption, and its monotonous narrative so eloquent of the writer's weariness, must have revealed, even to Mark Twain himself, that the literary life made greater demands upon intellect and imagination than, at that point, he could conceivably measure up to.

The frontier tradition, as all this suggests, could offer a writer no more than a start; but it was a good start, a start in the right direction. At the basis of western humor lay a gift for accurate observation and shrewd characterization— for realism, in other words. Longstreet defended the minuteness of detail in *Georgia Scenes,* and Crockett spoke of "the many small and, as I fear, uninteresting circumstances" of his narrative. They need not have apologized; every frontier tale, no matter how tall, relied on just such concrete observations. This realism not only gave point to exaggerations; it appealed in its own right to men whose lives depended on their ability to use their eyes. And Mark Twain was capable of it, as the early stories show even more fully than *Innocents Abroad*. Here was a virtue worth cultivating, a quality that could enrich our literature. But before the primitive realism of the frontier could take literary shape, even at the hands of a Mark Twain, a long course of discipline was necessary.

He seems to have known that something was wrong, and he was not unwilling to accept the guidance of those who might be able to remedy his deficiencies. Indeed, he was, if anything, too submissive for his own good, for his humility led him to believe, however uneasily, in the standards of eastern gentility. In Honolulu Anson Burlingame had prescribed "refinement of association" and "companionship among men of superior intellect and character": "Never affiliate with inferiors; always climb." Circumstances helped Mark Twain to obey the admonition. As if it were not enough for him to attach himself to Henry Ward Beecher, Charles Dudley Warner, and Thomas Bailey Aldrich, he became engaged to Olivia Langdon, a former invalid and a paragon of the accepted virtues of the Victorian era in eastern America, who celebrated their betrothal by helping him to prune away the crudities of *Innocents Abroad*. By the time he had settled in Hartford, tasted the joys of respectable wealth, and won recognition in England as well as at home, he had delivered himself into the hands of the genteel tradition. It could not suppress his inborn genius, but neither could it develop that genius, shape it, summon forth all its potentialities, conduct it to a level on which it could richly function. Could the genteel writers encourage Mark Twain's realism when they were themselves both less courageous and less keen-sighted than he? Could they help him to understand American life when they persistently ignored the forces that were shaping it? No, they could correct his grammar and chasten his exuberance, but they could give him no inkling of what it might mean, to a man with his talents and his experience, to be an American author in the Gilded Age.

Because there was so little in his own preparation, and so

little in the intellectual life of his time, to guide him, Mark
Twain could never satisfy himself that a literary career adequately expressed the powers that he felt within him. It is no
wonder, then, that he was restless, considered a variety of
vocations, speculated constantly, undertook scores of books
that he never finished, and prosecuted in the most dilatory
fashion the writing of such books as, often under financial
pressure, he deigned to complete. It is no wonder that, as
he more than once confessed, the joys of literature never
equaled the pride he had felt when he mastered the shoals
and windings of the Mississippi. Yet he did continue to write.
After *Innocents Abroad* came *Roughing It,* a better book and
a stronger testimony to the potentialities of frontier realism.
The year after its publication, that is, in 1873, he wrote *The
Gilded Age* with Charley Dudley Warner—a strange collaboration with strange results. And then, three years later,
came *Tom Sawyer,* in which he showed the possibilities,
good and bad, of a return to the scene of his childhood.
Thrice in the course of the next twenty years he returned to
the Mississippi Valley for material—in *Huckleberry Finn,
Life on the Mississippi,* and *Pudd'nhead Wilson.* The four
books of Missouri life, together with his principal piece of
satire, *A Connecticut Yankee in King Arthur's Court,* and
his major adventure in romanticism, *Joan of Arc,* are his
chief contribution to American literature.

He continued to write, and we should be considerably the
poorer if he had failed to do so. But it is doubtful if he ever
achieved all that he had given promise of doing or really deserved the high rank that was so readily accorded him.
There is, it is at least clear, no one of his books that is wholly
satisfactory, no one of his books that is quite so good as,
while reading the opening chapters, one expects it to be.
Tom Sawyer, at the outset, is not merely a glamorous evoca-

tion of the romance that boyish enthusiasm lends to life; it is a fine and subtle portrayal of the Missouri frontier. Yet it ends in the tawdry melodrama of conventional juvenile fiction. In the same way in *Huckleberry Finn,* after moving passages that celebrate the joys of loafing on a gently floating raft, after the swift narrative of the Shepherdson-Grangerford feud and the shooting of Boggs, after the robust humor of the episode of the Royal Nonesuch, comes the tedious and labored account of the rescue of Jim. We need not prolong the list, but who can forget the painfulness of the latter chapters of *Life on the Mississippi,* those commonplace notes on river towns, after the glorious record that, in the first part of the book, the author gives of his own river days? In book after book, after the most brilliant kind of beginning, Mark Twain crawls with undisguised weariness of soul to the closing page.

The imagination that can seize, as his so often and so effectively did, upon some trifling incident and catch its implications, is not necessarily an imagination equipped for the sustained development of a major theme. The literary attributes that lend brilliance to a descriptive paragraph or a brief narrative are not always able to maintain an entire novel upon a consistently high level. For what Mark Twain wanted to do, for the creation of a record of American life, for the expression of his own personality and experience, something was lacking. He had seen enough, and he could write, when he was at his best, much more eloquently than those contemporaries who rebuked him for his barbarism. But the imaginative power that sees hidden relations among the fragments observation reveals, that takes the fragments and shapes them into a whole, that builds towards some towering climax—that power was denied him.

Like Bret Harte and like the majority of his contemporaries, Mark Twain made no attempt to come to terms with the world in which he lived. Except *The Gilded Age*—and the exception is important enough to be given detailed consideration later, though it merely confirms our conclusions—not one of his major fictions concerns itself with the movements and events of American life in the latter half of the nineteenth century. For four of his books he made use, as has already been noted, of materials that belonged to his frontier childhood. In his principal satire he struck out against the evil of feudalism, evils that either had disappeared or were far less important than the sins of American industrialism. To disclose most fully the romantic and idealistic side of his nature, he told the story of the martyred Joan.

Yet it will not be maintained that Samuel Clemens was a recluse, sheltered from the hopes and fears of his contemporaries. He was, on the contrary, in the thick of current economic and political developments, participating as an investor in mechanical progress, occasionally raising his voice in presidential campaigns, making friends with Napoleons of finance as readily as with fellow-authors. The expansiveness that sent him seeking after fortune, the boundless optimism with which he sought it—these were of the essence of the American character in those giddy days. He knew what was happening in contemporary America, and he felt all that Americans were feeling; and yet for purposes of literature he looked back on a different kind of life. Life was so much simpler in the Missouri of the forties and fifties, and in a way so much finer. If there was poverty, no one realized it. If there was a caste system, there was no bitter competition on a pecuniary level. If there were the fearful dogmas of Presbyterianism, there were also the games of youth and the dances, songs, and stories. If there were crudity and violence in the village, there was beauty in the woods and on the river. And it was a world Mark Twain knew and understood and in which he had once had a recognized place. When he returned to that world, he escaped from the strain of conventional society, from the fear of treachery, from the everlasting demand for money. So strong was the temptation that it could have been resisted only if he had mastered, for literary purposes, the complex life of industrial America as he had mastered life on the Mississippi. If he had understood, if he had been at home in, the world of his own social interests, his own investments, his own ambitions, he might have written about it. The frontier humorist and realist might have become a great social novelist.

If we point out what Mark Twain might have become, it is neither to disparage the work he actually did nor to pass moral judgment upon him. But there is significance in our analysis because it was only by developing as a realist that he could develop at all. If such development was impossible, as it probably was, our regret must be the keener. For the alternative was stagnation. In minor ways Mark Twain made progress, but he never transcended the limitations of his tradition. And insofar as he failed to cultivate the realistic elements in that tradition, he was forced to rely on the humorous elements. He was, and knew he was, merely an entertainer.

As an entertainer he could scarcely be expected to regard the literary life as a serious enterprise. It is no wonder that he filled *Innocents Abroad* with surefire gags; that is what, so far as he knew, he was supposed to do. It is no wonder that he catered in *Tom Sawyer* to as wide a variety of tastes as possible, that he introduced in *Huckleberry Finn* devices the success of which he had tested, that he allowed burlesque to weaken the satire of the *Connecticut Yankee*. At times he willingly accepted the rôle of entertainer, but there were moments when he conceived of playing a nobler part. One night during the lecture tour he made with George W. Cable, he turned to his companion and said, "Oh, Cable, I am demeaning myself. I am allowing myself to be a mere buffoon. It's ghastly. I can't endure it any longer." Are we to suppose that he never recognized the resemblance between his functions as lecturer and his functions as author?

This awareness, however vague, of his failure to fulfil himself was expressed with peculiar force in his bitter condemnation of his lack of independence. Self-reliance, the great frontier virtue, always stood at the top of Mark Twain's hierarchy of values. When he wrote *Innocents Abroad,* the "cringing spirit" of the great painters seemed to him utterly contemptible: "Their nauseous adulation of princely patrons was more prominent to me and chained my attention more surely than the charms of color and expression which are claimed to be in the pictures." But a few years later, declaring that the river pilot was "the only unfettered and entirely independent human being that ever lived in the earth," he added this comment: "Writers of all kinds are manacled servants of the public. We write frankly and fearlessly, but then we 'modify' before we print." This became, indeed, a favorite theme in conversations and private letters. "For seven years," he said, "I have suppressed a book which my conscience tells me I ought to publish," and added, with bitter irony, "Yes, even *I* am dishonest." In an article, written in 1885 but first published in his autobiography, he listed "certain sweet-smelling sugar-coated lies current in the world," first of all the belief "that there is such a thing in the world as independence: independence of thought, independence of opinion, independence of action."

Obviously there is some connection between his shame at his lack of independence and his recognition of his status as a writer, and both of these facts have something to do with his growing pessimism. When he began life he shared the optimism of the time and place in which he was born, the frontiersman's confidence that he can enforce his will upon the surrounding world. Neither the loss of his position as river pilot nor his failure to make a fortune in Nevada seems to have diminished his hopes. Only after success of a kind had come to him, after he had seen much of life in the Gilded Age, did doubt and despair overtake him. And the character of his pessimism indicates something of its origin. The naïve joy that the sophomoric philosopher of *What Is Man?* takes in attacking the conception of freedom of the will is more closely related to the need for self-justification than it is to any fundamental understanding of determinism. The insistence on the chaotic meaninglessness of life perfectly reflects the author's bewilderment. "Byron despised the race," he said, "because he despised himself. I feel as Byron did, and for the same reason." The faith the frontier had nurtured was being destroyed, and its destruction was all the more rapid because the frontier itself was disappearing. By a different process Mark Twain learned the lesson that hunger and homelessness were teaching so many settlers in the West: the era of pioneer self-reliance had ended. The world that had given him birth and had nurtured him—not only as a man but also as a writer—was dying, and in the world that was taking its place neither the man nor the writer could feel at home.

The buoyant spirit that the frontier had created could not be wholly subdued; to the end jovial moods alternated with the hours of fury and despair, and the cynic of Stormfield could be transformed into the beaming idol of public gatherings. But, much as he might relish the approval of his contemporaries and expand in its warmth, at heart he knew what it was worth. When, at the end of his life, a friend said that he must be pleased with the constant evidences of popular affection, he gently answered, "Yes, they have liked to be amused." He had amused a nation; what more had he done? A good deal more, of course, but a good deal less than, all things considered, he had given promise of doing.

* * *

The frontier came closer to expressing itself in Mark Twain than in any other writer. Indeed, he stands almost alone as a literary product of its forces. But the regional movement in literature, of which both Mark Twain and Bret Harte were part, continued to dominate the decades after the Civil War. Sectional self-consciousness, though it had first expressed itself in Harte's *Overland Monthly* proclamation, was as strong in the older sections as in the new ones. It was, indeed, a phase of national development and a step towards national unity. The earlier writers of the East had been colonial rather than regional, and for a time eastern writers had transcended both regionalism and colonialism. But after the war New England was, and knew it was, only one region among many. Some of these regions were actually on the frontier, whereas others had been settled for centuries; but for each, whatever its history, the awareness of itself as a region resulted from the recognition of the existence of other regions and from a consciousness of a vaguely defined larger unit of which all were part.

Most of the regional writers had no sharp understanding of what they were doing, but at least one of them saw that, since the nation was in fact divided into sections, cultural homogeneity, like political unity, could come only through the development and expression of sectional interests. This man, Edward Eggleston, while the seventies were young and

Mark Twain and Bret Harte only at the beginning of their careers, went farther than either of them towards the creation of the regional novel. Former circuit rider, editor of papers for Sunday School pupils, author of much juvenile fiction, he had been reading Taine's *Art in the Netherlands.* "The artist of originality," he discovered, "will work courageously with the materials he finds in his own environment." He had long wanted to do something with the life he had observed as a boy and young man in Indiana; he had been jealous of New England's literary hegemony; now Taine told him that the path pointed out by local pride was the path all great literature must follow. The moribund *Hearth and Home* was on his hands, its pages waiting to be filled. He sat down and wrote a short story about a young Indiana teacher, a story that friends urged him to expand. For ten weeks he wrote, eagerly, convinced of the importance of his task, and *The Hoosier Schoolmaster* began its course as a serial.

In twenty years Eggleston followed this novel with six others about the middle border, but *The Hoosier Schoolmaster* remained his most popular work. He sloughed off, as time went on, much of the piety that is disagreeably obtrusive in his first book; he displayed in both *The Circuit Rider* and *The Graysons* greater skill in construction; he gained, as *Roxy* shows, more courage in handling the less pleasant aspects of frontier life. But he never surpassed the fundamental excellence of *The Hoosier Schoolmaster,* nor did he transcend its limitations. The book's faults are manifold: its piety, the implausible villain, the invisible heroine, the melodramatic plot, the incredible climax. It is the work of a preacher and an amateur, a man who had written for the edification of adolescents, who believed that "the story is the most effective of all literary forms in teaching truth, conveying interesting information and uplifting men's minds and souls." But it is also the work of a man who knew his material and was determined to treat it honestly. Eggleston was not defending Indiana, nor exploiting its picturesqueness, nor searching for amusing sectional types. His faults are faults of ignorance and inexperience, not of intention. He chose a situation that, without being remote from general human experience, took its shape from the peculiar qualities of life in Indiana. To the best of his somewhat meager ability he formed his characters after representative models. He employed dialect for purposes of realism, not for purposes of ornamentation. Taine need not have been ashamed of the convert that the exigencies of book reviewing had so surprisingly made: Eggleston had worked courageously with the material he had found in his own environment.

However inferior to them he may have been in natural talent, Eggleston offered in *The Hoosier Schoolmaster* a better model for sectional fiction than either Bret Harte or Mark Twain, and he went on with *The End of the World, The Mystery of Metropolisville, The Circuit Rider, Roxy,* and *The Graysons* to illustrate what knowledge and courage could accomplish. He saw the need for comprehensive treatment, and he avoided mere picturesqueness. But his eyes were focussed on the past. His virtue was that he did not romanticize the past, even though he called it the heroic age; his weakness was that he had no interest in the present and, except in a rather special way in *The Faith Doctor,* made no use of his experiences after leaving the frontier. Honest as he was, he could not fail to see that his function was historical rather than literary, and it was to history that he gave the last twenty years of his life.

There were others to devote themselves to the literary task that Eggleston had undertaken when, in 1871, he wrote *The*

Hoosier Schoolmaster. Two years later a New Orleans book-keeper, encouraged by Edward King of *Scribner's,* sent to the magazine a story called " 'Sieur George." Superficially he seemed more fortunate than Eggleston, for Indiana was poor indeed when compared with New Orleans, America's most picturesque city, rich in traditions, blessed with a long-established culture, populated with as colorful a mixture of races as could be found on the continent. It did seem a pity, as Cable later said, for such materials to go to waste. But the fertility of the literary soil was, especially for so untrained a writer as George W. Cable, a danger. Like Bret Harte in California, he was tempted on every hand by bizarre incidents, extraordinary characters, strange manners of speech, and he had only to reproduce this kaleidoscope to win popularity among a people eager for new sensations and in love with the eccentric. It would have been easy for him to become a dealer in picturesque trifles.

That he did yield to temptation the title of his first collection of stories betrays: *Old Creole Days*—New Orleans' romantic past, the twenties and thirties, when respected citizens engaged in smuggling, wild Irishmen led buccaneering expeditions, love-lorn youths pined for light-skinned quadroons that the law forbade them to marry, and gentlemen disinherited their sons for refusing to fight duels. But even in these stories there is a sober recognition of the bases of human conduct and a critical spirit that does not abandon itself to the grandiose absurdity of the theme. That spirit asserted itself even when Cable planned for his novel a picture on the grand scale of romantic Creole life. *The Grandissimes* is not merely a record of feuds and balls, of black revenge and lily-white love; it is, as H. H. Boyesen called it, a *Kultur Roman,* a substantial and detailed re-creation of New Orleans life at the beginning of the century, revealing, not at all in a complacent spirit, the effects of slavery and the caste system on the civilization of the times. The romantic element dominates the book, it is true, but not to such an extent that evil is ignored or suffering unrepresented. When, four years later, in writing his second novel, *Dr. Sevier,* the author chose to represent the period of the Civil War, he permitted his critical faculties to control its construction, based the story upon the abuses of vaunted southern virtues, and directly attacked the corruption and inefficiency of his native city. He could not resist the impulse to exhibit in tedious detail his facility in the variety of dialects to be heard in New Orleans, nor was he above the introduction of secondary plots that made room for whimsy, sentiment, picturesqueness, and piety. But the chief impression that remains is of the honesty and inclusiveness of his picture of New Orleans life and the basic austerity of his characterization of Dr. Sevier and the Richlings.

Soon after *Dr. Sevier* appeared, Cable left New Orleans and settled in Massachusetts. During the next decade he was occupied with his writings on southern problems, which were not well received in the South, and with his lecture tours, Home-Culture Clubs, and Bible classes. *Bonaventure,* the only work of fiction during the period, is composed of three slight sketches of Acadian life, written largely in the manner of his early tales. But after these ten years he gathered himself for another major effort, and in 1894 produced *John March, Southerner.* Cable had been changing. Early in the eighties, speaking at the University of Mississippi, he had pointed out the necessity of regarding southern literature as part of the national culture. The reception of his comments on the Negro, quite as much as his actual removal from New Orleans, had helped him to regard the South with increasing objectivity. Now, in this new novel, he proposed to turn upon southern life in the critical period of reconstruction the light of a thoughtful regard for the nation as a whole. With surprising clarity he saw the principal task of regional fiction and attacked it.

Unfortunately there were difficulties that he could not foresee. His great problem was to discover some vantage point, some intellectual eminence, from which the whole pattern of national life, with his chosen section in its proper position, could be discerned. Certain things he could see: he could recognize the stupidity of southern chauvinism and the necessity for southerners to adapt themselves to the situation the war had created; and at the same time he could see that the exploitation of the South's natural resources was bound to be accompanied by the corruption that had attended the march of business enterprise in the North. What he had to do was to understand the relations of the virtues and vices of both sections. In terms of the novel, he had to show that John March was right in opposing the old-fashioned southern gentry and allying himself with northern capitalists, and at the same time to show that the hero retained the highest southern virtues and acquired none of the northern vices. The problem was too difficult: the dice had to be loaded in favor of John and his victory granted him by an act of Providence. Even the characterization fails at the same point, for, though we are told that John March kept all the chivalrous qualities of his tradition the while he became a successful man of affairs, we are never allowed to see this combination of attributes in practice.

For most of the books that he wrote during the thirty years of life that remained to him, Cable returned to the New Orleans of his youth. More and more his critical acumen weakened, and he contented himself with either picturesque sketches or tales of adventure. He had tried and failed. The fact that he was the son of a merchant—and an unsuccessful one at that—could make him critical of the plantation aristocracy and help him to see the folly of its refusal to adjust itself to the inevitable march of industrialism. Speaking in a way for those elements in the South that had never shared the privileges of the slave-holders, he could temper his account of past glories with realistic details of the lives of the oppressed. But he could not escape from the provincialism of his upbringing, from the effects of narrow orthodoxy and the long exposure to southern values. He could not penetrate below the superficial manifestations of the change that was taking place. Nevertheless he tried, and that attempt entitles him to respect.

Other regionalists, and there were many by the time Cable was fairly established, were untouched by the ambition that impelled him to try to broaden his outlook till it included more than his own section. As Cable and Eggleston followed Bret Harte and Mark Twain, the interest in local peculiarities grew. Everywhere men and women were at work, each of them seeking to discover and record the qualities that distinguished the life of his section from the life of other sections. The chronicling of these peculiarities became an end in itself. Even New England authors, forgetting their literary heritage, followed the prevailing fashion. New England had, indeed, produced a pioneer of the regional movement: Harriet Beecher Stowe, fresh from the triumphs of *Uncle Tom's Cabin,* had planned, early in the fifties, a novel about the people of the Maine coast, a novel that, after certain romantic experiments, was published a decade later. This book, *The Pearl of Orr's Island,* and the collection of short stories, *Oldtown Folks,* that followed it, anticipated the methods of Harte and Eggleston, and, though they were overshadowed by the author's great polemic, prepared the way for the sec-

tional literature of New England. Mrs. Stowe brought upon
the literary stage certain actors that were to appear again and
again in the works of her successors: the eccentric, sharp-
tongued, kind-hearted spinster, the retired ship captain with
his tall stories, the village flirt, the saintly pastor. In certain
respects, it is true, she showed that she belonged to the group
of women writers who, in the period before the war, had
made pious didacticism palatable by coating it with sticky
romance; but her careful observation of familiar types, her
use of dialect, her elaborate exposition of local customs, and
her detailed description of the natural setting stamped her
as a precursor of sectionalism.

She soon had her following. By the end of the seventies
Rose Terry Cooke had begun her mild studies and Sarah
Orne Jewett had entered upon her apprenticeship. The
former, for all her sentimentality, could portray the more
salient traits of the New England character, and the latter
reflected with extraordinary subtlety the fragile beauties of
that bleak land. Neither, however, made any effective recognition of whatever was ignoble or sordid or otherwise unpleasant in the life of New England, and it remained for
Mary Wilkins Freeman, who joined their ranks in the eighties, to display the lonely spinster, the toil-bent farmer, and
the worn-out workman. She at least saw that the small town
had sometimes warped its inhabitants and that the intrusion
of industrialism had increased the difficulties of these simple
people. She could not, it is true, resist the temptation of the
happy ending; her unfortunates are always compensated for
their sufferings. But she had an eye for varieties of character
and types of experience that her contemporaries ignored, and
her stories made the record of New England life more nearly
complete.

As Mrs. Stowe, Miss Cooke, Miss Jewett, and Mrs. Freeman explored New England together, as Miss Murfree discovered the Tennessee mountains and their strange inhabitants, as Alice French ventured into the Ozarks, as Kate Chopin and Grace King supplemented Cable's pictures of New Orleans, as Thomas Nelson Page set down his impressions of Virginia before the war and Joel Chandler Harris preserved the folklore of the Negro, as section after section put forth its representatives and took its place in the literary sun, the power of regionalism seemed irresistible. If what was needed for the future of American literature was a change in the geographical distribution of authors and subjects, it had been accomplished.

The accomplishment was important. Even when their literary talents were relatively slight, these novelists and short story writers were interpreters, helping the people of one section to understand those of another. And far more important of course than any such semi-sociological function of sectional literature, was the fact that it was only by beginning with the country and people he knew that an author might express whatever insight he had into the nature and destiny of man. In their essence Whitman's prophecy and Harte's challenge were right. The conditions that had made possible all that the East achieved in the years before the war had gone, never to be restored in the East, never to be reproduced anywhere else. If literature was to be possible at all, it had to be on new terms, and the only hope of discovering what those terms might be lay in each author's first of all examining the life about him.

* * *

The promise of regionalism was never kept. Scarcely was the movement under way before its dangers were apparent; before it reached its apogee, its failure was inevitable. Look-

ing back on it to-day, we see the extent of its collapse and
the ridiculousness of its pretensions so clearly as to be almost
unable to understand how natural and proper its impulses
were and how great its promise must have seemed. The collapse of its dominant personalities symbolizes the catastro-
phe that overtook the movement. For twenty years Bret
Harte lived, an unhappy exile, in London, defending his
country but never returning to its shores, praising his coun-
trymen but unhonored by them, refashioning in a hundred
different ways the themes that had once stirred his com-
patriots. Estranged from his old friend, battered by bereave-
ment, plagued by the judgments of his own conscience,
Mark Twain journeyed from Hartford to London, from
London to Vienna, from Vienna to Florence, and back to
Hartford again, carrying with him a burden of doubt and
despair that he dared not share with a public that insisted on
regarding him as a high-class minstrel. Eggleston, who had
once so clearly stated the aims of sectional fiction, began to
scorn the novel as a means to the end he visualized, and
turned to history as a more adequate medium for recording
the experiences and preserving the spirit of the American
people. Cable, uprooted from the soil that had nourished his
best work, baffled in his brave effort to outgrow the limitations of his inheritance, sought to compensate for his remoteness from the main current by engaging in adult education and dissipating in a variety of petty reforms the ener-
gies that had once sustained his labors.

A sad and a significant spectacle. One thinks of Mary Wilkins Freeman, following *A New England Nun, A Humble
Romance,* and *Pembroke* with the soggy sentiment and in-
ept symbolism of *Six Trees,* with so clumsy a venture into
new fields as *The Portion of Labor,* with the repetitiousness,
the stylistic pretentiousness, the unconvincing complacency

of any of her later collections. Like Harte and Cable, she could not find another subject so congenial to her powers as that she had begun by attacking, and that subject proved incapable of extension and unfriendly to literary growth. Her fate was also that of Charles Egbert Craddock, as Miss Murfree called herself, who had honestly conceived and painstakingly wrought the tales of *In the Tennessee Mountains*. For an outsider she had succeeded remarkably well in seeing through the eyes of her mountain people, had contrived to exhibit the cruelty and narrowness of their lives without sitting in judgment upon them, and had caught the flavor of their speech without wantonly exploiting its eccentricities. But, as time went on and she returned again and again to her chronicles of the mountaineers, these talents failed to grow, and her old faults—stylistic mannerism, verbose description, uneconomical structure—did not disappear. She slipped from the high repute of her prosperous days as an *Atlantic* contributor into an oblivion that the regular appearance of new volumes only intensified. In that limbo of productive but forgotten authors she was joined by Octave Thanet—that is, Alice French—who wearied of the search for local color and at the end of the century turned to short-sighted and trivial problem novels.

As one can trace the downward curve of individual writers, so one can note the similar line that marks the movement of regionalism through the two closing decades of the century. In Louisiana, for example, Kate Chopin and Grace King—both writers of delicacy and precision—contented themselves with deft but fragile sketches. Miss Chopin had her brief moment and lapsed into silence; Miss King became more and more the antiquarian; neither ventured along the path that Cable had, for a distance at least, blazed. In New England Alice Brown, with her *Tiverton Tales* and

Meadow Grass, relying on romantic reminiscence and the reproduction of types, opened the way for Kate Douglas Wiggin, Grace S. Richmond, and Joseph C. Lincoln. In Virginia Thomas Nelson Page told story after story in which one loyal Negro is indistinguishable from another, all brave young masters are cut from the same pattern, and the beautiful young heroines are as alike as dolls in a toy store. In *Red Rock,* his major effort, he told a preposterous story, reeking with sentimentality, completely provincial in its point of view. James Lane Allen, John Fox, and F. Hopkinson Smith won further applause for the southern school of sentimental myopics. But in time the public was satiated. By 1900, though all the leading regionalists were alive and most of them productive, such discredit had fallen upon their movement that younger writers turned aside in disgust and even the populace transferred its allegiance to the historical romance.

The aim of the sectional writers, it is to be remembered, was to make imaginative use of the kind of life that was familiar to them, and their strength should have lain in a steady progress from an understanding of that life to a comprehension of the larger issues of American civilization. But how could such growth take place if they were not willing to examine the section as they found it, if their attention was fastened not on the present but on the past? Bret Harte was interested only in the California of the gold rush years; Mark Twain's best books portray the Mississippi Valley of his boyhood; Eggleston laid *The Hoosier Schoolmaster* in the Indiana of his youth and *The Circuit Rider* in the first part of the century, "the heroic age"; the New Orleans of Cable's earliest and latest stories is the Creole city of the first half of the century; the New England writers most frequently described an earlier generation than their own; Page chose the Virginia of antebellum days. They were not interested, these men and women, in understanding their respective sections as they were at the time they wrote; several of them—Harte, Mark Twain, Eggleston, Cable—had long since left the regions they described. What they wanted to do was to recapture the romantic past of boyhood impressions, the sectional life of the vanished era.

For the truth is that the kind of life these writers described no longer existed. The telegraph and railroad were, in the sixties, seventies, and eighties, making actual isolation a thing of the past. As many miles of railroads were built between 1868 and 1873 as had been constructed in the thirty years before the Civil War, and in the eighties 73,000 miles of track were laid down. Moreover, in those sections of the West devoted to agriculture, pioneer independence had become a myth, for the welfare of the farmers, with their specialized crops, depended on the state of industrialism and the condition of foreign markets. It is no wonder, then, that these farmers sufficiently modified their historic individualism to bind themselves into a large and sometimes effective political alliance. To describe the contemporary scene regional writers would have had to record the breakdown of sectional lines, the growth of extra-regional alliances, the increasing industrialization of agriculture, and the steady march of the factory across the continent. They would have had to show how machinery reduced the labor time spent in producing a bushel of wheat from three hours to ten minutes. They would have had to show how the farmer's sons and daughters went away to the city, to work in factories and mingle with the immigrants from other lands. They would have had to show how the shrinking of the public domain killed the optimism that had thrived while the westward pilgrimage went on. These changes the regional writers could not have ignored if they had made any vigorous effort to understand

and record contemporary life in the various sections, and sooner or later they would have found themselves trying to comprehend the forces that were shaping the nation. But this was precisely what they were instinctively avoiding when they located their stories in the past: for their purposes the sectional life of the past could be adequately understood; the life of the present was a different, a more disturbing, matter.

It is impossible not to see the effects of this habit of looking backward in the books of the period. Insofar as the regional movement represented a break with the romanticism of the early nineteenth century, insofar as it utilized the realistic elements in the frontier tradition, it was fruitful for American literature. But concentration on the past inevitably prevented the growth of realism and encouraged the development of romantic tendencies. Just as Bret Harte, far removed in time and space from the scenes he described, relied more and more on fantastic plots and absurd characters, so such writers as Page and Fox appeared who made little pretence of fidelity to fact. The frankly nostalgic note became common. "For we who have walked in country ways," Alice Brown wrote in *Meadow Grass,* "walk in them always, and with no divided love, even though brick pavements have been our chosen road this many a year." Grace King introduced *The Pleasant Ways of St. Medard* by saying, "What a pleasant world that was, to be sure, in which we were born fifty years ago in New Orleans; what a natural, what a simple world!" No author in such a mood could be expected to concern himself deeply with the honest reproduction and interpretation of the common facts of experience.

Concentration on the past also encouraged the attempt to exploit sectional peculiarities and thus invited the writer to concern himself with the superficial mannerisms of his re-

gion. Though at the outset the interest in dialect held out
the hope that literature might be rooted in the realities of
everyday speech, as time went on dialect was cultivated for
its own sake, as a kind of literary ornament, and attention
was distracted from the fundamental tasks of fiction. In the
same way the description of local scenery and the introduction of local customs became ends in themselves. Alice
French, for example, traveled the country over in search of
local color, and wrote impartially of Canada, Florida, South
Carolina, and Arkansas. The function of regionalism, as
Eggleston had defined it, was completely forgotten, and the
strange result was that the regionalists defeated themselves.
Instead of creating individuals representative of their respective sections, they manufactured literary types, characters that could not be distinguished from each other except
by superficialities of speech and clothing. The faithful but
forgotten spinster, the lovable vagabond, the reformed bad-
man, the misunderstood hero, and many another stock character display the same qualities and go through the same
actions whether they speak the language of Pike County or
Cape Cod, whether they drop their r's or multiply them.
The search for the eccentric had come full circle: seeking to
ignore the forces that were destroying sectional differences
and bringing the inhabitants of the various sections closer
together, the regional writers ended by losing all individuality of character in the monotonous sameness of conventional stereotypes.

Of course it cannot be argued that there was any easy alternative open to the regionalists. The understanding of historical forces that would have explained actual conditions in
any given section in the decades after the war was difficult
to attain. When, as sometimes happened, a writer sought
that understanding, he was almost certainly doomed to dis-

appointment. So Cable learned when he attempted *John March, Southerner.* So Mrs. Freeman discovered when she wrote *The Portion of Labor,* with its strange mixture of insight into New England character and childish ignorance of industrial conditions. These writers were what they were, and they carried with them into any literary field the burden of habits that regionalism had fostered. Mrs. Freeman had all her life been dealing with essentially tragic materials that she had refused to treat as tragic. She had, for example, furnished *Pembroke,* as sharp a study of New England crabbedness as has ever been written, with a happy ending that violated every premise she had laid down. It is no wonder, then, that she disposed in *The Portion of Labor* of problems of shop conditions, wage cuts, and strikes by ending the book with a collection of engaged couples, a meaningless conversion, and a handful of platitudes.

Certainly there was no one to help these writers to discover the one path out of their difficulties. The accepted heirs of the pre-war tradition enthusiastically welcomed the regionalists, but they could do nothing for them. The alliance between regionalism and gentility, symbolized in the collaboration of Mark Twain and Charles Dudley Warner, grew stronger and stronger, transcending the sectional boundaries that the writers emphasized. *Scribner's* welcomed Cable's work, and the *Atlantic* printed Charles Egbert Craddock's stories side by side with the contributions of its own New Englanders. Grace King moved easily from New Orleans' aristocratic literary club to the salons of New York and Hartford. It is, perhaps, to the credit of New York and Boston writers that they so willingly accepted these invaders, but the way was paved for that acceptance by the regionalists' submission to genteel standards. Praised for that studied picturesqueness that was one of their principal faults,

condemned for whatever harshness they ventured to introduce, the sectional writers found the weight of what they regarded as sound critical opinion on the side to which their
own timidities impelled them.

Their own weaknesses and the verdict of the polite critics
were reënforced by the will of the reading public. Book
buyers did not care to read about the contemporary scene and
contemporary forces; they liked these accounts of the kind
of life that was passing. The reading public wanted to be entertained. If we look for a key to the entire period, we find
it in that strange custom, so prevalent in the seventies and
eighties, of paying eminent men of letters great sums to appear on public platforms for the purpose of entertaining the
multitude. Whereas once the lyceum had been an important
American institution, a powerful force for adult education
and a vehicle that even Emerson was proud to employ, it
was now merely a substitute for the vaudeville stage. Mark
Twain and George W. Cable toured the country together,
appearing in every city that could pay their price—and for
what purpose? To read from their own works and make
people laugh. Mark Twain, Bret Harte, George Cable, Bay-
ard Taylor, and James Whitcomb Riley complacently followed in the footsteps of Bill Nye and Artemus Ward!

The public wanted to be entertained. At the top of the
scale the men whom industrial enterprise and speculation
had made fabulously wealthy built ornate villas, purchased
complete art galleries, bought their way into society, gave
banquets for horses and dogs, spent $600,000 for a necklace
or $75,000 for a pair of opera glasses, and transformed the
Waldorf Astoria into a replica of Versailles for their balls.
At the bottom of the scale men and women who worked
long hours in dingy shops and lived in disease-ridden tenement houses dreamt the great American dream of wealth to

come, and in the meantime sought their amusement at church socials or prize fights or P. T. Barnum's circus or in reading of the adventures of Diamond Dick and Nick Carter. And in between were the respectable members of the middle classes, who adorned the exteriors of their houses with gimcracks and gingerbread and the interiors with steel engravings, wax flowers, gold-framed ancestral portraits, and crocheted tidies. It was they who supported the monthly magazines and the priests of the genteel tradition. They, too, wanted entertainment. The women founded literary societies, made a cult of the obscurities of Browning, and twittered over diluted Emersonianism. They and such of the men as had time to read did not want to be unsettled by the close scrutiny of contemporary conditions. They wanted a literature that flattered their sense of their own distinguishing refinement and that gently took them away from whatever was unpleasant in their lives. They may even have had a genuine nostalgia for the simpler, more rugged, more colorful past, though certainly few of them would have cared to return to it. The honest portrayal of real life as it had been led was almost too much for them: Harte offended the Californians and Cable the people of New Orleans; there were librarians who wished Olivia Clemens had expurgated her husband's books a little more drastically; Eggleston alarmed some of his religious brethren; and some readers of the *Atlantic* found Mrs. Freeman unpleasantly harsh. They would surely have resented any attempt to show them what was going on before their faces and eyes. What they really wanted, and what they loudly applauded when they found it, was the romantic sentimentality of *Tiverton Tales, A Kentucky Cardinal, In Ole Virginia,* and *The Little Shepherd of Kingdom Come.*

By and large the impulse that inspired the creators of sectional literature was a desire to offer a way of escape, for themselves and their readers, from the complexities of contemporary life. The writers who participated in the movement were men and women of differing degrees of talent; the extent to which they abandoned themselves to flight varied; the forms of refuge they created were sometimes ignoble and sometimes rather fine. But not even the best of these writers, not even those whose works we are proud to preserve, realized their potentialities, and the movement itself failed to provide, as it certainly gave promise of doing, a natural transition to a national literature. Instead, it swiftly degenerated into a form of amusement for a vulgar age.

Chapter III

THE BATTLEFIELD

IT IS easier to understand why so many promising authors preferred to bury themselves in the comfortable past when we realize what happened to those who turned their attention to the uncomfortable present. For there were a few who sought, either as an isolated venture or as a settled program, to make imaginative conquest of the elements in American life that were shaping its growth. Such a frontal attack meant, of course, an excursion into either the sphere of business or the sphere of politics, and the invasion of one necessarily led to an invasion of the other.

The approach by way of politics was more attractive, if only because the American mind was more accustomed to thinking in political terms. The period after the war furnished, it is true, few statesmen-heroes, but the political scene presented situations so complicated, dramatic, and significant that the absence of genuine heroes could be overlooked. Yet few writers felt the temptation to use in fiction the events of the quarter century after Appomattox; there are perhaps half a dozen political novels written in the period, and of them only two still have readers. Both, as their titles show, were planned in an ambitious mood: Mark Twain and Charles Dudley Warner called their picture of the era *The Gilded Age,* and Henry Adams named the book in which he sought to dramatize the lessons of two decades of political experience *Democracy*. An opportunist like F. Marion Crawford might hastily exploit the superficial drama of government, subordinating honest observation to the fancies of a practiced romancer, as he did in *An American Politician;* but these were conscientious men, deeply concerned with the events they described and not unaware of the responsibilities of authorship.

What both *Democracy* and *The Gilded Age* describe is the demoralization of a nation. Time has revealed the extent, as well as the causes, of that debauch, and we cannot wonder that three sensitive and thoughtful men, such as Clemens, Warner, and Adams, were both horrified and fascinated by the spectacle. In less than a decade after the war the American public had been forced to recognize the corruption of municipal and state governments and of the federal government itself. The Tweed Ring, robbing the citizens of New York of at least twenty million dollars, had merely accomplished on a somewhat larger scale what similar rings had achieved in Brooklyn, Philadelphia, Chicago. The open buying and selling of votes at Albany could be matched at Springfield, Madison, or Topeka. A member of Congress from Massachusetts, observing that "there is no difficulty in inducing men to look after their own property," smoothed the way for the Credit Mobilier by offering his fellow Congressmen stock at a price well below the market value. The American minister to England sold his name to a fraudulent mining scheme for $50,000 in stock. General McClellan supported a project, whose dishonesty should have been transparent, for exploiting an alleged diamond field in California. The brilliant leader of the Republican Party, James G. Blaine, was involved in a dubious railroad development, and repeatedly lied to save himself before a congressional committee. Closer and closer the scandals came to the President himself, for his vice-president was involved in the Credit Mobilier bubble, his private secretary in the illegalities of the Whiskey Ring, his brother-in-law in the machinations of Jim Fisk and Jay Gould, and his secretary of war in a scheme for the sale of office. From top to bottom, in all its departments, the government of the United States was corrupt and inefficient.

This was the scene that Mark Twain and Charles Dudley Warner were contemplating in 1873, and it had changed but little when, seven years later, Henry Adams set down his impressions. After his return from the Holy Land Mark Twain had spent a few months in Washington, where the odor of corruption had filled his nostrils; Warner, for some time a practicing journalist, had a newspaperman's knowledge of what was going on. Neither had ever written a novel, but their lack of experience did not check their ambitions, and they planned nothing less than a comprehensive survey of the nation. Mark Twain, in the opening chapters, sketched the background of the story in the hopes of Squire Hawkins and the dreams of Colonel Sellers. Warner introduced two young easterners, caught by the speculative spirit of the age and deprived by its uncertainties of moral strength. Shifting from Missouri and the optimistic efforts of Sellers and his associates to exploit, at the federal government's expense, certain imaginary resources of the state, the story turns to Washington and the lobbying for Knobs University that is to make the Hawkins family's fortune. The novel also involves the discovery of a coal mine, the ambitions of a young Quakeress, a love story, a melodramatic shooting, and a bizarre murder trial. From east to west *The Gilded Age* stretches, one of the most ambitious novels written in the decades after the war.

The authors' problem was, obviously, to find a way of unifying this far-flung narrative with its variety of characters and its multiplicity of incidents. They did not solve it, as the uncertainty of its tone would be enough to show. It is disturbing to have to turn from Mark Twain's hearty narrative to the passages in Warner's romantic manner; it is worse to find the progress of the story interrupted by the crude burlesque and heavy-handed satire of the former and the pinched moralizing of the latter. Neither author, it is clear, was quite sure what attitude he should take towards the persons and incidents he portrayed. They were agreed in condemning the speculative spirit, and they were aware that it was that spirit that bound together the comic excesses of Beriah Sellers, the hypocritical dishonesty of Senator Dilworthy, the calculating unscrupulousness of Laura Hawkins, the careless expansiveness of Harry Brierly, and the resolute progress of Philip Sterling. But how they were to distinguish among the various manifestations of this ubiquitous spirit they did not know. Superficial evils they could attack: coarseness and snobbery in Washington society, dishonesty and greed in Washington politics. But what lay behind all this? How did it happen that so many Congressmen were venal and so many business men untrustworthy? Why was it that so relatively honest a man as Ruth Bolton's father found himself inextricably allied with rascals? Such questions Clemens and Warner were not prepared to answer. It was easier to turn to the most obvious kind of satire on the jury system, even though that involved a farcical climax to the sharply tragic story of Laura Hawkins. It was easier to soothe the sensibilities of a romantically inclined reading public by blessing Philip Sterling with a coal mine and a wife. It was easier—though Samuel Clemens' eagerness for quick profits was to cost him hundreds of thousands of dollars—to preach a sermon against speculation.

The collaborators made an ambitious attempt, and they succeeded in giving a valuable picture of the superficial aspects of the age they rightly called gilded. But a good novel requires understanding quite as much as observation, the kind of understanding that leads to mastery and to structural unity. For this, burlesque, melodrama, and even shrewd portraiture are poor substitutes. It is no wonder that Warner went back to his editorials and essays and compilations, and that Mark Twain, regarding *The Gilded Age* as an unfortunate and somewhat inexplicable misadventure, began his exploitation of boyhood recollections.

Henry Adams had had less opportunity for the observation of American life than Mark Twain, but he had been early introduced to the realities of politics, had devoted himself to the study of his nation's past, and had, when he wrote *Democracy,* spent several years in first-hand examination of men and policies in Washington. His education, if one can judge from his own record of it, had passed beyond the elementary stage. But whatever lessons he had learned had not sunk deep enough into his consciousness to shape his imaginative outlook on life, or even to prevent him from naïvely adopting the attitudes of his class. His book, more than one chapter of which unpleasantly resembles the society romance of the period, is more impressive as a record of manners in Washington's fashionable circles than as an analysis of the basic realities of political life. The dangers Adams sees are party loyalty and the spoils system, the elevation to high positions of ignorant and immoral men, the tendency to reduce all society to one low level, the snobbery of the newly rich, and the active dishonesty of powerful politicians. On the other hand, he expresses, both in his own person and through his chosen spokesman, a faith that, democracy being the logical outcome of past developments, the laws of the universe will somehow—he does not suggest how—bring order out of chaos and virtue out of vice. With such an outlook he could, of course, give no suggestion of the actualities of American politics, and there was nothing for him to do but, like the scholarly Mr. Gore, to repudiate political activity, and, like the disillusioned Mrs. Lee, to forget the problems of democracy in the contemplation of the sidereal system.

The path through the labyrinth in which Henry Adams and Mark Twain wandered now seems so plain that it is hard to believe they sought very diligently for it. The vulgarity and dishonesty they recorded and condemned were manifestations of a single phenomenon, the revolution that was taking place in American life. The exploitation of the natural resources of the continent, conducted in the interests of individual aggrandizement, was proceeding at a pace that day by day rendered the political machinery of the nation more and more inadequate. The exploiters, having gained control of both parties, employed that political machinery when it served their purposes, but when it failed to do so, they unhesitatingly and ruthlessly scrapped it. And, so long as the masses of people hoped for a share in the fruit of that exploitation, there was no hope of effective protest. Such remedies as civil service reform, proposed by men whose moral sensibilities were shocked, were irrelevant and futile. The only alternative was that this exploitation should take place in the interests of all the people and under the egis of a firmly conceived social purpose. At the moment there was no chance of the adoption of such a program, but the individual could either advocate it, with all the revolutionary concepts it involved, or he could reconcile himself to the

evils that existed. If—like Mark Twain and Henry Adams—
he could do neither, the result was confusion.

* * *

If, for reasons we have begun to understand, politics had
little attraction as a literary theme, industry attracted even
fewer authors. Despite the romantic rapidity with which the
great financiers and industrialists had risen to wealth and
power, despite the extent to which their achievements shaped
the ambitions of millions of Americans, the sixties and seventies slipped by, and no novelist had chosen to make a serious
study of that amazing national phenomenon, the multimillionaire. Not until 1885 was there an author courageous
enough to make the attempt, and even he shrank from the
implications of his task. It is useless to criticize William Dean
Howells for not making *The Rise of Silas Lapham* a different
sort of book; he was limited by his experience, his interests,
and the literary standards of his day. And yet, when one considers his desire to treat realistically the representative phenomena of his own civilization, and when one remembers
how constantly present to his mind the exploits of the money-
masters must have been, his book is only less astonishing, as
a revelation of the confusions and blindnesses of an obviously
intelligent man, than Henry Adams' *Democracy*.

Silas Lapham, as everyone will remember, had made his
fortune by exploiting a paint mine that his father had discovered before the war. He built up, it appears, a fortune of
perhaps a million dollars in the decade and a half after Appomattox. In the same period Rockefeller had laid his hands
upon ninety per cent. of the oil refineries in the country, had
seized most of the pipe lines, and had brought about the
monopoly that from the first was his goal. Commodore Vanderbilt, by manipulating the stock of the New York and

Harlem Railroad, by overcapitalizing the New York Central and Hudson River, and by beating Drew and Gould at their own game of buying legislators and judges, had created the first great transportation system and added at least eighty millions to his fortune. Andrew Carnegie, beginning quite as humbly as Silas Lapham and without even a paint mine in the family, had, through shrewd investment and a belated recognition of the importance of the Bessemer process, put himself in possession of a business that was soon to yield a profit of forty million dollars in a single year. Daniel Drew, Jay Gould, and Jim Fisk had calmly wrecked a railway system to advance their private interests, and they had aimed at and nearly secured a corner in gold.

Silas Lapham's record as a business man is comparatively clean: the most he can reproach himself with is having treated a partner with some severity; the principal charge his enemies can bring against him is the vulgarity of his advertising. Rockefeller had created his monopoly by taking advantage of his competitors' weaknesses, by resorting to deceit in the purchase of rival concerns, and by securing rebates from the railroads; at every step the rise of the oil industry had involved bloody battles and the incessant bribery of legislatures and courts. The fight between Vanderbilt and the combined forces of Drew, Gould, and Fisk had been carried on with legislators who merely waited for the highest bidders, with venal judges in the courts and gangsters in the trainyards. Elkins and Widener had built their fortunes by securing railway franchises from the government of Philadelphia, which they personally owned; their associate, the ex-convict Samuel Yerkes, had followed their example in Chicago. The great railroad magnates—Sage, Stanford, Huntington—robbed the government, the public, and their own stockholders.

The chief problem that occupies Lapham at the outset of the story is the establishment of social relations that will make his daughters happy, and the author's major interest seems to be in showing the situation that arises from the impact of a person of humble origins and slight education upon a polished, complacent, and firmly rooted society. Many of the great money barons did, of course, seek social rank, but they seem to have met no such obstacles as Howells throws in the way of the well-meaning Lapham. Jay Cooke and Daniel Drew had early shown the extent to which ostentatious philanthropy could create social respectability, and Carnegie and Rockefeller followed their example on a scale that made their donations seem the pettiest of alms-giving. On the other hand, Jim Fisk was indifferent to polite opinion, and found consolation in his mistresses, his opera house, and his company of sycophants; his death at the hands of a rival in business and love brought him a fine funeral with a regiment of soldiers and a two-hundred-piece band to escort the corpse to the grave. Morgan, one of the few chieftains who could boast of wealthy parentage and a higher education, made the best of both worlds, enjoying all the sensual pleasures that money could bring as well as the adulation of the aristocracy. In Boston, perhaps, where fledgling millionaires of industry and finance were rare, the sons of Plymouth Rock looked askance at paint stains, but in New York, where the victors gathered to enjoy their spoils, the odorlessness of money was well understood.

The climax of the story, one recalls, comes with Lapham's great decision: twice he is tempted to sacrifice personal integrity in order to keep his fortune, once when he has the opportunity to sell a worthless mill, again when an alliance with his principal rivals is possible if he conceals his financial status. Both times he is firm, and he ends with honor, if in poverty. Such a dilemma, so far as one can see, never disturbed for a moment even the more restrained generals of industry. The climactic decisions of their lives related to concrete problems of manufacture, transportation, and finance. After all, they were fighting for the resources of a continent, and staking with each day's engagement everything they had and hoped for. If they bothered to apologize for their methods, it was not in the terms of Lapham's morality, but in the terms of definite achievements: the reduction of the running time between New York and Chicago, the crushing of chaotic inefficiency in the oilfields, the emergence of the nation as the world's foremost producer of steel. They dealt, these men, with gigantic problems in a spirit of ruthless realism, and if some contributed greatly to the material growth of the nation, whereas others merely enriched themselves at the expense of their fellowmen, it is hard to see that the motives of the former were in any way different from those of the latter. One thing is clear, and that is that neither the great rewards nor the great achievements would have been possible if they had spent much time in meditating on the problems that distracted Silas Lapham.

It is ironic, but by no means surprising, that the first novel of post-war industry should have as its central character a business man who, in methods, outlook, and ideals, belonged to the generation before the war. Although in the early years of the industrial revolution the Laphams had flourished, creating small fortunes by the relatively honest conduct of a single enterprise, they could play but an inconsiderable part in the new era of amalgamation and large-scale exploitation. Lapham belonged to the past, and so, as a matter of fact, did the grandeurs of the Boston society that he viewed with awe. Equally remote, though that was less apparent at the time, was the romantic dilemma of the Lapham girls and Tom

Corey, which Howells placed, in the construction of the novel, on the same level as Lapham's great decision. Yet *The Rise of Silas Lapham* was considered too bold and too searching by many of its readers, and Howells almost boastingly counted the cost of his "frankness about our civilization."

The sort of thing that Howells failed to do is suggested—merely suggested—by *The Money-Makers,* a novel that appeared the same year with no author's name on its title page. In time it proved to be the work of a journalist, Henry F. Keenan, who had been inspired to write it by his indignation at *The Bread-Winners,* which also had appeared anonymously, though its author was subsequently known to be John Hay. The style is crudely pretentious, the characterization is rough and unconvincing, the conduct of the action is erratic; but such incidents as the discrediting of Fred Carew, the rise of Aaron Grimstone, the political progress of Senator Killgore, and the repression of the Valedo trade unions resemble too closely certain historical events to be disposed of as implausible or unrepresentative. Keenan had little talent for fiction, and his mild radicalism was no comprehensive philosophy of society; but he was willing to include in his book the sort of material Howells ignored. Was that, then, the alternative? Was it necessary to be frankly a journalist in order to use in fiction typical men and events of the era of big business? If so, one can understand the hesitations of a William Dean Howells.

* * *

Howells, in telling the story of Silas Lapham, paid little attention to his relations with his workmen, beyond saying that he treated them well and they were loyal to him. On that ground as on others Keenan displayed his greater awareness of the actualities of the economic struggle. But perhaps

Keenan would have been less likely to emphasize the honesty and idealism of labor leaders and the handicaps of labor organizations in their struggle against men whose money bought them the services of traitors and spies, called to their support the resources of government, and enlisted on their side the weight of respectable public opinion, if he had not had in mind as he wrote *The Money-Makers* the account of workingmen's activities that had been presented in *The Bread-Winners.* To one of Keenan's views the great popularity of that book seemed to require some sort of counterblast, and he did what he could.

After the appearance of *Democracy* in 1880, Henry Adams playfully accused his friend and neighbor, John Hay, of being its author; when, in 1882, the *Century* began to print *The Bread-Winners,* Hay took the opportunity to reciprocate. It made a pleasant jest between them, this fact that each had written a first novel and published it anonymously. The real joke they were not able, at that time, to perceive. *The Bread-Winners* was the last contribution John Hay, who had dreamt of being a poet and a man of letters, made to literature; an illustrious career as diplomat and politician lay before him. To Henry Adams, on the other hand, who had scorned authorship and coveted political honors, the years, though they brought no eminence in affairs of state, did eventually bring fame as an author.

When Hay wrote *The Bread-Winners* he already had something of a literary reputation. Though he had read law after his graduation from Brown in 1858, had served as Lincoln's secretary, and had spent five years in various European legations, he had never forgotten the ambition formulated in his college days. In the sixties he had written a number of poems in the vein of Longfellow and Lowell, but in 1870 he had put forth in his *Pike County Ballads* a much less conventional kind of poetry and had won much wider popularity. The following year had come a collection of essays on Spain, *Castilian Days*. By that time the young man, who was employed as an editorial writer on the New York *Tribune,* had not merely begun a literary career but had indicated the direction his subsequent activities might be expected to take. In his poems and essays he had revealed a mild interest in the revolutionary movements of Europe and a typically midwestern faith in the principles of republicanism. In his *Pike County Ballads* he had shown himself not indifferent to such peculiarly American qualities as could be observed on the frontier. One might, in 1871, have conceived of his writing a book on the theme of *The Bread-Winners,* but one could not have foreseen the attitude he took towards this theme.

That attitude was largely the result of events that took place between the appearance of *Castilian Days* and the writing of the novel. In 1873 Hay became engaged to Clara Stone, daughter of a wealthy Cleveland financier. After their marriage they lived in a house that Amasa Stone had built for them on fashionable Euclid Avenue, and Hay opened an office in which he was chiefly engaged in helping his father-in-law. In the summer of 1877, while Stone was in Europe and Hay was in charge of his interests, railroad strikes, accompanied by riots, shook most of the country's industrial centers, including Cleveland. After the panic of 1873 the railroads, many of them bankrupt because of the speculative policies of their directors, had repeatedly cut wages, and in July of 1877 most of the roads in the country announced a general ten per cent. reduction. The strike began in Baltimore and spread, spontaneously and rapidly, as far as the Pacific Coast. Riots and pitched battles followed, with Pittsburgh the scene of the most violent outbreak. Hay, realizing that such activities threatened his newly established position, wrote hysterical letters to Stone, telling him that the country was at the mercy of the mob, that a disgraceful surrender to the strikers seemed likely, and that the devil had entered into the lower classes. After the strike had been put down and adequate reprisals instigated, he resumed work on the life of Lincoln and his regular services to his father-in-law, but he continued to meditate upon the conditions so disturbingly revealed in the strikes and riots. The fruit of his meditation was *The Bread-Winners,* one of the earliest American novels of industrialism and certainly, as William Roscoe Thayer called it, "the first important polemic in American fiction in defense of Property."

The hero of the book is Captain Farnham, a retired army officer who conscientiously devotes himself to the administration of his fortune. By chance he meets Maud Matchin, a girl whose usefulness to society—presumably as a domestic servant or as the dutiful wife of some lowly workman—has been impaired by the misfortune of a high school education. Her father is an honest but ignorant carpenter, and his assistant Sam Sleeny is humbly courting Maud. Matchin and Sleeny, in their ignorance and despite their essential goodness of heart, fall victim to the villainies of Andy Offitt, "the greasy apostle of labor," who has organized the Bread-Winners. We are shown how a strike begins and spreads, and how corrupt and self-seeking rogues take advantage of honest workers, persuading them to go against their own interests. We also see how a strike is defeated. Farnham organizes a group of veterans to protect the property of the industrialists. They, on their part, are not sorry to close their factories for a while. "We want nothing better than ten days' rest," one of them says. "We want to repair our furnaces, and we haven't a —— thing to do." Farnham's volunteers prevent the mob from damaging the homes of the rich, and he displays great personal bravery and wins the lady of his heart. The strike collapses. One of the employers says, "We shall . . . reengage on our own terms, next day, as many as we want. . . . We shan't be hard on them." And there is nothing for Hay to do but to wind up the romance.

When *The Bread-Winners* was reissued in 1899, Hay, still anonymous, wrote a preface: he had not attacked the working class or even trade unions; he had merely tried "to give an absolutely truthful picture of certain phases of our social life." He had not intended Farnham and Offitt to be regarded as representatives of their classes; he had merely utilized certain actual events that had come to his attention. Few readers, apparently, were naïve enough to believe him; it was generally taken for granted that the novel was intended to be what Hay's biographer called it, a polemic in defense of property. Yet Hay in answering his critics had described his novel more correctly than his enemies and had put his finger more precisely on its basic fault. The weakness of the book, both as polemic and as fiction, is its remoteness from the central facts of the industrial struggle. Farnham is certainly not a typical business man; he is simply the cultivated, courageous hero of popular romance, endowed for the purposes of the story with a sense of social responsibility. Offitt is not the kind of man who organized American labor in the years after the war; he is the bad man of Sunday School fiction. The struggle reduces itself to the immemorial struggle, so dear to melodrama, between good and evil, and in the end to little more than a personal conflict between the handsome leading man and the altogether unspeakable villain.

If, then, we confine our judgment to the characters *The Bread-Winners* presents and the story it tells, we find it a trivial book. It is trivial because, as Hay pointed out, it is not in the least a reflection of existing industrial conditions. Hay knew that he was attempting something new in American fiction; he subtitled his book "A Social Study." But he shrank from the implications of his task. Whether we assume that he deliberately chose to misrepresent the situation he had observed in 1877 in order to make a better case for the property owners in their fight against labor, or give him the benefit of the doubt by accepting his own interpretation of his intentions, we see that his people are unreal and his plot ludicrous because they are unrelated to the realities of American life in the seventies. It was impossible to describe even "a commonplace soldier, with a large property," if one refused to take into consideration the economic processes of the time. It was impossible to describe even "a little society, organized for his own ends by a criminal," if one paid no attention to the real grievances of the workers, the actual mechanism of strikes, and the extent and ideals of labor associations.

It is amusing to note in passing that Hay was considerably less realistic in his account of the conditions of labor than that arch romanticist and sentimentalist, Elizabeth Stuart Phelps. In 1871 the popular author of *Gates Ajar* applied herself to the task that Mrs. Gaskell, Charles Kingsley, and other novelists had earlier undertaken in England, the task of arousing Christian sympathy on behalf of the oppressed workers. Miss Phelps's faith in pious benevolence may not inspire respect, but she did have intelligence enough to study the reports of the Massachusetts Bureau of Statistics of Labor before writing *The Silent Partner*. When she describes the blacklisting of Bijah Mudge, the death of Bub Mell in the jaws of a machine, the home life of Sip Garth, or the general effect of a wage cut, she writes of what she knows. Such documentation does not make the novel a piece of literature, nor does it render Miss Phelps's theories any less ridiculous, but it at least suggests that John Hay might have known something about the labor movement if he had cared to.

Obviously he did not care to, and for very good reasons. The young westerner who had had his share of the idealism that went into the organization of the Republican Party had become the son-in-law and associate of Amasa Stone, railroad magnate and ally of John D. Rockefeller. The attitude of the author of *The Bread-Winners* is, at every point in the story, the attitude of a man of property. The fact that he did not embody his assumptions in any general reflection of the current scene is not, as he desperately tried to make it, a defense of his novel; it is the betrayal of his impotence as a writer. But if he failed as a fictional apologist for the *status quo,* his talents did not go unused nor his efforts unrewarded. Leaving literature behind him, he rose rapidly until he became Secretary of State. The posthumous collection of addresses shows that, though he could still speak on literary themes, he was at his most eloquent when praising the Republican Party as the creator of American prosperity. Not a doubt assailed him as he lauded McKinley, interpreted our occupation of the Philippines as a sacred mission, and defended the seizure of Panama. There was no real need for an apt apologist to bother with the intricate problems of the social novel.

*   *   *

When one considers the list of failures, it is no wonder that most of the ventures in the field of politics and economics are isolated experiments. If one excepts Judge Albion W. Tourgee, a violent partisan and ardent propagandist, whose novels of the Reconstruction were accepted, not altogether unjustly but much to his displeasure, as historical romances, there is only one writer who, persistently and as a matter of principle, devoted himself to the life of his own era. *The Rise of Silas Lapham* is not an isolated experiment; it is a fair sample of its author's work. Whatever else may be said of William Dean Howells, he was the one writer of the period who was convinced that "every inch of this America is interesting," and who acted on that conviction. Regardless of his limitations, it is only fair to observe that he wrote about more aspects and more important aspects of life in the United States than either his contemporaries or his predecessors. Cooper had written of Indians and sailors; Hawthorne had been at home only in a world of his own imagining; Melville had explored the Pacific. Howells refused to be so limited: he wrote of East and West, of villages and metropolises; he wrote of farmers and business men, journalists and doctors, Bohemian artists and Back Bay aristocrats.

In the novels of rural life in New England Howells shows himself almost as shrewd as the best of the regionalists and far less likely to deal with the purely idyllic. As a study of the New England character nothing could be better than the last chapter of *The Lady of the Aroostook*. Both *Annie Kilburn* and *A Traveler from Altruria* portray the trouble-breeding impact of summer visitors on the life of a small village. The effect of the city on the kind of character the country has formed is the theme of *A Modern Instance* and *The Minister's Charge*. Two of Howells' most impressive characters are village radicals and eccentrics—Squire Gaylord in *A Modern Instance* and Ralph Putney in *Annie Kilburn* and *The Quality of Mercy*.

In the city, especially Boston, Howells is even more at home. As one reads his books, noting the recurrence of certain characters in novel after novel, one appreciates his understanding of the kind of society that city produced in the days of its decline. There are played-out aristocrats such as

Corey and Bellingham, substantial men of affairs such as
Hilary and Halleck, eccentric and impractical reformers such
as Miss Vane, frivolous but well-intentioned young women
such as Clara Kingsbury, serious-minded young men such as
Hilary's son and Halleck's, conscientious ministers such as
Mr. Sewell, mildly discontented business men such as Basil
March, ambitious reporters such as Brice, and unscrupulous
reporters such as Hubbard and Pinney. Howells sees their
virtues and limitations, the Bostonian bias in their way of
thinking, their relation to the compact society of which they
are part, and in the novels and parts of novels that deal with
Boston he is not far from creating a convincing world.

New York, as Howells quickly realized, was not so easy to
master as Boston, but he made a brave effort "to use some of
its vast, gay, shapeless life" in his fiction. *The World of
Chance* and *The Coast of Bohemia* limit themselves to the
lives of publishers and artists, but *A Hazard of New Fortunes* aims at nothing less than a portrayal of the city's magnificent variety. Howells' choice of Basil March, one of his
favorite Bostonians, as central character, is wise: nothing in
the book is better than the chapters in which the Marches
simply wander about the city, noting its buildings and its
people. But these stanch Bostonians, it is made quite clear,
are not the only persons who have been attracted to the
metropolis, and we find in the novel the middle-western millionaire Dryfooses, the upstate Leightons, and the almost pro-
fessionally southern Colonel Woodburn and his wife and
daughter. The characters happen to be linked together by
their common interest in a magazine, *Every Other Week,*
but they are representative of thousands of New Englanders,
Westerners, and Southerners, caught in the whirlpool of
commercialism, and the various attitudes they take towards
the spirit of business enterprise are representative attitudes:

Fulkerson is its prophet; Conrad Dryfoos is its victim; March tries to be its detached critic; Lindau, immigrant and socialist, is its bitter enemy; Colonel Woodburn is a survivor of the system it has destroyed. No other American novel of the nineteenth century, except possibly *The Gilded Age,* can be compared in its scope with *A Hazard of New Fortunes.*

Howells knew what he was doing. When, in 1879, Henry James pointed out that America had "no sovereign, no court, no aristocracy, no church, no clergy . . . no country gentlemen, no palaces, no castles nor manors," and patiently asked what was left that the novelist could deal with, Howells replied, "We have the whole of human life remaining, and a social structure presenting the only fresh and novel opportunities left to fiction." These are words there should have been someone to say, someone who voiced not a youthful nationalism but a serious esthetic conviction. And, as his career was to show, Howells had a right to say those words if anyone did. He devoted his life to showing that America was rich in materials for the artist, not merely picturesque fragments out of the colorful past of the frontier, but great movements, dramatic characters, vivid situations.

Yet it is impossible to maintain that Howells made the most out of these materials, that he did for America what Tolstoy did for Russia or Zola for France. Whenever one reads a novel by Howells, one feels, as has already been observed in connection with *The Rise of Silas Lapham,* that he has not quite forced his way through to the center of the situation he has chosen to deal with. One feels, so to speak, that he is either asking the wrong questions or giving the wrong answers. In *The Quality of Mercy,* for example, he is asking whether a defaulter should repent, not why a business man is false to the trust that has been placed in him. In *Annie Kilburn* he wonders how the rich can help the poor, not how rich and poor happen to be in their relative stations. On the other hand, *Dr. Breen's Practice,* raising the question of women in medicine, confuses the answer by ending the book on a sentimental note. Similarly, *A Modern Instance,* which is concerned with divorce, fails to state the problem in its most representative terms, and, by turning Bartley Hubbard from a likable poseur to a contemptible rascal, distracts attention from the major issue.

Silas Lapham, one is further forced to admit, is also representative of Howells' work in that, though the material is typically American, the emphasis falls on elements of experience that do not quite correspond to the major movements in the life of the nation. In *A Hazard of New Fortunes* the reader, feeling that something important is being neglected, becomes impatient with the amount of attention devoted to the progress of the magazine, the home life of the Woodburns, and the various love stories. In *Annie Kilburn* there is far too much about amateur theatricals and far too little about the conflict between Gerrish and Peck. And there are the many novels, such as *April Hopes, The Coast of Bohemia, The Story of a Play,* and *The Vacation of the Kelwyns,* that, though good enough in their way, never once suggest a valid reason for Howells' having chosen to write them. There is something ironic in his making so little use of the wealth of resources of which he boasted to Henry James. Indeed, much of the time, instead of exploiting those resources, he was content to pose the kind of problem that James was posing, to much better effect of course, in terms of the established society and traditional culture of Europe. "My way," he said in 1904, "is still the byway."

It is, moreover, clear that Howells had not sufficiently mastered the civilization of which he was part to be able to deal incisively even with minor issues. In *A Hazard of New For-*

tunes the characters are confronted with the commercial spirit, but, whether they go with it, are broken by it, or seek to remain aloof from it, they do not understand it. Neither did Howells, and it is no wonder that, as he said, the novel "seemed to flounder along on a way of its own." Emerson, Melville, and Whitman have been called seers; that is the last thing one would think of calling matter-of-fact, easy-going William Dean Howells.

In his aims Howells was the kind of novelist America needed, and our literature would in many respects be poorer if he had not lived; but it is his aims that are important. For them we can be grateful, and we cannot too harshly condemn the failure of his actual achievement since we can so easily explain it. On the one hand, his experience was limited to a degree that was fatal to his ambitions as a novelist of contemporary America, limited by the kind of life he led and also by a certain deliberate unwillingness to look about him. On the other hand, he was a product of his age and subject to the confusions of that age. For Howells to have done what he really wanted to do he would have had to transcend personal, moral, and intellectual limitations of a sort that, as a matter of fact, no one in the years of his prime could transcend.

He was born in Ohio, raised in a family that had won its culture by its own efforts, and filled with literary ambitions before he reached manhood. In the Ohio of the late fifties any young man who thought of making literature looked hopefully towards New England. Thither the youthful journalist cast his envious gaze, dreaming day and night of becoming a contributor to the *Atlantic*. Thither he went in the flesh, for a short visit, when he was but twenty-three. He met Lowell, Hawthorne, Emerson, Thoreau, and—in New York—Whitman. It is significant that only one man of the five made a strong impression upon him, and that the one was Lowell. Hawthorne was kindly but, as always, remote; Thoreau somehow chilled the youth despite the bond of their admiration for John Brown; Emerson he did not understand; Whitman seemed, then as later, a barbarian. But Lowell—Lowell was not merely courteous and helpful to the youth; he represented everything that Howells, who had shared his family's struggle to maintain cultural standards in the face of poverty, recognized as his goal.

So it was again when Howells, returning from Venice, whither he had been sent as a reward for his campaign biography of Lincoln, found himself actually upon the staff of the sacred *Atlantic*. Hawthorne and Thoreau were dead; of Melville he had apparently never heard; Whitman, he remarked, made him tired. Of course Emerson was there, admittedly an Olympian, but remote, untouchable. Lowell, on the other hand, was approachable, friendly, a great and good man, Howells said, a man of the richest nature, a man of genius. He embodied for Howells the great New England tradition, he and Longfellow and Holmes. Howells differed from them in literary theories, and later in social theories, but he never lost his reverence for them or his sense that their lives must serve as models for his.

He had felt as a youth that he was "not formed to battle with life," and he had shrunk from the harsher side of a reporter's duties. The years of the war he passed in Venice. And then he returned to spend fifteen years as an editor of the *Atlantic* and a resident of Boston or Cambridge, associating daily with the custodians of the genteel tradition and accepting their conception of the literary life. Even when he went to New York it was as a recognized man of letters whose goings and comings were in literary circles. No college professor could have been more securely cloistered, more completely protected from contacts with the rough realities of politics and business. Of captains of industry he saw nothing except when he sat as honored guest at their literary dinners. Of farm laborers or city workers he saw as little; he observed them, of course, as he had observed the peasants and beggars in Italy, but in their lives he had no share. He wrote for the most part about gentlemen, preferably Boston gentlemen, and there is no doubt that he understood them and their wives uncommonly well. But from the greater part of that rich world he described to Henry James he was absolutely barred.

And from much in American life he was not sorry to be shut out. Here again his association with the respectable literary men of New England re-enforced the tendencies that had originated in his Ohio home. Of his prudishness there is only too much evidence. His first visit abroad convinced him that Americans were "manlier and purer" than Europeans, and it was his prayer that "America may grow more and more unlike Europe every day." On his return he defended Harriet Beecher Stowe's life of Lady Byron, and rejoiced that she had shown how "base, filthy, and mean" Byron was. Even the upright Charles Eliot Norton could not measure up to the standards of purity he enforced in the *Atlantic*. He rejoiced that his own books could be read by his children: "My children are my censors, and if I wished to be wicked, I hope they would be my safe-guards." Much as he admired Zola, he felt obliged to hide his books, and he maintained that even artistically they were vitiated by "the bad French morality." When Gorki, visiting the United States with a woman who was not legally his wife, found himself the object of attack, Howells, though sorry the Russian had been troubled, would not defend him. "He is a

simple soul," he observed, "and a great writer, but he cannot
do impossible things."

In *Criticism and Fiction*,[1] moreover, Howells sought to give
his poor provincial prejudices the dignity of esthetic principles. He argued that reticence does the artist no harm, for
books that have dealt "with love that was chaste, and with
passion so honest that it could be openly spoken of before
the tenderest society bud at dinner" have been "all the more
faithfully representative of the tone of modern life." A sincere man, with no gift for sophistry, he did not hesitate to
reveal his true position: "If the novel were written for men
and for married women alone, as in continental Europe, it
might be altogether different. But the simple fact is that it
is not written for them alone among us, and it is a question
of writing, under cover of our universal acceptance, things
for young girls to read which you would be put out-of-doors
for saying to them, or of frankly cutting yourself off from
the pleasure—and it is a very high and sweet one—of appeal-
ing to these vivid, responsive intelligences." And that, for
Howells at least, was conclusive. Even the literature of the
past, written "before an ethical conscience began to inform
it, or the advance of the race compelled it to decency,"
should, he believed, be made to conform to "the tone of
modern life." "I hope the time will come," he wrote in *My
Literary Passions*,[2] "when the beast-man will be so far subdued and tamed in us that the memory of him in literature
shall be left to perish; that what is lewd and ribald in the
great poets shall be kept out of such editions as are meant
for general reading. . . . At the ends of the ends such things
do defile, they do corrupt."

[1] Copyright 1891 by Harper and Brothers; copyright 1918 by W. D. Howells.
Quotations made with permission of Mildred and John Mead Howells.

[2] Copyright 1895 by Harper and Brothers; copyright 1922 by Mildred Howells
and John Mead Howells, with whose permission quotations are made.

It was not enough that Howells should be shut off, by training and profession, from vast sectors of American life; he must deliberately blind himself to still other elements in American experience. Yet we must not put too much of the responsibility for his faults on his seclusion and blindness; the nature of his approach to his material was also to blame. Howells called himself a realist, and within the rather narrow limits that have been indicated it was as a realist that he wrote. But the kind of realism that he believed in was inadequate for the task he had set himself, and behind that failure of method was a failure of understanding.

The type of novel Howells wrote is implicit in his two volumes about Italy, his first published work except for the Lincoln biography and the book of poems he wrote with J. J. Piatt. The success of *Venetian Life* and *Italian Journeys,* in which he presented the fruit of his observations during his four years in Venice, led him to wonder if the same method could not be applied to material nearer home, and he wrote *Suburban Sketches,* which differs from the earlier books only in the fact that it is based on observations made in Cambridge. It was a short step thence to *Their Wedding Journey,* with sketches of a railroad station, a hot day in New York, a trip on the Hudson River, and the scenery at Niagara Falls, and with a thread of narrative on which the sketches hang. The same formula served for *A Chance Acquaintance, The Lady of the Aroostook,* and *A Fearful Responsibility.* Not until he wrote *Dr. Breen's Practice* was Howells ready to dispense with his descriptions of travel and to unite his characters in a dramatic situation. The brief sketch had developed into something like the novel, and the novel itself, in the form of *A Modern Instance,* was just around the corner.

Gradually Howells had developed a definite and almost

unique type of novel. He had no theory at first, but in time the theory was formulated, and expressed in *Criticism and Fiction*. He scorned, of course, the improbable incidents of the romantic novel; he repudiated as well the grotesqueries and exaggerations of Dickens and the commentaries of Thackeray. Of his contemporaries he chiefly admired the Russians, for they knew how "to forbear the excess of analysis, to withhold the weakly recurring descriptive and caressing epithets, to let the characters suffice for themselves." But he made no attempt to reproduce the intensity of Dostoyevsky or the sweep of Tolstoy. He preferred a more modest, more placid kind of fiction, and it is by no means strange that, among English novelists, Jane Austen won his heartiest admiration. American conditions, he believed, invited "the artist to the study and appreciation of the common, and to the portrayal in every art of those finer and higher aspects which unite rather than sever humanity." "The talent that is robust enough," he wrote, "to front the every-day world and catch the charm of its work-worn, care-worn, brave, kindly face need not fear the encounter."

To front the every-day world was precisely what, all his life, Howells tried to do. From the Negro maid and the horse-car conductor in *Suburban Sketches* to Parthenope Brook and Alvin Kite in *The Vacation of the Kelwyns,* his characters are ordinary, if not always completely representative, Americans, faced with ordinary situations. They meet and marry, or they meet and separate. They write plays or preach sermons or manufacture paint. Howells was afraid of neither coincidence nor anticlimax. If a man and woman met and nothing came of their meeting, that was only what one could expect of life. If it was the merest accident that brought success to a struggling author, that was the sort of thing that happened in a world of chance. Howells did not keep a scrap-book, as Charles Reade is said to have done, but he was quite as scrupulous in checking the facts of his novels by the facts of observation.

Such a conception of the novel was not likely, it is clear, to summon forth all Howells' powers; though it encouraged the growth of observation, it discouraged the exercise of the will and the imagination. "Ah!" he once wrote, "poor Real Life, which I love, can I make others share the delight I find in thy foolish and insipid face?" Not, one is inclined to answer, without discovering beneath the folly and insipidity such capacities for joy and sorrow as link even the most commonplace of persons with the rest of mankind; not without finding, in the lives of the most foolish and insipid persons, the operation of the forces that shape the destinies of all. The realist, Howells said in *Criticism and Fiction,* "finds nothing insignificant; all tells for destiny and character; nothing that God has made is contemptible. He cannot look upon human life and declare this thing or that thing unworthy of notice any more than the scientist can declare a fact of the material world beneath the dignity of his inquiry. He feels in every nerve the equality of things and the unity of men; his soul is exalted, not by vain shows and shadows and ideals, but by realities in which alone the truth lives." But truth, neither for the artist nor for the scientist, is merely a matter of observation. Just as the scientist must seek relationships, must find the bearing of one fact upon another in order to comprehend either, so the artist must perceive, in his examination of this event and that event, some hidden pattern.

Nevertheless, this theory of Howells' was, though he did not recognize it as such, a necessary compromise between the demands of literary integrity and the difficulties of his era. It was essential that he should cling to the importance of the isolated observation, since he could perceive no all-embracing pattern. His work had to be more or less dull, more or less trivial, more or less confused, if it was to be honest. Had he been aware of a fundamental unity in American life, had an adequate social philosophy helped him to see the significance of what he described, had he possessed what we sometimes call vision, observation would have fallen into its properly subordinate place. As it was, fidelity to fact was his one great virtue and within limits he made the most of it.

Howells' interest in social problems began, naturally enough for the son and grandson of abolitionists, with participation in the crusade against slavery. But at the end of the Civil War he assumed, like so many of his generation, that all the nation's problems had been settled, and contentedly devoted himself to a literary career. In time, of course, as the scandals of the Tweed Ring and the Grant administration forced themselves upon his attention, he saw that he had been mistaken, but he accepted the prevailing custom of blaming our political ills upon the immigrant, and dismissed his worries from his mind. He wrote Rutherford B. Hayes's campaign biography, and he praised *The Bread-Winners.* He lived in comfort and peace, and he assumed that other people did the same. Not, in fact, until into the eighties did he become disturbed by the injustices of the system of which he was part. But he was after all the son of struggling westerners, and he had been brought up to believe in equality of opportunity, social and cultural as well as political. He could not indefinitely conceal from himself what was happening in America. The trial of the Chicago anarchists in 1886 shocked and stirred him. Hesitantly, and yet very bravely, he took his stand and accepted the consequences. His reading of Tolstoy sharpened his discontent with the existing order, and he began to describe himself as a kind of socialist. "Our competitive civilization is a state of warfare," he told Edward Everett Hale, and he wrote Mark Twain, "There is no longer an American Republic, but an aristocracy-loving oligarchy in place of it."

His social views are fully recorded in two books that take their place with the scores of Utopian novels written in the decade before and the decade after 1900. *A Traveler from Altruria* is primarily a criticism of the organization of society in America, written from the point of view of a member of a perfect society. In *Through the Eye of the Needle* the Altrurian returns to his native land, taking with him an American wife, whose letters to a friend describe the customs of that pleasant country. Altruria, we learn, after passing through a competitive stage, abolished private property and substituted social equality. Each citizen is required to work three hours a day, which is sufficient to provide all with the necessities of life. The remainder of the day is the citizen's, to spend as he likes, and it is in this period of voluntary labor that the nation's many works of art are produced. The needs of the people are slight: food—a purely vegetarian diet prevails; shelter—the climate has been changed so that this is an inconsiderable problem; clothing—there is a graceful but unpretentious national costume. They are very religious, and there is a devout sense of the brotherhood of man.

Pretty as all this is, it has, one can see, very little to do with the realities of the American problem. Howells was, in the first place, concerned with ends rather than means, and, except for his insistence on the peacefulness of the change, he paid little attention to the methods by which such a society might be created. In the second place, he carefully eliminated the whole question of industrialism by assuming that the Altrurians were for the most part able to dispense with machinery and by neglecting to tell how such machinery as they had was made and operated. In the third place, he assumed that social stability depends on a spiritual attitude, to which objectors are converted, rather than on any concrete program of production and distribution.

There is only one point at which Howells was able to relate the life of Altruria to his own American experience: he repeatedly calls attention to the fact that there are no domestic servants in Altruria. This emphasis reminds one of the extent to which he discusses the relations between servants and masters in his novels. Suddenly one realizes why this question so constantly concerns him: it is one social problem that actually touched his own life. And there is Howells—a kindly man, disturbed by the humiliations of butlers and maids, grieved by such sufferings as he might see on the street, depressed by obvious cases of the miscarriage of justice. It was all very unpleasant, but what could he do? He could not take to making shoes as his beloved Tolstoy had done; he saw that that helped no one, and besides, as he remarked with more bitterness than was customary with him, he preferred to "wear a fur-lined overcoat, and live in all the luxury my money can buy." He could not, after these long years of isolation, lead a political party or throw in his lot with the labor movement. He could not even—and this is the tragedy —free himself enough from the habits and prejudices of his upbringing and his manner of life to see the problem clearly.

Howells' socialism was at best the vague reaction of a well-intentioned, sensitive man to the contemporary spectacle of misery and greed. There is something pathetic in the joy with which he writes a friend that he has been to a socialist meeting and found it "as quiet and orderly as a Sunday School." We owe a dozen of his best books to the fact that, as he wrote Stedman in 1888, the economic phases of American life had become increasingly important to him. But that interest did not lead to an understanding of economic forces.

That is why Howells could not strike to the center of American life; that is why the issues in his books are never clear; that is why the persons and events he describes always seem to be not quite perfectly realized. That is why *The Rise of Silas Lapham* is not truly a novel of American industrialism, why *A Hazard of New Fortunes* fails to give a satisfying picture of New York in the eighties, why *A Traveler from Altruria* is only one more Utopian novel. That is, in short, the principal explanation of Howells' inability to make us feel that here is a master.

Limited by his way of living and his views on morality, confused in his thinking and condemned by that confusion to work with superficial phenomena, Howells was grievously handicapped in his attempt to make an enduring record of the life of his country and his time. Yet he tried, and it is to his credit that he tried so persistently. On certain important questions he saw the truth and held to it. He saw that the primary concern of American authors must be American life, and he practiced what he preached. He saw that the basis of fiction must be honest observation and a passion for truth. He had no fear of the commonplace, and it required merely courageous unconventionality to make his type of realism a useful instrument for the recording, if not for the interpreting, of the American scene. He was not too narrow-minded to praise Zola, and he did much to popularize Turgenev, Dostoyevsky, and Tolstoy in the United States. He aided and encouraged H. H. Boyesen and Hamlin Garland; he had words of praise for Crane, Norris, and Herrick. Wrong as he was on many issues, weak as he was at many points, he was, through the seventies, eighties and nineties, a force that impelled American literature, however hesitatingly, however feebly, in what history has shown to be the right direction.

Chapter IV

FUGITIVES

IN 1871, with his usual perspicacity in the statement of dilemmas, Henry James, after describing Howells as one who could write "solely of what his fleshly eyes have seen," went on, "For this reason I wish he were 'located' where they would rest upon richer and fairer things than this immediate landscape. Looking about for myself, I conclude that the face of nature and civilization in this our country is to a certain point a very sufficient literary field. But it will yield its secrets only to a really *grasping* imagination. This I think Howells lacks. (Of course *I* don't!) To write well and worthily of American things one need even more than elsewhere to be a *master*. But unfortunately one is less!"

How extraordinarily right James was, not only about Howells but also about America! We have seen why America would yield its secrets only to a really grasping imagination and have realized what mastery would involve. We have seen, too, why the nation was unlikely to produce masters: the impact of industrialism on a country only beginning to create an art and literature was necessarily more devastating than such a blow could be for nations with firmly established cultures. We can understand why flight, born of a desire to escape from a scene too unpleasant to contemplate and a situation too complicated to understand, was so common in the Gilded Age. It remains now for us to ask ourselves what, in its happiest form, flight could do for a writer.

When Sarah Orne Jewett was a girl, New England was changing. Cities were developing; huge, ugly buildings housed hundreds of employees; smoke blotted out the sky and soot mingled with the daily bread. Slowly industrialism pushed its way into the farming country, capturing the little towns, planting factories by every waterfall. The newly rich sought the beautiful mountains and lakes of New Hampshire and Maine, and their urban ways were discords. Many of the village people went away to the cities; others, touched by prosperity, abandoned the ways of their fathers. "It was easy," Miss Jewett later wrote, "to be much disturbed by the sad discovery that certain phases of provincial life were fast waning in New England. . . . While it was impossible to estimate the value of that wider life that was flowing in from the great springs, many a mournful villager felt the anxiety that came with these years of change." She felt that anxiety and, while still in her twenties, wrote *Deephaven* so that, in literature if not in fact, the life she loved might be preserved.

Fully conscious of what she was doing, she carefully represented in the book those aspects of life in a Maine village that she wished could endure. Because she sympathized with that life so instinctively and had participated in it so gladly, she wrote of it in *Deephaven* with a vividness that even now lights up the commonplaceness of Miss Carew, Captain Sands, and the other inhabitants of the little seaport town. Her knowledge of Maine customs, Maine people, Maine scenery, and Maine ways of speech was always, of course, a source of strength. From the days when her father took her about with him on his trips to his patients in the vicinity of South Berwick to her last visits to the little town, she watched and listened to and loved its people. Like Nan in *A Country Doctor,* she felt from the first a kind of vocation, but where Nan's call was to medicine hers was to literature. She began writing when she was in her teens and had contributed a story to the *Atlantic* by the time she was twenty. And she wrote, after one or two false starts, quite simply, out of the fulness of her knowledge. For her there was no problem of investigation such as had confronted Howells; the world she wrote of was her own world.

If she had a problem, it was, at first, that of putting a certain distance between herself and her material, in order to acquire literary poise. But that problem, too, was easily solved. There were no financial barriers to keep her from knowing the world outside of South Berwick. Boston was open to her, and, with Annie Fields as companion, she could soon count Longfellow, Lowell, Aldrich, and Howells among her friends. There was travel also: England, with visits to Arnold and Tennyson, Paris, Italy, Greece, the West Indies. And there were books, not merely the classics of her own country and England, not merely her beloved Thackeray, the Brontë sisters, Donne and Herbert, but the French and Russians also, Tolstoy and Turgenev, Zola, Daudet, Maupassant, Bourget, and Flaubert. If she knew South Berwick, that was not all she knew, and if she was provincial, she was provincial by choice.

With this equipment—the close, sensitive knowledge of the people she wrote about, and the awareness of a larger world of culture and refinement—she went tranquilly about her work, carefully selecting whatever served her personal needs and her literary purposes. "Écrire la vie ordinaire comme on écrit l'histoire," she copied out of Flaubert and pinned on her secretary. That is what she tried to do. But to write about ordinary lives as if one were describing the great pageant of history one must see in ordinary lives something of the grandeur and significance of historical events. That gift, so far as a certain limited kind of ordinary life was concerned, Miss Jewett had. In a story called "By the Morning Boat" the departure of a boy for Boston is so presented to us that we find it as exciting as he and as moving as his parents. The trip to Topham Corners in "The Hiltons' Holiday" makes itself felt as something epochal, the equivalent, let us say, of a trip to Europe, as indeed it was to the little girls. All that Helena Vernon means to the poor servant girl in "Martha's Lady" is communicated to us with the poignancy of Martha's own emotion. That sense of importance, which Miss Jewett so successfully conveys, is the product of insight based on sympathy. She understood and respected the tranquil dignity of Eliza in "Miss Peck's Promotion," the happiness of the self-sacrificing invalid in "The Life of Nancy," the simple mysticism of Sylvia in "A White Heron." It is because she knew how much these virtues meant to her, and could arouse in the reader a kindred response, that she rose so far above the merely nostalgic, sentimental regionalists. *The Country of the Pointed Firs,* a kind of miracle in pastel shades, varying between a delicate humor and a delicate pathos, is, within its limits, the finest American achievement in its *genre* and a work of which we can be permanently proud.

But one is always conscious of Miss Jewett's limitations. She was lost the moment she stepped outside her Maine villages, whether she wrote of Boston, or Irish immigrants, or the American Revolution. More important, she was safe, even in Maine, only within her chosen emotional range. The stronger feelings, the more violent passions, the more harrowing griefs, she could not portray. Her methods, however suitable for the portrayal of pathetic situations, failed when she was confronted with tragedy. In "The King of Folly's Island," for example, a dying girl is condemned to isolation by her father's stubbornness and robbed of her one glimpse of the larger world by the departure of a summer visitor; Miss Jewett softens here and modifies there until the outlines of the situation are lost and the anguish of the girl becomes pale and meaningless. In "The Landscape Chamber" a fierce pride and an irrational fear blur out weakly into mere idiosyncrasies. The family curse that is the theme of "In Dark New England Days" would be credible only in an atmosphere of savage hatred that the author cannot create. It is well that Miss Jewett usually ignored the harshness in rural life, for all her weaknesses were revealed whenever she forced herself to contemplate it.

There is, in short, nothing that we can admire her for except those delicate powers of perception that, under favorable circumstances, she could exercise so fruitfully. In other respects she was merely a New England old maid, who had a private income, traveled abroad, read the *Atlantic Monthly,* and believed in piety, progress, and propriety. She may have read Turgenev and Flaubert, Voltaire and Donne, but she praised Thomas Bailey Aldrich for his "great gift and genius of verse," called Tennyson the greatest man she had ever met, and thought *Pendennis* superior to *Anna Karenina* because more Christian. Like her dear friends, Mr. Lowell and Mr. Arnold, she believed that "the mistake of our time is in being governed by the ignorant mass of opinion, instead of by thinkers and men who know something." The Spanish-American War was, for her, "like a question of surgery . . . we must not mind the things that disgust and frighten us, if only the surgery is in good hands." A few years before she died she read Mahan's *Influence of Sea Power on History.* "One thing is so nice," she wrote Mrs. Fields, "about the fleets that are attacked having the best chance."

Her delicate powers of perception, however, give to the best of her work a richness, an authenticity, and a dignity that are too rare to be scorned. It was precisely because she so placidly disregarded what lay outside her little world that she could concentrate so effectively upon it. It was because she instinctively rejected characters, situations, and emotions that were not congenial to her that she could let her imagination play so calmly and sympathetically over the lives she chose to record. We may grant that she is only a minor writer, that the kind of pleasure her work offers only remotely resembles the effect of great literature, that the insight she gives us into men and women is only fragmentary. We may grant that her attitude is essentially elegiac, and that she writes of a dying world of old men and old women. We may even grant that her aims were virtually those of the other regionalists. But there is a difference. For a moment her people live and breathe. For a moment, as we yield to her art, we feel that here is a master, though a master of a tiny realm. Calmly, but with both instinctive determination and conscious artistry, she selected from the decaying New England about her the elements she admired, and out of them created a little world, not merely for the purposes of her stories but also for the needs of her personality. She found her refuge.

* * *

In the same letter in which he gave his estimate of Howells and his analysis of the writer's problems in America, James said, speaking thus at the very outset of his career, "To write a series of good little tales I deem ample work for a life-time. I dream that my life-time shall have done it." "It is art," he wrote the year before he died, "that *makes* life, makes interest, makes importance, for our consideration and application of these things, and I know of no substitute whatever for the force and beauty of its process." "The daily drama of his work," Percy Lubbock says, "was like a mystery to which he was dedicated. . . . He threw his full weight on the belief that supported him and it was never shaken. That belief was in the sanctity and sufficiency of the life of art." For half a century James preached and practiced this doctrine. It sustained him in the face of popular indifference, personal suffering, and social isolation. It dictated his place of residence, shaped his opinions, and determined his daily regimen. It is apparently the one subject on which he either felt deeply or thought long. Men have lived by many creeds less satisfying than Henry James's belief in the sanctity and sufficiency of art.

The doctrine can have had but few adherents in any age or place, but it is peculiarly surprising to find in the little band an American of the post-war decades. Only an unrepresentative American of that day could, one feels sure, have belonged to such a company. Unrepresentative Henry James, thanks in large measure to his father and grandfather, undoubtedly was. His grandfather had made a comfortable fortune in business, had invested his money wisely, and had left his descendants free to live as they saw fit. This boon permitted one of the descendants, Henry James the elder, to believe that the most important thing in life "was just to *be* something, something unconnected with specific doing, something free and uncommitted." For him, growing to manhood in an age when theology was still the principal concern of American intellectuals, this meant the privilege of cultivating independence in religious matters to the point of eccentricity. For one of his sons it meant devotion to art.

Everything conspired to keep the younger Henry James from throwing himself into any contemporary struggle. The family did not remain in one place long enough to permit of strong local attachments, and in his most impressionable years he was abroad. When the Civil War broke out, ill health prevented his participation. He had, then, uncommonly few ties to America when, in the latter sixties, he began to consider literature as a career, and he was conscious, as few of his contemporaries could have been, of the necessity of choosing between the United States and Europe. Twice he set out to learn for himself what the latter could offer, once in 1869 and again in 1872, but both times he returned. Europe was undoubtedly richer, more satisfying, but "the great fact for us all there is that, relish Europe as we may, we belong much more to that than to this, and stand in a much less factitious and artificial relation to it." It even seemed that "in our great unendowed, unfurnished, unentertained and unentertaining continent" it ought to be possible "to turn out something handsome from the very heart of simple human nature." He was trying hard to convince himself, but in 1875 he gave up the struggle and set out for Paris.

When, a few years later, James wrote in his biography of Hawthorne an implicit defense of his expatriation, he said, "The best things come, as a general thing, from the talents that are members of a group; every man works better when he has companions working in the same line, and yielding the stimulus of suggestion, comparison, emulation." In his own mind it was the absence of fellow-worshippers at the shrine of art that drove him from America. Yet in Paris, where he met Turgenev and Flaubert and their associates, he was unhappy. "I have seen almost nothing of the literary fraternity," he wrote Howells, "and there are fifty reasons why I should not become intimate with them. I don't like their wares, and they don't like any others; and besides, they are not *accueillants*." There was nothing for it, then, but London, whither he went. Soon he convinced himself that he had discovered the milieu he sought. "I feel now more at home in London than anywhere else in the world," he wrote. A breakfast with Lord Houghton and John Morley, dinner with Tennyson and Gladstone, the Oxford-Cambridge boat race, dinner at Lady Rosebery's—these were evidence that he belonged. Of course he had his moments of doubt: "I am still completely an outsider here," he wrote his brother in 1878, "and my only chance for becoming a little of an insider (in that limited sense in which an American can ever do so) is to remain here for the present." But after all, he had dined out one hundred and seven times in one season, and he had no reason to despair of the future.

It was in this period, flushed with his joy in the active social life so recently opened to him, that James wrote his *Hawthorne* with its famous list of the institutions America lacked: "No sovereign, no court, no personal loyalty, no aristocracy, no church, no clergy, no army, no diplomatic service, no country gentlemen, no palaces, no castles, nor manors, nor old country-houses, nor parsonages, nor thatched cottages, nor ivied ruins; no cathedrals, nor abbeys, nor little Norman churches; no great Universities nor public schools —no Oxford, nor Eton, nor Harrow." In short, no leisure class. That was what Henry James wanted. Both as a person and as a writer he needed the sanctions that an established class could lend to his individual tastes and activities. That is what he thought, in England in the late seventies, he had found. If the remainder of his life was a progressive disillusionment, if he was more and more forced back on his faith in the sanctity and sufficiency of art, that need not concern us now. He thought he had found a way of life that would permit him "just to *be* something, something unconnected with specific doing." He thought he had found a society that would provide him with the themes he preferred to write about. He thought he had found a group that would yield "the stimulus of suggestion, comparison, emulation." Everything that he wanted and needed and could not have in America now seemed to stretch before him.

The forces that sent James to England were the forces that determined his theory of the function of art and his conception of the proper field for literary activity. In both respects the peculiar course of his life strengthened tendencies that were rooted in the economic situation and cultural habits of his family. For James art was not a form of action but a form of enjoyment, and the artist was not a participant but an observer. He had not taken part in any of the great movements of his day, not even in that supreme struggle that had absorbed so many of his contemporaries. And since he potentially belonged to and certainly shared the ideas of the leisure class, which by definition has no economic function, non-participation seemed to him a virtue rather than a fault. In the same way, his conviction that the novelist should deal with the phases of life farthest removed from the basic struggles for existence is evidence not merely of the limitations of his own experience but also of the influence on him of the standards of a class that refused to justify its existence in terms of anything that it did. Upon these two conceptions James elaborated a superstructure that is still a marvel to novelists and a joy to critics. Out of the idea of the artist as observer came his whole preoccupation, in its way so fruitful, with the question of the novelist's point of view. It made him an ingenious experimenter and, within his limitations, the sharpest of observers. His interest in what Lubbock calls "the results and effects and implications of things" encouraged in him a subtlety that no American writer has equaled. Yet he could not transcend the ideas and principles, the prejudices and blindnesses, of "the little world of urbane leisure." He was often vexed with that world and its standards, but, as Percy Lubbock has said, "at the moment of greatest revulsion he never suggests that the claims may be fraudulent after all, or that this small corner of modernity is not the best and most fruitful that the age has to show." Indeed, James could scarcely have repudiated that world without repudiating all that he had been and done.

So far as his writing was concerned, James could not, of course, plunge at once into the life of the British leisure class, with which he had chosen to affiliate himself. The theme that occupied him during the first decade and a half of his career was the international, as "The Passionate Pilgrim," fruit of the visit he paid to England in 1869, had announced. The people he best understood were Americans, "other apprehensions being," as he later said, "absolutely bolted and barred" to him. The scenes he best knew were in Europe. The particular kind of American he could, out of his own experience, most fully comprehend was the kind that came to Europe. Therefore, from Clement Searle to Isabel Archer, James's characters make their way across the Atlantic, gaze with rapt surprise upon the European scene, and are humbly initiated into the mysteries of a superior civilization.

James's choice of material is thus easily understood, but his attitude towards it has no such obvious explanation. In "The Passionate Pilgrim," balancing Searle's longing for Europe with Rawson's eagerness to visit America, he seems to be telling us, with a baldness of which he must later have been ashamed, that the advantages are not all on one side. He repeated himself in his first novel, *Roderick Hudson,* weighing the hero's losses and gains, and contrasting Mary Garland's simplicity with Christina Light's sophistication; and in *The American* his admiration for the businesslike Christopher

Newman was so marked that Howells hailed it as a sign of spiritual repatriation. In "Madame de Mauves," "The Reverberator," and even "The Siege of London" his sympathies and ours are with Americans, and "Lady Barbarina" and "An International Episode" contain direct criticisms of the bad manners of British aristocrats and their indifference to art. And it is always the distinctively American characters that he selects for our appreciation; for expatriates—one thinks of Gilbert Osmond, the Countess Gemini, Madame Merle, and Mrs. Touchett in *The Portrait of a Lady*—he has little but scorn.

Though he deliberately aimed at fairness, striving not to let his own alienation from the United States prejudice his accounts of his fellow citizens, it was not merely objectivity that led James to portray his native Americans as fresh, intelligent, and above all else honest. If he went to England because there was no class in America to which he could be loyal, he turned back in spirit to America because he could not be completely assimilated by the British leisure class. There was not only the fact that he was an American; there was also the fact that he was an artist. For many decades the British aristocracy, whether one looks at that section of it that is actively occupied with the administration of the state or at the section that constitutes the leisure class properly so called, has not been deeply concerned with art. This indifference, this abnegation, as he regarded it, of one of the great duties of a leisure class, James resented. No matter how many dinners he went to—and the number considerably diminished in time—this resentment effectively separated him from the people whom, on so many other grounds, he admired. To a certain extent, both because of the insularity of the English and because of discrepancies in taste, James could not be a participating member of the British leisure class, and to that extent he remained conscious of his American backgrounds. When he depicted the radiant virtue of Mary Garland and Isabel Archer, the emerging fineness of Francie Dosson, the sensitiveness and intelligence of Christopher Newman, the dogged loyalty of Caspar Goodwood, or the dignified honesty of Mr. Wentworth, he was reminding himself of all the resources on which, as American, he could count.

To this divided loyalty we owe James's peculiar fitness for the portrayal of the international scene. In his treatment of this scene he made constant progress, sloughing off the crude documentation of *Roderick Hudson,* the implausible melodrama of *The American,* and the diffuseness of *The Europeans,* until, in *The Portrait of a Lady,* his strength and lucidity beautifully revealed themselves. From the introduction of Isabel at Gardencourt to her sad departure thence to rejoin her husband in Florence, we participate in this drama of an awakening mind. For the first time James gave himself leeway, building solidly both his places and his people, allowing ample time for the character of Lord Warburton to define itself, giving Henrietta Stackpole opportunity to disclose the fineness beneath her barbaric surfaces, permitting Madame Merle to display all the brilliance that so charms the ingenuous Isabel, preparing step by step for the heroine's encounter with Gilbert Osmond. No earlier creation of James's rose in so solid and dignified a structure, and none could show characters so varied and so thoroughly understood.

Just before writing *The Portrait of a Lady,* James had published a novelette, *Washington Square,* in which, for the first time since the juvenile *Watch and Ward,* he occupied himself exclusively with American characters against an American background, as if, in the maturity of his powers, he had decided to give America another try. The book is admirably planned and sustained, but it is all too clear that James is making the best of a bad matter. Writing to Howells, in defense of the thesis he had advanced in *Hawthorne,* he spoke of *Washington Square* as "a tale purely American, the writing of which made me feel acutely the want of the 'paraphernalia.' " It may be justly pointed out that this thin little tale makes not the slightest effort to use the grandeurs that America could offer, but we must recognize that it was this sort of material James could and wanted to deal with, and that the 'paraphernalia' was indeed lacking. Like Isabel Archer, Catherine Sloper is deceived by a superficial impressiveness, but the difference between their stories is measured by the difference between Gilbert Osmond and Morris Townsend, between Madame Merle and Mrs. Penniman; Isabel's story is tragedy and Catherine's little better than farce. The background of *The Portrait* is rich and intrinsically attractive; that of *Washington Square* is empty and dull. The conversation is accurate but banal, and in general the style is severe and colorless. If this was the best he could do in America, it is no wonder James could see little hope for success if he continued in that direction.

Yet he was willing to try again, and within a few years he had published *The Bostonians.* The temporal conjunction of this book and *The Princess Casamassima* suggests how eagerly he was seeking to escape from bondage to the international theme, for if *The Bostonians* is purely American, *The Princess Casamassima* is, despite the princess' own origin, purely European. Neither ranks with James's best works, and the reasons for the two failures are somewhat similar. In both he was less concerned than usual with the leisure class, and in both he ventured, contrary to his usual practice, into the field of social theories. So far as material went, he was not too badly off in *The Bostonians,* for he had had considerable opportunity to observe Boston society in its decline, but for the analysis of the conflicting opinions involved in the story he was quite unfitted because of his ignorance of the fundamental issues in the struggle for feminine independence, and he had to resort to a conventional and unconvincing resolution of the dilemma he set forth. In *The Princess Casamassima* his predicament was even more marked. What he proposed to do was to defend civilization against the attacks of the dispossessed majority by demonstrating that this majority has a stake in the finer things of life, as cultivated by the privileged minority. This thesis forced him to deal not only with ideas that he did not grasp but also with types of character he did not understand. The only way for him to conceal his ignorance was to make his hero, Hyacinth Robinson, completely exceptional both as a member of the working class and as a radical; he did succeed in making Hyacinth plausible, but in doing so he defeated his fundamental intention.

James had tried, and by his own high standards had failed. There are fine characters in both books: Miss Birdseye, Selah Tarrant, and Dr. Prance in *The Bostonians;* Miss Pynsent, Anastasius Vetch, and Madame Grandoni in *The Princess*. In the latter, moreover, there is the subtle portrayal of Hyacinth's development and the genuinely romantic picture of the princess. But neither book is "done" as James intended to "do" his subjects; they could not be because they involve varieties of experience he was incapable of understanding. The qualities he so effectively analyzed in *The Portrait of a Lady,* for example, could not, in these books, be isolated from other qualities that baffled him. The life he was describing, especially in *The Princess,* was too close to its basis to be within his range.

There remained one field for him to occupy, and he made haste to explore it. In *The Tragic Muse* he concerned himself, as he had not done in *The Princess Casamassima,* with the kind of Englishman he had personally known. The result is—unfortunately for the high hopes with which he had undertaken the experiment—the dullest and least moving of his longer novels. On one side *The Tragic Muse* is moderately convincing, for James could always write eloquently of the appeal of art. But on the other side—the side that should have displayed his knowledge of English life—it is lamentably deficient. Nick Dormer's political career never seems a real temptation, or even a real alternative, for the reason that the political life of England is never presented to us as a comprehensible and important form of human activity. Whether we consider Nick's vaguely patriotic emotions, Mrs. Dallow's ambitions, Peter Sherringham's diplomatic vagaries, Lady Agnes' hysterical appeals on behalf of her deceased husband's ideals, or Mr. Carteret's devotion to election statistics, the whole political scheme of things is vague and meaningless, a cross between a beguiling game and a sacred mystery. Into the basic desires of the aristocratic administrators of England, their methods and aims, we are never given a moment's insight, and yet on a knowledge of all that the success of the book, as a presentation of a conflict and its resolution, clearly depends. In the year that *The Tragic Muse* was published, James wrote Howells, "One thing only is clear, that henceforth I must do, or half do, England in fiction—as the place I see most to-day, and, in a sort of way, know best." Those qualifying phrases, "half do" and "in a sort of way," may have meant no more for James, with whom such expressions had become a mannerism, than they usually did; for us they are altogether significant. It is no surprise to find him writing his brother, *"The Tragic Muse* is to be my last long novel. For the rest of my life I hope to do lots of short things with irresponsible spaces between."

For five years he devoted himself to the theater, spurning "the pale little art of fiction." His professed motive, to make money, can scarcely be credited, and Percy Lubbock must be right in saying that he really wanted to acquire a following, to win for himself the kind of recognition that had been promised by his earlier successes but subsequently denied. Again he failed, and in what was for him a singularly humiliating way. He returned to the novel in 1897 with *The Spoils of Poynton* and *What Maisie Knew,* which he followed with *In the Cage* in 1898, *The Awkward Age* in 1899, and *The Sacred Fount* in 1901. All of these books are located in England, but not one of them throws any light on English life. James had no intention of repeating the mistake he had made in *The Tragic Muse,* and he painstakingly isolated his characters from the social conditions in which they presumably have their roots. In *The Spoils of Poynton,* which charmingly reflects James's love of beautiful objects rich in tradition, the isolation may be justified, and in *What Maisie Knew* the method of presentation, so ingeniously maintained, demands such isolation. But one becomes suspicious when one finds the working class heroine of *In the Cage* a lady by birth, a snob by inclination, and a thoroughgoing Jamesian in her habits of thought and speech. Doubt grows as one discovers, upon going below the technical brilliance of *The Awkward Age,* that its persons have no visible connection with the rest of London society and exist as human beings only on what may be called a Jamesian level. And when one comes to *The Sacred Fount,* one is forced to conclude that James has moved into a realm that bears scarcely any relation to life as it is lived on this planet. In this realm a woman drains her husband of his youth and a man drains his mistress of her intelligence; the principal concern of most of the guests at a week-end party is the attempt to discover who the second woman, the mistress, is; this investigation is carried on according to tacitly accepted but rigid rules, and it is assumed to be of absorbing interest and real importance; the participants in the chase are capable alternately of the most astounding subtlety and the profoundest stupidity, and none of them seems to have any interest in life aside from this inquest. Such reckless disregard not merely of the findings of psychology but of the facts of everyday observation suggests how far James was willing to go in order to deal with his own kind of problem exclusively in his own terms.

To the same conclusion we are brought by the short stories that we find in such volumes as *The Lesson of the Master* (1892), *Embarrassments* (1896), *The Soft Side* (1900), and *The Better Sort* (1903). They are less distressing than the novels, for one is accustomed to taking more for granted in the short story. Indeed, in their own way they are superb, whether James develops some macabre theme as in "The Turn of the Screw" and "The Way It Came" or writes a parable as in "The Beast in the Jungle" and "The Great Good Place," whether he paints a portrait as in "Glasses" and "The Birthplace" or builds to a dramatic climax as in "The Tree of Knowledge" and "Paste," whether he works with the short story proper or with "our ideal, the beautiful and blest *nouvelle.*" But where is such a life led as he describes? Even in the stories of writers and artists, in which James might have had the advantage of first-hand knowledge, there is nothing one can denote as realism. After all, who has ever known such artists? Where are the Hugh Ververkers, the Mark Ambients, the Neil Paradays, the Overts, Limberts, Dencomes, Delaways? The question occurred to

James, and he answered it: "If the life about us for the last thirty years refuses warrant for these examples, then so much the worse for that life. The *constatation* would be so deplorable that instead of making it we must dodge it: there are decencies that in the name of the general self-respect we must take for granted, there's a kind of rudimentary intellectual honour to which we must, in the interest of civilization, at least pretend."

But this is the purest romanticism, this writing about what ought to be rather than what is! And it is to exactly that that James had come. Failing to find a satisfying standing ground in America, unable to obtain more than a foothold in England, he effectively removed himself from the soil of both countries, abandoning the realistic principles he had heartily expounded in his first enthusiasm for Balzac, Flaubert, and Turgenev. That he was consciously a romanticist cannot be assumed. The very fact that he returned to the international scene for his later novels is evidence of his ingenuousness and good faith. But his long alienation from his native land, though it had not enabled him to master Europe, had robbed him of that awareness of American responses to European sights and people that had informed his earlier work. He had to dodge more than one deplorable *constatation* and to take decencies and much else for granted. What, to all intents and purposes, he asked from his readers was the willing suspension of disbelief.

The three late novels—*The Wings of the Dove, The Ambassadors,* and *The Golden Bowl*—display the height to which James's peculiar virtues had been raised. They are "done" as nothing earlier had been; there is not a moment in them when he has not complete control of character and situation. And yet one needs only to compare them with the earlier international novels to recognize the price he had

paid for perfection. Milly Theale in *The Wings of the Dove*
is another Madame de Mauves, another Isabel Archer; but
Isabel emerges from a recognizable domicile, passes through
a series of credible adventures that contribute to a natural
development, and meets her apparent defeat at the hands of
human beings with human motives, whereas Milly is pure
innocence confronted by the essence of sophisticated, selfish
intrigue. Christopher Newman and Roderick Hudson were
Americans of their time, coming from more or less representative situations and endowed with more or less typical
manners; Strether in *The Ambassadors* is not an American,
but merely a receptive barbarian, whose one attribute is the
preparation of his mind for the impressions it receives, not
in any spot recognizable on the map, though James does call
it France, but in "the great good place." And *The Golden
Bowl,* with its extraordinary dialogue and its interminable
hair-splitting, depends on the reader's granting James's assumption that Maggie is a person of unusual simplicity and
innocence, though her every thought and deed reveal a
falseness beside which Charlotte's so-called duplicity is posi-
tively admirable.

When he finished *The Golden Bowl,* James's work as a
novelist was virtually ended. He threw himself into the preparation of his collected works, with their extraordinarily
revealing prefaces, published an account of his visit to the
United States in *The American Scene,* and wrote two volumes of autobiography. His ambition was unflagging, and
in 1908 he occupied his mind with a plan for an American
novel, a novel wholly located on American soil. In 1909 he
began work on it, and in 1914 it took shape as *The Ivory
Tower.* The published fragment and his notes for the remainder help us to understand the workings of his mind.
On the one hand, it seemed to him quite possible to write

a novel about American business men without any knowledge of business conditions: "I haven't proposed," he stated in his notes, "at all to be definite, in the least, about financial details or mysteries—I need hardly say." On the other hand, he proposed to make the book a vindication of the leisure class. At the very outset the weary millionaire Betterman admits that he likes Fielder because the latter has "never done three cents' worth of business." And in the end Fielder was to triumph over the unscrupulous Horton Vint by sheer indifference to Vint's scheme of values. Thus James planned his revenge; he would show how business men could be humbled by a person who was, quite simply, a man of leisure.

James gave up *The Ivory Tower* when the war broke out, and though he returned to an earlier undertaking, *The Sense of the Past,* his chief interest was in the war. He threw himself into war activities with the most amazing fervor, in view of his age and the state of his health, and his zeal on behalf of the Allies surpassed the zeal of most Englishmen. It must have been gratifying to him to feel that at last he had identified himself with the people in whose midst he had established himself, and to celebrate his success he became a British citizen. Fortunately death came long before the danger of disillusionment.

Henry James's career was over. He had not been altogether unhappy, for what was for him the greatest interest in life remained vital almost to the end. But in many respects his career had been less than satisfying. After the first successes he had written for a smaller and smaller audience: "I have felt for a long time past," he wrote Howells in 1895, "that I have fallen upon evil days—every sign or symbol of one's being in the least *wanted,* anywhere or by anyone, having so utterly failed." Nothing seemed to remedy the situation, and he resigned himself to writing for the sake of writing. "In our conditions," he said, "doing anything decent is pure disinterested, unsupported, unrewarded heroism." But he did want some sort of appreciation. In how many of his stories we find unrecognized geniuses—"The Figure in the Carpet," "The Next Time," "The Middle Years," "The Author of Beltraffio," "The Death of the Lion," "Broken Wings." Each of these geniuses, however, finds one person who understands him. That was what James wanted—not mere appreciation of his technique, for that was not altogether lacking, but an understanding of the mysterious figure in the carpet. He wanted some one to understand him as he did not, in reality, understand himself. He wanted some one who could point out where, in the universal scheme of things, such work as his belonged. He wanted some one to justify him.

There have been men who thought they understood James and tried to state the justification of his career. There has been a kind of James cult. But the majority of readers, however thoughtful and patient, have rejected him. Have they not been wise? No one can deny that considerable insight went into the writing of the earlier novels, and even in the later books there are moments when a subtle power of observation and understanding makes itself dazzlingly apparent; but for the most part James's novels and tales seem completely remote from the lives of the vast majority of men. And why should one read a novel if it does not give him a sense that he is moving, with enhanced powers of perception and a greater certainty as to direction, through the strange world of which he is part? It is all very well to praise James's technique, but could one not fairly characterize the literary processes we have been describing as a game? Is not James's world a world of almost complete abstractions, in which he invents the situations and the people, and only the technique is constant. Grant that he was a master of the game, and that the game, if one consents to abide by the rules, is fascinating to play; it is still a game.

The trouble is not that James wrote about the leisure class. One can write of any minority, however vastly removed they may seem to be from the rest of mankind, in such a way as to make their lives interesting and of first importance. One can even, as Proust has indicated, write of the leisure class as a member of the leisure class, without severing oneself from the interests and needs of one's fellowmen. The trouble is that, in a sense, James did not write about the leisure class; he did not, that is, fully and convincingly re-create leisure class life. The omissions in his novels are altogether significant. Even in the earlier novels, for example, we are seldom shown by what means characters are supported; either there is no indication of a person's economic status, or we are told that he has become rich by virtue of "a native financial faculty of the finest order." James, indeed, boasted that he had no understanding of the American business man. And yet some knowledge of economic processes is obviously essential to the interpretation not only of America but also of England, not only of business men but also of landed gentlemen, prosperous widows, and practicing artists.

But that is not all. In James's world the people, though some of them die, do not suffer from ordinary ills, and no gross physical suffering is ever present in their lives or even to their sight. They are mysteriously preserved from the spectacle of poverty, and, with an exception or two, they apparently assume that everyone in the world is as happily placed as they. They talk a strange language, such as one has never heard spoken. Their lives involve the subtlest nuances of thought and emotion, and they are capable of the most minute distinctions in problems of conduct. On the other hand, the clearest moral issues are often clouded for them, and they sometimes act with a perversity that can scarcely be accounted for. Though they occasionally engage in adultery, they give no evidence of physical passion. They never seem to read books, and the educational processes they have gone through are usually vague; yet they are perfectly at ease in the discussion of literature, art, or history. They accept the stupefying routine of the society in which they mingle, but personally they are sensitive and subtle. How, we may legitimately ask, are we to relate such lives as these to such lives as ours? We know there are aristocrats in England; we know there are millionaires in America; we assume that these people live in the same world as we do, and that that fact would be revealed in an adequate presentation of them. In James's novels, alas, they seem to—and indeed they do—live in a world that is almost totally different.

It would be wrong to suggest that any of James's books—even such absurd novels as *The Sacred Fount* and *The Outcry*—are completely unreal; but their contacts with reality are too fragmentary and too tenuous for them to have more than secondary value. He had begun his career with certain conceptions of life and literature that prevented him from making any effective attempt to understand his own country. Thus driven abroad, he tried to identify himself with the British leisure class. If he could successfully have done so, his whole career would have been different, but such identification was impossible, not only because he was an American, but also because his standards of leisure class life, formulated in terms of his own interests and desires, separated him from the actual British aristocracy. This disappointment might have made him a critic of his class, and indeed he did attack minor faults; but his tastes and his hopes were too

deeply rooted in "the little world of urbane leisure" for him
to wish to destroy it. So placed, he could only create a more
ideal leisure class in his imagination, and devote all the resources of his art to portraying it in his novels and tales.
For him, as for the characters in one of his stories, "literature was a game of skill, and skill meant courage, and courage meant honour, and honour meant passion, meant life."
His refuge was not England but the realm where art was
sacred—and sufficient.

* * *

Henry James's grandfather had made money and left his
descendants free to live as they saw fit; Emily Dickinson's
grandfather devoted himself to the advancement of evangelical Christianity in the Connecticut Valley and bequeathed to
his family the responsibilities of that cause. Though he chose
the law rather than the ministry, he was the mainstay of the
local church, and his great achievement was the founding of
Amherst College as a bulwark against infidelity. His son Edward inherited his father's practice along with his obligations to church and college. His failure to join the church
until he had reached middle age argues, perhaps, the existence in him of some such spirit of rebellion as was to manifest itself in his daughter, but it did not prevent him from
loyally serving both that institution and the college. From
the first lawyers had constituted the secular arm of the
Puritan theocracy, and Edward Dickinson took his duties
seriously. He was chosen to Congress, and he was called
Squire by his fellow-townsmen—an honor probably as pleas-
ing to him as any within their power to bestow.

By the time Emily was born the Puritan theocracy had
made its last stand; it was no longer able, as the Unitarian
schism showed, to dominate New England. Its foundations
were tottering: the cultivation of the land to the westward

struck at the prosperity of its small farmers; its merchants were losing their power at sea. The building of textile factories in Lowell and Lawrence marked the beginning of a new era. Yet Amherst, in 1830, was still a Puritan village, with its life centered in the church and the church-controlled college. The new currents of life had thus far left it untouched; Edward Dickinson, stalwart defender of the old order, was largely responsible for the coming of the railroad in 1853.

In such an environment Emily naturally occupied her young mind with religion, and her early letters bear much testimony to the seriousness of her affirmations and her doubts. At the age of sixteen she was lamenting her failure to make her peace with God and asking a friend to pray for her. After a college revival she regretted that she "did not give up and become a Christian," and the death of Leonard Humphrey filled her with solemn thoughts of the hereafter. With her reflections there mingled, it is true, both suggestions of doubt and touches of mild irreverence; but it may be questioned whether, either in her pious or her profane moods, she greatly differed from other young women of her day. Certainly thoughts of religion did not darken her life; she could be gay and even giddy. She engaged in such social life as Amherst afforded, and even the most intuitive of her friends must have believed that she would, in due season, marry some minister, lawyer, or teacher, and settle down in conventional domesticity.

By some event, still a mystery, that path was closed to her. In one sense what happened does not matter. Reading the letters we can see that, as Colonel Higginson observed, "the mystic and bizarre Emily is born at once between two pages," and that is enough to confirm the tradition that somehow love was aroused and frustrated. How Emily would have adjusted herself to domesticity we cannot surmise; it may have been well both for her and for poetry that the adjustment did not have to be made. As it was, she turned to solitude. There were inner resources for her to rely upon, fortunately for us, for otherwise she would have been one more New England old maid, of the kind Mrs. Freeman so often described, instead of the most distinguished poet of her generation.

For a person of Emily Dickinson's intensity no compromise was possible: either she accepted the active life of the average woman of her day, or she lived in and for herself. For her as a poet, in other words, solitude was imperative. The spirit of her age, of those momentous years between 1850 and 1880, could only have interfered with such an imagination as hers. In other ages, perhaps even in the period of Emerson, she could have found some nourishment in the life about her, but by the time her poetic powers were ripe, that was impossible. Presumably, after her love had proven fruitless, she wanted to live as she did live and write as she did write; it is, however, worth observing that, whether she knew it or not, she had no choice.

If we want proof, we need only turn to the work of those poets who were in the public eye in the post-war years. They enjoyed their popularity and went to their graves believing they had enriched the literature of the world. To be their kind of poet in the Gilded Age was not to live in a garret; on the contrary, Americans were eager, as Henry James pointed out, to bow down and worship the man of letters. If poetry was musical, graceful, and easily understood, if it reflected the current morality, if it sounded like Tennyson, and if it avoided the expression of personal passion, the promulgation of religious heresy, and the use of any theme that had not been sanctified by at least two generations of poetic tradition, its author was highly esteemed and well rewarded.

The appreciation of art had become a mark of social distinction. The church was no longer at the center of American life; politics had been debauched; business was not quite respectable. Poetry helped the moderately prosperous Americans who read it to forget the gross struggle for material goods, and yet it did not hinder their participation in that struggle. So long as it was completely removed from the great affairs of the day, poetry had an enormous appeal, even reaching, at one end of the scale, some of the malefactors of great wealth and, at the other, some of their humble victims.

Plenty of persons appeared to meet this demand for polite poetry, foremost among them Thomas Bailey Aldrich, with Taylor, Stoddard, Stedman, and Gilder not far behind. Precocious, talented, genteel, Aldrich devoted himself to enamelling discreet trifles and, on occasion, to voicing in portentous odes his faith in the righteousness of the Republican Party and the superiority of the Anglo-Saxon race. The others were as willing slaves as he, and their poetry like his never shook off its chains.

By contrast the homely humor and pathos of the dialect poets are a relief. The popularity of Bret Harte, the success of John Hay's handful of Pike County ballads, and the long-continued vogue of James Whitcomb Riley suggest that the polite poets may have been praised more than they were read. And it can at least be said for these men that they sometimes spoke with authenticity of life as it was being lived. Riley, like the urban poets, voiced a complacency based on ignorance, blindness, and self-deceit, but his sympathies were with the common people, and he gave little comfort to those who wanted to be convinced of their own superiority.

For a person with a capacity for original perception and a longing for individual expression, neither the genteel poetry of the city nor the self-consciously rude poetry of the country could have been attractive. E. R. Sill, for example, though he leaned towards respectability, was driven by self-distrust out of the beaten paths of the Aldriches and Gilders, and wrestled in solitude with his own problems. Sidney Lanier, perhaps because he was a southerner, was outspokenly critical of commercialism. He could declare,

> *If business is battle, name it so:*
> *War-crimes less will shame it so,*
> *And widows less will blame it so.*

But all he could propose was to substitute love of art for love of money. In practice that meant that poetry should be a refuge from the pressing problems of life, and as if to justify this evasion, Lanier elaborated his theories of the parallel between poetry and music. His own verse is musical enough, but too often it is nothing else.

The qualities that raised Sill and Lanier above such artificers as Aldrich were the qualities that made Emily Dickinson tower over the other poets of the period. Since she was forced into solitude, as we have seen, her age spoke in her poems only negatively, only in their omissions. The positive content comes from Emily herself, from her observations and from the influences of her childhood, which was of another age. Many of her poems are undistinguished: her loneliness did not nourish a capacity for self-criticism, and she left not only much work that is crude in expression but also some that is conventional in conception. But she reminds one, nonetheless, of the great poets: her experience, though limited, was intense; her perceptions, though active in but a small field, were original.

Emily Dickinson's theology has, obviously, little significance to-day, but her religious experiences are not without interest, simply because she describes and interprets them so personally and honestly. In her poems one feels the vitality of both Puritanism and the revolt against Puritanism; they are alive for us because they were alive for her. Emerson's doctrine of self-reliance takes on substance by virtue of its immediate reality for a real person, even though self-reliance meant for that person merely an isolated life in Amherst, Massachusetts. And what is true of her religious experiences is true of all the others that figure in her poems. Like Thoreau she could find importance in the simplest events of nature, and she was perhaps even more successful than he in communicating her sensitive perceptions to her readers. The limited observations of field and garden furnished themes for many poems and images for many more. And there was, of course, a whole field of experience, closed to Thoreau, that Emily returned to time after time in her poetry. We may not know who her lover was or why she never married him, but surely no American poet has written so movingly of love and renunciation. Sometimes she spoke with the utmost simplicity; sometimes passion merged with religious aspiration in a cry of fierce and almost agonizing intensity. The exaltation of the mystic is in most of her poems, whether her theme is life or death, heaven or hell; but that exaltation rests upon a singularly intense response to altogether human joys and fears.

To compare Emily Dickinson's poetry with the verse of her contemporaries is almost to deal with incommensurables. Though her themes are often metaphysical, her poems contain none of the platitudinous discourses on philosophy that Lowell introduced into his odes. Not only are her love poems free from sentimentality; they never suggest the slightest awareness of the romantic, prudish doctrines of contemporary respectability. She wrote of birds and flowers as if no one had ever written of them before. Literary conventions did not exist for her; as a poet she was quite untroubled by public opinion. Everything in her work is immediate, personal, and honest.

And yet the poetry of Emily Dickinson is undeniably fragile and remote. The discovery of her work is, for any sensitive reader, an exciting event; one responds eagerly to so complete a revelation of personal experience. But, close as her life comes to the lives of her readers, it touches them at very few points. It is as true of her as it is of Sarah Orne Jewett or Henry James that her strength is her weakness. The fact that she would not publish her poems in her own lifetime, though she was not unwilling to have them published after her death, indicates, among other things, that she was aware of the impossibility of coming to terms with her own age. By this gesture she severed herself from the Gilded Age more effectively than Miss Jewett could do in her Maine village or James in his home at Rye. This permitted her to avoid all the contamination of an era of uncertainty and of false values, but at the same time it meant that she could have none of the vigor that is found in an artist for whom self-expression is also the expression of the society of which he is part.

As Henry James somehow complements Howells, so that, as Emerson once said of Hawthorne and Alcott, the two of them might make one real man, so Emily Dickinson complements Walt Whitman, and the two of them, one feels, might make one poet. Where Whitman was merely expansive Emily Dickinson was intensive, but where she was narrow he was broad. And, though she did what she set out to do more effectively than he, just as James wrought more finely than Howells, the future was not with her, nor with James, but with Howells and Whitman. As one weighs the faults and the merits on both sides, one sighs with Emerson, "So many promising youths and never a finished man!"

Chapter V

STRUGGLE AND FLIGHT

"Perhaps some day—say 1938, their centenary—they might be allowed to return together for a holiday, to see the mistakes of their own lives made clear in the light of the mistakes of their successors; and perhaps then, for the first time since man began his education among the carnivores, they would find a world that sensitive and timid natures could regard without a shudder." Thus Henry Adams concluded his *Education*. Rhetorician to the end, he perhaps exaggerated his hope, as throughout the book he had overstated his despair; but he expressed for his contemporaries their vague expectation of a deliverance they would not live to see, as he had expressed, so very fully, their bewilderment and realization of defeat.

It was not because they were peculiarly timid or abnormally sensitive that so many men of the late nineteenth century shuddered at the spectacle of contemporary civilization; it was because they increasingly felt the hostility of that civilization to the values they had accepted. The beginnings of a vital American culture had come with the decline of the mercantile class and the emergence of the small business man and the independent farmer. The doctrine of self-reliance Emerson preached was put into practice, if not quite in the way that Emerson desired, and the triumph of democracy, as sung by Whitman, seemed, when Lincoln was elected President, a not unattainable dream. Because their roots were in the same soil, because they had fought side by side for what seemed to be the same ends, men of letters and men of affairs were, in the years after the Civil War, by no means hostile to each other. Evidences of the alliance are everywhere to be found: Howells wrote two campaign biographies; Howells, Hay, Harte, Lowell, Motley, and Taylor held diplomatic positions; one of Mark Twain's closest friends was Henry Rogers, of Standard Oil; George W. Cable was entertained at Andrew Carnegie's estate in Scotland; literary lions of all sizes regularly adorned fashionable dinners given by New York millionaires. Many authors were critical of particular politicians and particular business men, but they were slow to attack the political and economic system itself.

Gradually distrust grew. Lowell, confused as he was, came, as we have seen, to recognize that the ideals he had advocated in his youth were farther than ever from realization. Mark Twain became more and more cynical. Howells, who only a decade before had eulogized the Republican candidate for President, was startled into skepticism by the murder of the Chicago anarchists. George William Curtis, child of Concord and Brook Farm, turned desperately to civil service reform as a method of saving government from complete corruption at the hands of business. And the younger generation of writers repudiated, almost unconsciously, all ties with the dominant class. Bellamy dreamt of a socialist Utopia; Garland allied himself with the revolting farmers; Boyesen preached sermons on the moral costs of the rise to wealth; and Lafcadio Hearn fled to Japan.

In the decade from 1890 to 1900 writers began to realize that they could no longer assume a community of interest between themselves and the rulers of America. The majority of nineteenth century authors had accepted in all good faith the belief that American democracy meant equal opportunity for all citizens. They had expounded the doctrine of individualism, the duty of each person to develop his own talents. They had believed that intellectual integrity was and must be the basis of politics. And then they discovered that the very persons who had talked most loudly of democracy, individualism, and honesty when the old order was yielding to the new, had straightway created a system in which special privilege was the rule, the individual was helpless, and duplicity was essential to success. The leaders of industrialism had changed; the ideals that had seemed so real to them while they were rising to power no longer had any significance so far as they were concerned. But authors and artists still clung to those ideals, though to do so led to a repudiation of the social system they had helped to create.

That there was reason for alarm in the nineties is obvious. If Grant's administration had revealed the dangers of political corruption, and the depression of 1873 with the strikes of 1877 had disillusioned believers in peaceful industrial progress, another depression, a series of strikes, and a prolonged reign of graft had driven home the lesson. The evidences of financial inequality were before every eye, and it required little discernment to recognize the forces that would rapidly widen the gap between the possessors of great wealth and the masses of the people.

It is not to be supposed that the novelists and poets of the nineties saw with perfect clarity the outcome of existing tendencies or sought any fundamental remedy for the evils about them. They merely exercised their prerogatives as individualists and sought to break away from the existing order. For many of them—Hearn, Harland, Saltus, and eventually Crane—this repudiation was expressed in a departure from America. For others—Garland, Bellamy, Boyesen—it took the form of criticism of particular aspects of social organization. But all of them felt—some consciously, others unconsciously—that they had little in common with either the avowed or the real rulers of the nation.

Of the critics not the least acute was Henry Adams, who had the advantage of having been born an outsider. Both his great-grandfather and his grandfather had held office at times when the balance of interests permitted them to act with considerable independence, and the Adamses had come to regard governing as their particular function. His father, Charles Francis Adams, had deliberately looked about him to find a party that could use him and that he could use, and his selection of the Free Soil Party led to his appointment as Minister to England. Thus it was natural that Henry Adams, writing his brother from Germany in 1858, should say, "There are two things that seem to be at the bottom of our constitutions; one is a continual tendency towards politics; the other is family pride." Politics was the only career he could seriously consider. In religion he had little interest, and he felt his talents for business were slight. As for literature, he said he would rather die than bring low the name of Adams by becoming "a writer of popular sketches in magazines; a lecturer before Lyceums and College societies; a dabbler in metaphysics, poetry and art." Law was the path to politics, and he studied law. In Washington, before his father sailed, he enjoyed the sense of power that he derived from being in the midst of wartime activity, and in England he took his duties seriously, more seriously than he was willing to admit when he wrote the *Education*. When he returned to America, he was disturbed by the changes that had taken place, and he quickly realized that in such an administration as Grant's there could be little place for an Adams. Yet he at first tried to wield an indirect influence through journalism and later returned to Washington, after seven years at Harvard, gravitating to a capitol, as he said, by a primary law of nature. Though he became increasingly doubtful of his own chances and increasingly contemptuous of politicians, he did not cease to hope for the emergence of "our party" until the death of his wife destroyed, for many years if not forever, all personal ambition.

If the Emersons thought they were born to be educated, the Adamses thought they were born to hold political power, and Henry shared the family conviction. But the ruling class in America in the decades after the Civil War had no use for the Adamses, a fact not wholly to the discredit of the family. It is not to be supposed that the Adamses were deeply concerned for the masses of the people, but they had their own standards, which made them unacceptable to the industrial capitalists. In his *Education* Henry speaks of the antipathy between Quincy and State Street, an antipathy based on the fact that the financiers could find more serviceable tools than the Adams family. Although Brooks Adams blamed the decline of the family on the rise of democracy, Henry saw that this could not be the explanation since it was obvious that the masses were not in power. What a politician needed, he realized, was the ability to serve the masters of capital while giving the masses the impression that he was serving them. Being unwilling and perhaps unable either to help the capitalists or to delude the people, he found no opening in politics.

Henry Adams correctly attributed his failure to achieve the only kind of career he desired to the maladjustment between his type of character and the social situation in the United States in his lifetime. But that maladjustment in no small measure explains his success as a critic. On the one hand, his interests forced him to occupy himself with the contemporary scene, and on the other hand, they kept him at a certain distance from it. It is in a way extraordinary that he did not accept any of his several opportunities to escape from a situation so unfavorable to his development and so unflattering to his self-esteem. He might have settled down as an expatriate dilettante in Europe; he might have remained in the Far East; he might have occupied himself exclusively with medievalism and spent his days in the security of the twelfth century. But, though he was tempted many times, he always returned to his study of American life, and the result was one of the most enlightening books in our literature, *The Education of Henry Adams.*

Early in the *Education* Adams says of himself, "He and his eighteenth-century troglodytic Boston were suddenly cut apart—separated forever—in act if not in sentiment, by the opening of the Boston and Albany Railroad; the appearance of the first Cunard steamers in the bay; and the telegraphic messages which carried from Baltimore to Washington the news that Henry Clay and James K. Polk were nominated." Here, of course, is the keynote of the book: Henry Adams grew up in a new world, a world created by the rise of industrialism. Few people were aware of what was going on: "Even the violent reaction after 1848, and the return of all Europe to military practices, never for a moment shook the true faith. No one, except Karl Marx, foresaw radical change." But when Adams and his family returned from England after the war, they could not ignore the course of events: "Had they been Tyrian traders of the year B.C. 1000, landing from a galley fresh from Gibraltar, they could hardly have been stranger on the shore of a world so changed from what it had been ten years before." "The world," he wrote, "after 1865, became a banker's world." In 1892 he found few protestants against "a banker's Olympus,"

and the repeal of the Silver Act a year later was final evidence
of the power of the financiers: "All one's friends, all one's best
citizens, reformers, churches, colleges, educated classes, had
joined the banks to force submission to capitalism." "The
whole mechanical consolidation of force . . . ruthlessly
stamped out the life of the class in which Adams was born,
but created monopolies capable of controlling the new ener-
gies that America adored." That mechanical power was to
shape the world Adams fully recognized, and he tried to
make his peace with the new deity in his hymn to the
dynamo. That the capitalists would control that power in
their own interests he also saw, and, though he offered no
open resistance, he refused to grant his approval.

Few men in America, even in 1907 when the *Education*
was written, saw so clearly what was happening. Adams, as
he says, had "in a half-hearted way, struggled all his life
against State Street, banks, capitalism altogether." Yet it
seemed to him that, at that particular stage, the kind of system that had been created "must be run by capital and by
capitalist methods." He could only regret the fact and count
the cost. He was rather sorry for the capitalists, pathetic
figures for the most part, who could do nothing with power
when it came to them. He was certainly sorry for the American people, "wandering in a wilderness much more sandy
than the Hebrews had ever trodden about Sinai." Education
had been debauched, he saw, partly because in its traditional
form it did not contribute directly to financial success, partly
because the capitalists controlled the colleges and would not
brook criticism. Art had been affected, both by changes industrialism had brought about and by the confusion of values
involved in capitalism. Older codes of ethics had been completely invalidated.

Henry Adams observed all this and tried to understand

how it had come about. The *Education* is by no means a complete picture of the period: he scarcely mentions the labor movement, the revolt of the farmers, or the suffering of the masses of the people. He was incapable of broad sympathy, and the actual cost of capitalism in terms of sweat and blood meant little to him. He frequently refers to Marx, and at one point says of himself, "By rights, he should have been also a Marxist, but some narrow trait of the New England nature seemed to blight socialism, and he tried in vain to make himself a convert." One doubts if he tried very hard: his case against capitalism was that it had destroyed the prestige of the Adams family and ruined the political prospects of Henry Adams. His book was largely an apology, an attempt to justify himself by showing that his failure was not his fault, and this accounts for the tiresome affectation of humility, the occasional touches of self-pity, and the recourse to cheap cynicism, as well as for the indifference to the oppression and the rebellion of the working class. But if Adams was not an admirable man, he was an interesting one, and the *Education* gives one an excellent idea of the development of American thought from about 1800 to 1925. The first ideas that he imbibed were not those of his generation, not those current in the forties and fifties in Concord and the more intellectual portions of Boston; they were, as he stated, eighteenth century ideas, the ideas of his great-grandfather. Very rapidly he caught up. In England he became acquainted with the writings of Lyell and Darwin, Comte and Marx. On his return to America he began his study of capitalism, and, because he remained outside the struggle for wealth and power, he went a long way towards understanding America in the decades after the war. Finally, with the breakdown of personal ambition, he arrived at an attitude that has only become common in the last fifteen years. It is amazing to note at how many points Adams anticipated the writers of the twenties, and it almost seems as if his work had been written, as theirs was, at a time when capitalism was rapidly decaying. He worshipped force, boasted of his ennui, complained of the sexlessness of Americans; he preached the general futility of action and the particular hopelessness of political effort; he made elaborate generalizations, not in order to influence the age in which he lived but merely to amuse himself; he pointed out the value of Catholicism as a refuge from struggle and a bulwark against change. It is little exaggeration to say that *The Education of Henry Adams* carries us from the adolescence of American industrial capitalism to its senility.

* * *

All his life Adams remained indifferent to the movements that sought to remedy those evils of capitalism he so clearly saw. As the challenge of transcendentalism and Utopianism, still resounding in his youth, left him unmoved, so the concrete struggles of laborers and farmers meant nothing to him. He read *Capital,* but he paid no attention to the rise of socialism in America. The organization of the Socialist Labor Party in 1877, the growth of anarchism in the eighties, and the emergence of the Socialist Party under Debs in the nineties did not touch his life. He was equally indifferent to Ira Steward's campaign for the eight-hour day, the rise and fall of the Knights of Labor, and the establishment of the American Federation of Labor. Greenbackism and Populism he regarded merely as curious phenomena, and he paid little attention to either Henry George's denunciation of the landowners or Henry Demarest Lloyd's attack on the monopolies.

But all these movements existed, to testify that, however

passivity might become an Adams, there were others who would not—who could not afford to—accept defeat so placidly. In 1888 the growing forces of revolt found literary expression in Edward Bellamy's *Looking Backward*. A practicing journalist, author of several romances, he set himself to work in 1886 "to reason out a method of economic organization by which the republic might guarantee the livelihood and material welfare of its citizens on a basis of equality corresponding to and supplanting their political equality." Where his sympathies lay he had already made clear in *The Duke of Stockbridge,* a novel of Shays's Rebellion, which appeared in a Berkshire newspaper in 1879. Though he was very much an amateur when he wrote it, he showed that the historical novel might be more than a polite diversion, and he demonstrated, by presenting the case for the oppressed farmers and workers of the period after the Revolutionary War, his friendliness to those who in his own time were struggling against their exploiters.

The practice *The Duke of Stockbridge* and his other romances had given him undoubtedly helped Bellamy when he came to write *Looking Backward*. Crude and unessential as the narrative now seems, with its circumstantial account of Julian West's long sleep and its systematically interpolated references to the progress of his love affair, it was to no small extent responsible for the book's wide circulation. Readers picked the book up as seekers of amusement and laid it down converts. Though Bellamy made no claim to originality, the book and its sequel, *Equality,* gave hundreds of thousands of Americans their first understanding of the possible achievements of socialism. Bellamy did not repudiate the machine, as Howells virtually did in *A Traveler from Altruria.* He not only saw the creation of an ordered society as the result of industrialism, but also recognized that such a society would avail itself more fully than could any capitalistic state of the possibilities of machinery. In the year 2000 every able-bodied person works; everyone receives the same income; distribution has been rationalized; farms have been collectivized and industrialized; domestic labor has practically been abolished; the productivity of industry has been immeasurably increased. If it had no other importance, *Looking Backward* would be significant as a work based on the confident assumption that the machine is not the enemy but the potential servant of mankind.

But Bellamy's insight into the possibilities of the social control of industry did not free him from the prejudices of his training and his economic position. Not only did he predict a peaceful transformation from capitalism to socialism; he expected that transformation to take place under the leadership of enlightened members of the middle class. It is significant also that social conditions in the year 2000 are presented exclusively through the eyes of professional men, doctors, teachers, or ministers; we are told of the happy lot of the working man, but we never see the new order from his point of view. As we shall see, this curious and quite unconscious omission on the part of the first American writer to set forth the advantages of socialized industry was characteristic of socialistic novelists in the decades that followed. Progress was made but very slowly.

The value of *Looking Backward* to its own period, however, should not be underestimated. It was widely read, and led to the formation of Nationalist Clubs and the founding of the *Nationalist* and the *New Nation,* and was followed by scores of other Utopian books. Ignatius Donnelly, veteran campaigner for the farmers, predicted in *Caesar's Column* bloody revolution and ultimate chaos. In *The Great Awakening* Albert Merrill staked all his hope on monetary reform.

Bradford Peck, a merchant, wrote *The World a Department Store* to announce the triumph of the co-operative movement and the Christian spirit. Henry Olerich advocated "practical co-operative individualism." H. W. Hillman in *Looking Forward* pointed to electricity as the agent of change. Though none of the Utopists adequately analyzed the economic and political situation, and though many of them were mere faddists with fantastic proposals, the rise of Utopian literature did focus public opinion on the possibility of changing the social order, challenging both complacency and cynicism and counteracting the tendency to work for petty reforms and to be satisfied with halfway measures. Some of the Utopists advocated a return to agrarianism, but most of them followed Bellamy in demonstrating the necessity and the possibility of the humanization of industry. In the midst of suffering, confusion, and hopelessness they rallied to a great standard, to the assertion that man could control the productive forces. If their zeal was accompanied by ignorance, they nonetheless raised their voices on the side of justice and used such weapons as they had in the great battle of the age.

*   *   *

That battle was going on on many fronts, and at the time Bellamy published *Looking Backward* it was raging in the Middle West. The farmers had not shared in the prosperity of the post-war years, and yet the West felt the depression of 1873 quite as sharply as the East. In the Patrons of Husbandry and the Greenback Party they recorded their discontent, but the good crops of the early eighties led them to abandon their struggle. In 1889, however, the wheat crop was only one-third of what it had been in 1885, and money was scarce and interest rates high. Countless farmers, attracted to the West by land agents' promises of prosperity, labored from sunrise to sunset, only to deliver the fruits of their toil into the hands of bankers and railroad magnates. Though agricultural production grew, the lot of the farmer did not improve, and the proportion of tenant farmers increased. It was no wonder that organizers of the People's Party, campaigning up and down the agricultural states, met with a response that suggested the enthusiasm of the crusades. It was not a narrow nor a fantastic program they advocated: they wanted financial reform, an income tax, postal savings banks, public ownership of the means of transportation and communication, and the restriction of the possession of land to actual producers. The farmers became conscious not only of their own ills but also of the oppression of other classes, and they proposed measures that they believed would protect the downtrodden everywhere.

It would have been strange if that wave of revolt, so charged with emotion, had not had its literary effect. Its spokesman was Hamlin Garland, who, in the late eighties, returned to Minnesota after two or three years of self-education in Boston. He looked about him, and for the first time he really saw the middle border. He saw his family and their neighbors, defeated, downhearted, degraded. "I perceived beautiful youths becoming bowed and bent," he afterwards wrote. "Some of my playmates opened their acrid hearts to me. . . . Every house I visited had its individual message of sordid struggle and half-hidden despair. . . . All the gilding of farm life melted away. The hard and bitter realities came back upon me in a flood." And he not only saw; he felt, surging within himself, the bitter resentment that was rousing the West to action. Joseph Kirkland, who had written two painstakingly accurate novels of rural life, *Zury* and *The McVeys,* told Garland that he was the first dirt farmer in literature and should make the most of that fact. Kirkland was wiser than he knew: Garland's power sprang from his identification with the farmer's cause. Ed Howe, who had published *The Story of a Country Town* in 1883, knew and portrayed the harshness of life on the middle border, but he was a bitter, disappointed newspaper man, whose bitterness set him apart from instead of allying him with his neighbors. Garland came from a farming family, had worked on a farm, had farmers for friends and neighbors, and he made their cause his cause and their enemies his enemies.

In his play, *Under the Wheel,* Garland's sympathies were all with the Edwardses, who, escaped from the slums of Boston, have been led to the West by the extravagant promises of unprincipled speculators, to be beaten down by the harshness of nature and the greed of men. Crude as the play is, the scene laid in the boomer's office is effective propaganda, and the climax of the fourth scene, when hail comes instead of the longed-for rain, is moving drama. And though the tragedy of the Edwards family is complete, the play holds out promise to the farmer. "Courage," one character says, "you will yet live to see the outposts of the enemy carried, and Linnie will live to see a larger and grander abolition cause, carried to a bloodless Appomattox, the abolition of industrial slavery. . . . Over us the shadow still hangs, but far in the west, a faint, ever-widening crescent of light tells of clear skies beyond."

It was in this spirit that Garland wrote the stories in *Main-Traveled Roads* and *Prairie Folk,* though he made no such attempt at direct propaganda as he had made in his play. The former is dedicated "to my father and mother whose half-century pilgrimage on the main-traveled road of life has brought them only toil and deprivation." As we read of the unhappiness of the woman in "The Branch-Road," the contrast between Howard and Grant in "Up the Coolly," the reception of Ed Smith in "The Return of the Private," Haskins' defeat in "Under the Lion's Paw," we know what toil and deprivation are. Garland does not neglect the humor and kindness of the people of the middle border, but he places these pleasanter characteristics against a background of dull, monotonous, ceaseless struggle. The stories are not merely honest—and honesty was rare at the time they were written; they are stirring stories, by virtue of the power of the protest that is implicit in them. And there is some of the same power in passages of *A Spoil of Office* and *Rose of Dutcher's Coolly.*

Reading *Crumbling Idols,* a collection of literary essays, one sees that Garland never fully realized why he had written so surely and soundly in his short stories. His conscious aim was simply to do for the middle border what other local color writers were doing for their sections; that his alliance with the most vital force in his region had made his work superior to that of the ordinary sectionalist he never understood. He protested against slavish subservience to tradition, but he was as much in bondage to Victorian prudishness as any of his contemporaries. He praised the heroism of labor and called for the abolition of special privilege, but he also glorified the sturdy individualism of the pioneer and preached the doctrine of success. His veritism was no stronger than Howells' realism, and his acceptance of the most sentimental of the regionalists indicates the superficiality of his theories.

Perhaps it was because Garland so imperfectly understood what he had done that he abandoned so readily the high ground on which he at first established himself. After the first five or six years of literary activity his career is almost pure tragedy. Reading his many autobiographical volumes, we find that even as a boy he felt the urge of the pioneer to better his circumstances: he wanted to succeed, to raise himself and his immediate family out of the slough of poverty. In accordance with this ambition he went east to prepare himself for literature. When he returned, equipped with standards by which to measure the misery of middle border life, and armed with the revealing theories of Henry George, his sympathies reached out beyond the Garlands and the McClintocks to embrace the whole class to which they belonged. This zeal made not merely a reformer but a writer of him. He no longer fumblingly sought for subjects and methods; his life had a center, a purpose, that concentrated all his experience and imaginative power. The result was the finest stories yet written of American farm life—direct, comprehensive, moving, and savagely honest.

The fiction thus inspired laid the foundation of a literary career, and gradually Garland realized his ambition for his family. Though far from wealthy, he found himself on the road to comfort and respectability. Accepted in literary and academic circles, he became fastidious and a little contemptuous of dirt and disorder. "The reform impulse was steadily waning," he wrote, describing the middle nineties. "*Looking Backward,* like *Progress and Poverty,* was a receding, fading banner." He forsook Populism and Bryanism for more respectable causes, and good naturedly confessed that his days of controversial writing were over, that he was "in league with the capitalistic forces of society." Young writers such as Norris and Dreiser he only half-heartedly accepted; on the other hand, his own acceptance by the academicians was a constant joy.

He yielded to the temptations of the new popular magazines with their higher prices. S. S. McClure candidly advised him, "Drop your literary pose," and he did his best to obey. When he established himself in Chicago and his family on the old Wisconsin homestead, his ties with the struggling farmers were broken. "The pen," he said with pardonable pride, "had proved itself to be mightier than the plow. Going east had proved more profitable than going west." But this deracination involved the finding of new themes, and these he sought in the farther, wilder West. "I perceived," he wrote, "that almost any character I could imagine could be verified in this amazing mixture." He embarked upon a career as romantic novelist, and, as he has boasted, anticipated Zane Grey. Between 1900 and 1917 he wrote a series of highly colored tales of western adventure, with one or two experiments in the novel of psychic experience and an occasional venture in the profitable field of juvenile fiction. But during these years he was unhappy and restless. His novels achieved no spectacular success, the money that his new responsibilities and tastes demanded was not forthcoming, and his creative powers grew constantly feebler. Finally he began to write his autobiography, emphasizing the heroism of the pioneer rather than the cruel realities of agrarian oppression, and throwing over everything the charm of reminiscence. When at last *A Son of the Middle Border* was published, and was greeted by Howells' flattering review, the road to success was open. Garland had found a way to utilize the only vital experiences of his life while maintaining his new standards of respectability. Other autobiographical volumes followed, each one a step to greater comfort and a more impeccable standing. The rebel had vanished. "The poor are almost obsolete," he wrote in one of his autobiographies. In another he referred to "the all-conquering genius of Mussolini." And in the campaign of 1932, speaking as "a theoretical radical," he endorsed the candidacy of Herbert Hoover.

It is interesting to speculate as to what might have happened to Hamlin Garland if he had kept his loyalty to the humble, hapless farmers of his early stories, and had extended his loyalty to embrace urban as well as rural laborers. He might have avoided the whole period of unhappy experimentation in romanticism, and he might have ended, not as a complacent and garrulous chronicler of past glories, but as the great novelist he once gave promise of becoming. But the seeds of failure were there from the first. Perhaps the sources of his ultimate defeat were not far removed from the sources of his first victories. The embattled farmers were themselves individualists, each forgetting the cause of his class once his own success was achieved.

* * *

Most of the authors who revolted against the indecencies of capitalism in the nineties found no allies. And yet violent disgust with all forms of contemporary civilization—the kind of disgust young men were feeling throughout the western world—drove them to make some violent gesture of protest. Lafcadio Hearn made his gesture when, in 1890, he sailed for Japan.

Hearn had landed in America in 1869, a boy of less than twenty, full of admiration for Gautier, Loti, Merimée, and the Flaubert of *Salammbô* and *St. Anthony*. Temperamental peculiarities and physical defects made it difficult for him to adjust himself to American life. He was unhappy in Cincinnati, where he served his apprenticeship as a newspaper man, and he fled hastily to the warmer climate and more colorful customs of New Orleans. At first he rejoiced in his deliverance, but it took only a year or two to show him that the older, pre-industrial civilization, which had given the city so much of its charm for him, could not endure. It was, he

quickly realized, a city of the dead, and such romantic qualities as it had were mere symptoms of its moribund state:
"What remains is something horrible like the tombs here,—
material and moral rottenness which no pen can do justice
to."

But economic necessity kept him in New Orleans until, in
1887, literary success brought release. A brief visit to New
York sent him frantically to the West Indies. For the moment Martinique, with its warmth and its women, its customs and its color, was balm to his soul, but soon dissatisfaction was gnawing at him. Such a life as he was leading
meant, he quickly discovered, the cessation of literary activity. After all, he was a product of civilization, and what he
was seeking was more, and not less, than civilization in the
United States could offer him. But as soon as he returned to
New York, he burst out in a letter to a friend, "The moment
I get into all this beastly machinery called 'New York,' I get
caught in some belt and whirled around madly in all direc-
tions until I have no sense left. . . . Everything seems to be
mathematics and geometry and enigmatics and riddles and
confusion worse confounded: architecture and mechanics
run mad. One has to live by intuition and move by steam. I
think an earthquake might produce some improvement. . . .
This is frightful, nightmarish, devilish! Civilization is a
hideous thing. Blessed is savagery!" Not long after he sailed
for Japan.

At first there was great enthusiasm—for "the poor simple
humanity of the country," for "their gods, their customs,
their dress, their bird-like quavering sounds, their houses,
their superstitions, their faults." In time came dissatisfaction
and the desire to return to America or perhaps to Europe.
Personal misfortune and a growing recognition of the impossibility of adapting himself to Japanese ways entered into

this restlessness, but its principal cause was the realization that Japan was yielding, and must yield, to the march of industry. Hearn's old enemy was catching up with him. But with this new disillusionment came the discovery of the futility of flight and the admission of defeat. "More and more," he wrote Ellwood Hendrick, "I see how terribly tragical modern life is becoming." "I think civilization is a fraud," he said in another letter, "because I don't like the hopeless struggle. If I were very rich I should perhaps think quite differently—or, what would be still more rational, try not to think at all about it." He saw precisely how the rise of industrialism was undermining institutions and changing values: "In this industrial epoch it (religion) is the servant of the monster business. . . . Business has its fixed standard of hypocrisy; everything above or below that is to be denounced by the ministers of the gospel of God and business." "Love, honor, idealism, etc., these can no longer be supreme or absorbing motives. . . . We have first to learn how to live inside the eight-day clock of modern life without getting caught in the cogs. . . . The genuine is only good for the agricultural districts." "The Western business man is really a very terrible and wonderful person. . . . He represents insatiate thirst of dominion, supreme intellectual aggressive capacity, faultless practical perceptivity, and the art of handling men exactly like pawns. But he represents also Order, System, Law. . . . One thing is dead sure: in another generation there can be no living by dreaming and scheming of art." In 1896 he wrote Page Baker, "You think I am misanthropic—no, not exactly; but I do feel an intense hatred for the business class of Northern mankind."

He even understood how industrialism had affected his own career. He had written book after book of sketches, never attempting the novel and seldom the short story, though in *Chita* he had displayed considerable skill in narrative. To an inquiring correspondent he wrote: "Why do not men like myself write more fiction? For two reasons. The first is because they have little knowledge of life, little *savoir-vivre,* to help them in the study of the artificial and complex growth of modern society. The second is that, unless very exceptionally situated, they are debarred, by this very want of knowledge and skill, from mixing with that life which alone can furnish the material." "Fancy a good romance about Wall Street—so written that the public could understand it!" he exclaimed in another letter. "There is, of course, a tremendous romance there; but only a financier can really know the machinery, and his knowledge is technical. But what can the mere *littérateur* do, walled up to heaven in a world of mathematical mystery and machinery!" Thus isolated from the fundamental forces in contemporary life, the novelist, he saw, was impotent.

The same perspicacity illuminates his analysis, both in his letters and in his books, of his adopted country. In old Japan, he records, "the business of money-making was held in contempt," and persons who lived by purchasing and reselling goods were placed in the lowest class and regarded as inferior to artisans and peasants. Under the patriarchal system there was no misery, as a consequence of poverty, except such as might come through war or famine. As the clan system broke down, poverty appeared, and after the introduction of industrialism there were half a million operatives on the verge of starvation. Yet, he clearly saw, Japan could not resist the onrush of industrialism, since it could not compete with western nations on any other basis. In either case, either with victory through industrialization or defeat through lack of it, the older civilization that he loved was doomed.

Neither for Japan nor for America could Hearn see any

hope. His distrust of industrialism had become so deep-seated that he could not conceive of its ultimately benefiting mankind. His own revolt had been so intense and so persistent that only the attitude of revolt commended itself to him as intelligent. His first intellectual awakening had come through the reading of Spencer, and he was as loyal to Spencer's ideas, which he tried to fuse with Buddhism, as he was to Gautier's style. He dreaded what he called the coming slavery: "Bellamy's ideas will be partly carried out, but in no such paradisaical manner. . . . The edifice is even now being reared in which every man will be a veritable slave to the State,—the State itself a universal monopoly, or trust. Then every life will be regulated to infinitesimal details." "The rule of the many," he wrote Ernest Crosby in 1904, the year of his death, "will be about as merciful as a calculating-machine, and as moral as a lawn-mower. . . . It will mean the most insufferable oppression that ever weighed upon mankind."

Hearn died a desperately bitter man. His life had been one long flight, and in the end he learned that flight was futile. The terror of the machine could not be escaped and, he believed, could not be subdued. His writings, though voluminous, are curiously insubstantial, and his prose is delicate to the point of weakness. Even his best stories and sketches collapse under the burden of pointless decoration. Yet he was tenacious in the pursuit of his own goals, and wiser than his generation. Great talents seem to have been latent in him, and his failure to use them is a measure of the strength of the forces against which he struggled.

Lafcadio Hearn came to know what he wanted and why; Ambrose Bierce was baffled to the end. Just after Hearn's departure for Japan, Bierce suddenly spoke, in *Tales of Soldiers and Civilians,* later called *In the Midst of Life,* to a larger audience than that which had followed his contributions to the newspapers of the Pacific Coast. What impressed readers was the chilly disinterestedness with which Bierce, in this book and its successor, *Can Such Things Be?*, treated the most terrifying experiences. If they had looked carefully, they would have detected his secret. Bierce's stories were inhuman because their author believed that art had no relation to life. His theories of literature were as mechanical—and as false—as his theories of diction. What he was interested in was the climactic moment, for the sake of which he manipulated his puppets with little regard for psychological laws. So long as he could carry the reader with him to the unexpected dénouement, he was content. Only such situations as could be shaped to fit his theories interested him; not finding many, he wrote relatively few stories and even in those repeated himself.

Bierce came from a large family of what he later called "unwashed savages," and his boyhood must have been far from pleasant. After the Civil War, in the course of which he acquired an exhaustive knowledge of the possibilities for evil in the human race, he went to California, where he became a journalist. Essentially an idealist, he set out to attack hypocrisy and rascality wherever he found them. Already disillusioned by the war, he struck out blindly, making little effort to understand the causes of the evils he attacked, and permitting himself to be drawn into the battle of personalities that was constantly going on. Three years in London did not clarify his mind, and he returned to take up the fight precisely where he had dropped it. He was a good fighter, and he laid about him with considerable effect, but he remained a journalist, of not the finest sort.

In the midst of this pigmy warfare he wrote his two books of short stories, thus varying the literature of protest with the literature of escape. His protest was vigorous and heart-felt, but misdirected and useless. His escape was by way of a theory of literature that insists on the bizarre and surprising. For years he had been building up a philosophy that arranged human activities in various compartments, each unrelated to the others, and thus he constructed a defense against forces too strong to be met in open battle. Born of the experiences of wartime and the frustration of a youthful idealism, his conviction of the futility of life gave birth in turn to his conception, so effectively practiced, of the short story.

For cynicism to follow the defeat of early hopes is common enough and not too serious; for it never to be outgrown is tragedy. Bierce remained a sophomore, though a sophomore of talent. Personal disaster—estrangement from his wife and the loss of two sons—did nothing, of course, to lessen his bitterness. The coming of fame and the growth of a little group of disciples only made him pontifical, and he tried to rationalize the collapse of his hopes and to dignify his prejudices by calling them a philosophy. Convinced by the collapse of his own ideals that all idealism was false, he set himself up as a reactionary. To justify his own failure to abolish the evils he had fought against, he posed as an individualistic foe of all reformers. His cynicism became an affectation, but bitterness remained, and to the end it was directed quite as much against himself as against his fellowmen. In 1913 he sought Mexico and death.

One hesitates to turn from such men as Hearn and Bierce to so palpable a charlatan as Edgar Saltus, but he, too, was a representative product of the romantic nineties. A conscious follower of European fashions, he first made a reputation as a popularizer of Schopenhauer, and then wrote a series of slim little novels dealing with murder, suicide, and adultery in New York society. For nearly forty years his books appeared—society novels, historical romances, collections of essays, poems, translations. He had a certain subterranean reputation during his life, and after his death, in 1921, a few critics, recognizing him as an ancestor of theirs, praised him. He diluted for American consumption the theories and methods of the European decadents, protested in his febrile fashion against Victorian taboos, and, like Bierce, prepared the way for the noisy pessimists of the twenties.

The attack on the stolid middle class came from many sides. Richard Hovey, who had startled Dartmouth in the eighties by proclaiming his admiration for Whitman and damning the polite poets, allied himself with Bliss Carman, a young Canadian, and together they produced the three *Vagabondia* books. They were critical of commercialism, and they could work themselves up to something like revolutionary fervor, but they had nothing to write about except their loudly reiterated faith in the joys of being alive. Self-conscious Bohemians, they belabored the Philistines and celebrated the pleasures of wandering with the wandering wind, but it is doubtful if the boyish boisterousness of their songs about wine and women deceived many of their readers. The Spanish-American War diverted much of Hovey's energy into the production of patriotic bombast, and he was engaged in writing a series of Arthurian poems, experimental in form but conventional in theme, at the time of his death.

Presumably the middle class did not object to the kind of attack to which the Vagabonds subjected it; certainly it was not, in this period, left wholly uncomforted. Romanticism may sometimes express a deep individual disgust, but it may also be manufactured to meet a popular need. Hearn, Bierce, and Saltus were scarcely popular writers, but there were plenty of romantic novelists who correctly gauged the public temper and were rewarded accordingly. Great masses of the people—in the lower middle class and the more comfortably situated sections of the working class—were eager to forget the disturbing questions of strikes and starvation, populist revolts and capitalist consolidations. They wanted books that would take them far away from the troublous times in which they lived, and in stories of the American Revolution, Graustark, or feudal England, they found what they wanted. The vogue of local color waned, and what Carl Van Doren calls rococo romanticism took its place. Several of the regionalists changed to the current mode, and many new writers—Churchill, Chambers, McCutcheon, for example—rose to popularity, and were even taken seriously by the critics. One of the most popular, for a time, was Henry Harland, author of *The Cardinal's Snuff Box* and co-editor of the *Yellow Book*. That a man who contributed so largely to the romantic deluge should also have been identified with the publication that most fully expressed the literary impulses of *fin de siecle* England points to the common basis of the sentimental and the sophisticated revolt.

* * *

Even the tawdriest of the romanticists testified to the growth of restlessness and disgust, but even the most talented of them could not transmute the increasing bitterness into creative force, and the romantic revival was short-lived and ineffectual. The future was in the hands of the followers of Howells, men who carefully examined and faithfully recorded the life about them. What was needed was not less honesty than he had shown but more. The hope for American literature was that, as dissatisfaction grew, it would breed courage and lead to understanding.

Hjalmar Hjarth Boyesen had courage, enough at least to

argue that novels should deal with the fundamental realities of American life and to try to practice what he preached. Born in Norway, a close student of the European naturalists, and a teacher of Germanic literature at various American universities, he began his literary career by writing on Norwegian themes, turned to criticism, and finally, in the nineties, wrote three sociological novels of the American scene. As early as 1886 he attacked the boarding-school standard of criticism, denouncing the subservience of the writer to "his final judge, the young American girl, . . . the Iron Madonna who strangles in her fond embrace the American novelist." So long as authors catered to boarding-school tastes, he observed, they could not make serious excursions into the rich fields of politics and industry. He was willing, like Howells, to accept current moral taboos, but he could not countenance the absence of seriousness in fiction and the failure to use the novel for social criticism. In his own novels he tried not only to present an accurate picture of contemporary life but also to judge that life by the standard of personal integrity. In *The Mammon of Unrighteousness* he compared two brothers, one an idealist and the other a ruthless seeker after political honors. In *The Golden Calf* he described the course of a worthy young man who bit by bit surrendered his ideals in the quest for wealth. And in *The Social Strugglers,* a lighter and less searching but better written novel, he satirized the battle of the newly rich for social position.

There can be no doubt that the phenomenon Boyesen described, the disintegration of idealism as a result of the desire for success, was common in the eighties and nineties, and his denunciations of the bitch goddess were eloquent. He discovered, however, as many later writers were to discover, that an ethical theory is not necessarily the best clue to the understanding of a nation. His bad characters are stronger, more interesting, and more convincing than his good ones; they may deserve to be condemned, but to condemn is not to explain them. Obviously he had understood part of the change that was going on, but not enough to make his characters fully representative. Earnestness and indignation had done what they could, but something more was needed.

Boyesen was not the only writer of the nineties who reminded his contemporaries that they should count the cost of business success. In his more urbane manner Henry Blake Fuller made the same challenge. After denouncing the realists, and offering the strange preciosity of *The Chevalier of Pensieri-Vani* as an example of the kind of literature that interested him, he himself turned realist, and in *The Cliff-Dwellers* and *With the Procession* wrote brilliantly of everyday life in Chicago. More sophisticated than either Howells or Boyesen, quick in observation, a subtle and resourceful stylist, Fuller seemed likely to develop a richer and more flexible method than any of his predecessors. His portrayal of the rise and fall of George Ogden in *The Cliff-Dwellers* is circumstantial without being dull, and his treatment of the Marshalls and the Bateses is sympathetic without being uncritical. He had, however, none of Boyesen's power of indignation; he had merely a mild academic disdain for greed and snobbishness. With such an attitude growth was impossible, and perhaps it was the realization of this that led him to abandon the field of the social novel as suddenly as he had entered it.

Neither so earnest as Boyesen nor so talented as Fuller, Harold Frederic contrived to make some contribution to the progress of realism. He did it, one suspects, largely by virtue of the energy and resolution that took a poor country boy and made him London correspondent of the New York Times. At first he wrote, in *Seth's Brother's Wife,* of the people he had known on farms and in newspaper offices in western New York. Then he turned to the historical novel and made *In the Valley* far superior to its genre by utilizing a solid knowledge of the economic and racial issues involved in the Revolution. *The Copperhead* and the stories in *Marsena,* dealing with life in the Mohawk Valley during the sixties, show the effects of the Civil War on the lives of the people at home. By the time he had written these books Frederic was ready for a major effort, and in *The Damnation of Theron Ware* he made it. In his account of village life and his pictures of village characters he showed that, despite his long absence from his native valley, its people and their ways were still strongly fixed in his memory. And against this background he unfolded a tragic story that has been repeated in every generation in every region of America, the story of the man whose sudden realization of a world outside his experience, a world of intellectual and moral flexibility, results in personal disaster. There are innumerable questions that Frederic leaves unanswered; there are depths of character that he does not explore; but *The Damnation of Theron Ware* remains the finest portrayal of an evangelical minister in American literature and one of the best accounts of small town life. Frederic died soon after its publication, but *March Hares* and *The Market Place* suggest that he would never have surpassed it.

Boyesen, Fuller, and Frederic all indicated the possibilities of realistic fiction, but none of them had any direct influence on later writers. Of the decade's realists only Stephen Crane has had a following. If he was less sensitive than the others to social abuses, he did extend the bounds of realism as they had not done. He defied taboos they held sacred, and the readers and the writers of America have not forgotten their debt of gratitude. "I understand," he wrote, "that a man is born into the world with his own pair of eyes, and he is not at all responsible for his vision—he is merely responsible for his quality of personal honesty. To keep close to this personal honesty is my supreme ambition." Crane's virtues as a writer come from the honesty and the clarity with which he recorded what he saw; his weaknesses are the result of his failure to discover why he saw as he did.

In his most personal utterances, his poems, we see his intense and precocious bitterness. In *The Black Riders* he is the naked, bestial creature who eats his own heart. His revolt, directed against the God of his father and against the moral code of his generation, is the revolt of a man who has found life far less desirable than it had been represented as being, and who scarcely knows whether to blame the putative creator or his fellowmen. In *War Is Kind* he is less concerned with the Deity and more with human stupidity and corruption. He no longer protests for he recognizes the blank indifference of the cosmos, and his sense of human frustration is so strong that he has little room even for pity.

Though we know too little of Crane's early life to be able to determine the genesis of his bitterness, we have seen enough of conditions in the period of his youth to have some understanding of such states of mind as his. He once said to a friend, "You can never do anything good esthetically—and you can never do anything with anything that's any good except esthetically—unless it has at one time meant something important to you." In the work by which we best know him Crane remembered this: it was not mere objectivity that guided his pen, but a bitter awareness of the importance—to him—of the materials with which he dealt.

Crane's first book, *Maggie,* expressed not merely his hatred and fear of the slums and their inhabitants but also his irritation with the treatment those phenomena received at the hands of his fellow-writers. When Gilder questioned the book's grammar, which is certainly not beyond question, Crane cut him short: "You mean that the story's too honest?" That men could regard the slums condescendingly, ignoring their hideous squalor and sentimentalizing the vile men and women who lived in them, was an offense he could not forgive. He did not hesitate to make Maggie the stupid victim of stupid brutality, nor to make her brother a braggart and her mother a drunkard. He set down precisely what he saw, and he saw what he did because he was driven by a violent hatred, an almost physical loathing, for poverty and suffering. "In a story of mine called 'An Experiment in Misery,'" he wrote, "I have tried to make plain that the root of Bowery life is a sort of cowardice. Perhaps I mean a lack of ambition or to willingly be knocked flat and accept the licking." He hated the poor because they could consent to the ugliness of their surroundings, the brutality of their lives, the defeat of their hopes, because they continued to live on such terms. He saw in them the depths to which a human being might fall, and trembled at the abyss thus opened before him.

Hatred is a healthier emotion for the artist than pity. The hideousness and cowardice were there, and Crane's sensitiveness to color and sound and smell permitted him to describe them and to arouse the reader as he was himself aroused. Yet though we know what sort of person Maggie seems to Crane to be, we never know what sort of person she appeared to herself. As in "George's Mother," the author stands on the outside. He could not enter into his characters' lives because he did not understand them, and he did not understand them because he did not understand how they had come into existence. We see them merely as they present themselves to Crane, a symbol of everything he feared. As a result there is something dry and harsh in all Crane's work, even in *The Red Badge of Courage.* Here the description is peculiarly effective, and the irony is intense. Well might Crane feel, when he had actually seen war, that he had been surprisingly right. But not only is the bitterness misdirected; as in *Maggie,* the events of the story never quite touch us. Crane felt the horror of such events, and that was his strength; he could not understand their significance, and that was his weakness.

The Red Badge of Courage made Crane famous at the age of twenty-four; it did not help him to find himself as an author. The magazines were open to him now, and he wrote voluminously, sometimes of the slums, sometimes of war, in his Whilomville stories about boys. With no clear purpose of his own, he was unusually open to suggestions from others, and he tried his hand at many themes. His wandering life paralleled the course of his literary tastes. In the end he turned, as did so many of his contemporaries, to England, where, at the age of twenty-nine, he died. Much of his later work is slight and ineffective. Perhaps it was because disease already gripped him; perhaps it was because it was increasingly difficult for him to find anything of real importance to him. He had never tried to orientate himself; the expression of his bitterness, which was almost miraculously possible for him in his early twenties, had seemed enough. To the end of his short life the world remained to him a blank mystery, full of hateful objects, and, unless he had transcended that attitude, unless he had learned to understand as well as to record, he would never have surpassed his earlier work. Yet we must not forget that in that early work he had broken some of the intolerable bonds that restrained the American novelist. For the sake of artistic integrity he had challenged some of the most sacred taboos. If it remained just as difficult for the artist to understand the world in which he lived, it was easier for him to record whatever he saw.

Crane's courage has entitled him to much praise from our contemporaries, and his pessimism has been congenial to many of them. That may explain why the aridity of his writing and the lack of understanding have been overlooked. He has been singled out among his contemporaries for admiration, and other writers, no less limited, certainly, but of comparable historical importance, have been neglected. Yet Crane does very well as a symbol of the writers of the nineties—talent that flares bravely and is cruelly extinguished; blind, bitter blows against dark evils; struggle and flight, suffering and death.

Chapter VI

THE YEARS OF HOPE

Poor boys did become multimillionaires in the decades after the Civil War, and the stories of their successes were told and retold in the homes of factory workers and farmers. The chances came only to a few, the great chances to a very few; but the gambling spirit of the frontiersman still ran high. Everywhere attention was focussed on the victories; the failures were ignored. Schools, newspapers, churches, all impressed upon the average citizen that this was the land of golden opportunity. And the prizes were there, to be seen, to be worshipped, to be worked for. It was the great American dogma: any man could achieve success—concrete financial success—wealth, leisure, power.

Acquiescence in the dogma had not been quite universal: factory workers had challenged their exploiters and, with the strength of union, forced concessions from them; the farmers, after much suffering, had demanded legislation to control the railroads and had revolted against the bankers; laborers and small business men, educated by their own experience and by such books as *Wealth Against Commonwealth,* had secured a law to restrain monopoly. Whenever men believed that the paths to success were hopelessly blocked, whenever they felt that the odds were overwhelmingly against them, they were ready to protest. Their protest was usually aimed at little more than minor alterations of the rules of the game, but it was a protest, and it grew as time passed.

Bryan was defeated in 1896 and again in 1900, but, if the reformers could not elect a President, they could and did capture state and local governments. Such men as Joseph Folk, Robert LaFollette, and William S. U'Ren successfully challenged long-established political rings, and Golden Rule Jones and Tom Johnson showed that, if all cities were corrupt, not all were contented. The demand grew for the direct election of senators, woman suffrage, and a tax on incomes. States revised their constitutions, experimenting with the initiative and referendum and passing laws for the protection of workmen. And, by accident, the reformers did get a President, Theodore Roosevelt, who in his first message to Congress demanded greater regulation of the trusts, the extension of the powers of the Interstate Commerce Commission, and a conservation policy. His fight against the Northern Securities Company and his interference in the anthracite strike of 1902 convinced the progressives that he was their man, and in 1904 he was re-elected.

Roosevelt's actual achievements were slight. Despite all his talk about trust-busting, his administration brought fewer suits against monopolies than did Taft's. He did secure the passage of the Hepburn Act and the Pure Food Act, and he made a vigorous struggle for the conservation of natural resources, but these were only minor restrictions on the activities of the malefactors of great wealth. He had neither a philosophy of government nor a grasp of economics. His adoption of a reform platform was not wholly opportunistic, for his sympathies were with the middle class, but, as his conduct in the depression of 1907 showed, he had no intention of destroying the power of the great industrialists and financiers. He was able to give an impression of spontaneity and even of moral enthusiasm in everything he did, but actually he swayed this way and that before the impact of conflicting interests.

The progressive movement was scarcely more consistent than its leader. Even LaFollette, whose understanding of economic tendencies was far more profound than Roosevelt's, failed to realize that the issue was not one of men and laws but one of economic forces. The reformers wanted to throw the bad men out of office and put good men in, but they did not try to eliminate the sources of corruption. They wanted to restrict the powers of the very wealthy, but they refused to devise means for such a reconstruction of society as effective restriction demanded. Essentially, though they called themselves progressives, their eyes were on the past, on the days before capitalism had congealed, when the evidences of opportunity were everywhere apparent, when small business men could be independent and comfortable, when professional men had no masters and enjoyed the respect of their fellows. Their efforts were strenuous, but they were fighting against the logic of history.

A great many working men regarded the situation exactly as the middle class reformers did, but there were other workers, just as there were some men in the middle class, who began to wonder if reform was possible. The Socialist Labor Party, which had grown steadily in the late eighties and early nineties, began to lose its prestige after 1898, but the Socialist Party, organized under the leadership of Eugene Debs in 1901, made a respectable showing in 1904 and 1908, and in 1912, with two progressive candidates in the field, polled 900,000 votes. At that time the movement published five English dailies, eight foreign language dailies, two hundred and sixty-two English weeklies, thirty-six foreign language weeklies, ten English monthlies, and two foreign language monthlies. Its propagandists were active, and their books appeared in impressive numbers.

Most of the socialists were completely opposed to violence, and the others believed in it only as a last resort. But some radicals were not so convinced that change could be accomplished by political methods. The Industrial Workers of the World was founded in 1905, and in a little more than a decade had issued over a million membership cards. Its leader, Bill Haywood, by no means disregarded political struggle, but he believed also in direct action, and his attempts to organize one big union, his recommendation of sabotage, and his battles for free speech made his organization hated and feared from Massachusetts to Oregon. Many of his followers went farther than he in condemning politics, and the movement expressed the growing disgust of many workers with attempts at parliamentary reform. The successes of the I.W.W. indicated, more clearly than the vote for Debs, the growth of revolutionary sentiment.

The pattern of American life in the years from the Spanish-American War to the outbreak of the World War is curiously complicated, and literature follows that pattern, with all its complexities. Just as the movement of revolt was the most vital political force in the first decade of the twentieth century, so the novel of revolt was the most important literary phenomenon. There were, to be sure, authors enough to satisfy the vanity of the successful, and authors enough to entertain all those who wanted to forget their troubles; but their books have served their purpose and rotted away. The work of the critical observers of American life, however, has remained, at least as an influence on our literature. For nearly fifty years novelists had failed to come to grips with the great economic and political movements, and suddenly a whole generation of authors appeared who accepted the challenge. Their attitudes, as diverse as those of their political counterparts, ran the gamut from mild reformism to revolutionary ardor. And as these various attitudes expressed themselves, it became possible to judge the value of each for the author who was trying to understand and re-create the life of his country and his era.

*   *   *

Frank Norris, his brief career crowded into a few years just before and after the beginning of the century, sounds the motif of the new literature: the intensification of realism and the closer identification of realism with social purpose. Born of a comfortable middle class family, educated in Paris and at Harvard, as well as at the University of California, he at first accepted the ideas of prosperous, conservative business men such as his father. In his college days he referred scornfully to the *canaille* and wished that all radicals might be "drowned on one raft." He admired Cecil Rhodes, was prepared to take part in the Jameson Raid, which occurred at the time of his visit to South Africa, and regarded the outcome of the Spanish-American War as a triumph for Anglo-Saxon ideals. Captains of industry such as C. P. Huntington seemed to him romantic figures, and he once said: "Had Mr. Carnegie been alive at the time of the preachings of Peter the Hermit he would have raised a company of *gens d'armes* sooner than all his brothers-in-arms, would have equipped his men better and more effectively, would have been first on the ground before Jerusalem, would have built the most ingenious siege engine and have hurled the first cask of Greek fire over the walls."

At the outset Norris was a conservative in politics and a romantic in literature. As an art student in Paris in the late

eighties he discovered Froissart, and out of that discovery
came a poem, *Yvernelle,* published in 1890, when the author
was only twenty. A year or so afterward he came upon Kipling, and the effect of that experience he has recorded in the
autobiographical *Blix.* It was only a little later that Zola began to influence him, and he started writing *McTeague* and
Vandover and the Brute. But it was Kipling that dominated
the first novel Norris published, *Moran of the Lady Letty,*
and the romantic spell was never completely exorcised.
"Vitality is the thing after all," he said. "The United States
in this year of grace 1902 does not want and need Scholars,
but Men." To the end he quarreled with realism, saying that
it "stultifies itself" and "notes only the surface of things";
loyal to the cult of action, he was scornful of Howells' placid
still-lifes.

And yet Norris is remembered for his contributions to
American realism. *McTeague,* which was begun in 1893, was
finished in 1899, the year in which Norris published *A Man's
Woman,* the last of his purely romantic novels. *McTeague*
marked as great an advance over *Maggie* as *Maggie* had
marked over *A Modern Instance.* Norris was less direct than
Crane, less emancipated from prejudice; he did not drive so
surely to his objective. But he built solidly out of intimate
knowledge and a not unsympathetic understanding of his
people. He said of *Maggie:* "The author . . . is writing from
the outside. Mr. Crane does not seem to *know* his people.
He does not seem to have gotten down *into* their life." That
charge could not be made against *McTeague.* We overlook
the book's faults—the moralizing of the scene in which the
dentist kisses his unconscious patient, the forced humor of
the picnic, the failure to prepare us for Trina's miserliness,
the explosive melodrama of the ending; we forgive all that
because of the description of McTeague's daily life, the build-

ing in which he has his office, Polk Street, the Sieppe family, the dentist's friends. Through a multitude of petty details Norris gives us McTeague and his world.

The truth is that Norris had gradually changed his outlook on life. After his father's divorce in 1894, his income was reduced, and after his return from South Africa in 1896 he went to work on the San Francisco *Wave*. Though he retained many of his conservative prejudices, just as he retained many of the literary devices of the red-blooded romanticists, he acquired a measure of sympathy for what he called the People. On the basis of this sympathy he began to construct a theory of literature. The novel, he argued, is the characteristic mode of expression of the twentieth century: "The Pulpit, the Press and the Novel—these indisputably are the great molders of public opinion and public morals to-day." "The novelist to-day is the one who reaches the greatest audience. Right or wrong, the People turn to him the moment he speaks, and what he says they believe." Therefore, he maintained, the novelist is responsible to the people: "A literature that cannot be vulgarized is no literature at all." "It is all very well to jeer at the People and at the People's misunderstanding of the arts, but the fact is indisputable that no art that is not in the end understood by the People can live or ever did live a single generation." The novelist fulfils his responsibilities, Norris continued, only when he devotes himself to a high purpose: the novel may be "a great force, that works together with the pulpit and the universities for the good of the people, fearlessly proving that power is abused, that the strong grind the faces of the weak, that an evil tree is still growing in the midst of the garden, that undoing follows hard upon unrighteousness, that the course of Empire is not yet finished, and that the races of men have yet to work out their destiny in those great and terrible movements that crush and grind and rend asunder the pillars of the house of the nations." The novel serves this purpose when it portrays life in such a way as to enlighten the reader, when it "draws conclusions from a whole congeries of forces, social tendencies, race impulses, devotes itself not to a study of men but of man."

McTeague did not wholly conform to this theory, and certainly it did not satisfy the needs of Norris' temperament. It illustrated his belief that "no piece of information—mere downright acquisition of fact—need be considered worthless," and it showed how much "a receptivity, an acute sensitivity" could do for a writer. But he had said that the highest type of novel "draws conclusions from a whole congeries of forces," and he could be content with nothing less. The task required, he felt, an enormous canvass; only an epic would suffice. And so he planned his trilogy. There was to be enough action in it to satisfy his own romanticism; it would grow out of the lives of the plain people and it would appeal to them; it would be honest and exact but never dull; it would reveal the pattern underlying seemingly unrelated events and thus would influence men's thoughts and deeds. All that Norris thought literature should be he proposed to make his *Epic of the Wheat.*

Though the second volume, *The Pit,* falls far below Norris' conception, the first, *The Octopus,* is not wholly unworthy of the name of epic. Woven out of a dozen strands, it achieves the dimensions necessary for the adequate portrayal of a great economic struggle. It depicts a movement by depicting people, scores of them, all caught up in the battle between the wheat-raisers and the railroad. On page after page, in analyses of character, in descriptions of ranchers' meetings, of wheat fields, of fighting, Norris gives us the substance of a struggle that, in its fundamentals, was nationwide. He had at least one quality of greatness: he could seize upon the central issues of his time and create people in whose lives those issues were reflected.

Yet *The Octopus* can scarcely be called a great book; it is too confused, and in the end too false. Norris' growing sympathy with the people made him sorry for the dispossessed ranchers, and he could even become indignant at their misfortunes. But on the other hand, he admired the romantic boldness of Collis P. Huntington, who appears in the book under the name of Shelgrim. Moreover, he had talked with Huntington, as Presley talks with Shelgrim, and he could see no flaw in the railroad president's argument that the way of the railroad was the way of progress. Somehow he had to reconcile these conflicting sympathies if he was to make his novel an interpretation of life. His reading of Zola had introduced him to determinism, which he had employed as a literary device in both *McTeague* and *Vandover and the Brute,* though he seems never to have understood its philosophic implications. And a deterministic version of the apologies of the captains of industry, as stated in Shelgrim's interview with Presley, provided him with his method of interpretation. One recalls Presley's meditations at the end of the book: "Men—motes in the sunshine—perished, were shot down in the very noon of life, hearts were broken, little children were started in life lamentably handicapped; young girls were brought to a life of shame; old women died in the heart of life for lack of food. . . . *But the WHEAT remained.* Untouched, unassailable, undefiled, that mighty world-force, that nourisher of nations, wrapped in Nirvanic calm, indifferent to the human swarm, gigantic, resistless, moved onward in its appointed grooves. . . . Falseness dies; injustice and oppression in the end of everything fade away. Greed, cruelty, selfishness, and inhumanity are short-lived; the individual suffers, but the race goes on. . . . The larger view always and through all shams, all wickednesses, discovers the Truth that will, in the end, prevail, and all things, surely, inevitably, resistlessly work together for good."

This is consoling doctrine, and no doubt it seemed to Norris to answer his purposes. The thoughtful reader, however, finds Presley's rhapsody the most disturbing kind of anticlimax. As a theory it is ridiculous, and it destroys the emotional effect of the book, for it means that the contemptible Behrman has worked as surely for good as the noble Derrick, the impulsive Annixter, or the violent Dyke. Moreover, the consequences of this philosophy are found on page after page. How many problems Norris leaves unsolved: Magnus Derrick's ethical dilemma, the whole question of the use of violence, the place of the poet in such a struggle as that between the railroad and the ranchers! And how far he is from a consistent interpretation of character! For example, in interpreting Magnus' downfall he wavers between the view that his surrender is ignoble and the view that it is inevitable. Presley hovers on the edge of the struggle, now repelled, now drawn in, and at last takes refuge in his mystical optimism. The confusion permeates even the minutiæ of the book: we are asked to believe that Vanamee has a sixth sense, that Annixter is capable of a miraculous transformation under the influence of pure love. Norris' old romanticism creeps in again and again, sheltered by the incoherence of his philosophy. Even the method is confused, for austere realism often yields to overt melodrama and careful objectivity to special pleading.

But if in *The Octopus* an impressive novel is marred by such defects, in *The Pit* a fine theme is ruined because of them. In *The Octopus* Norris was at least concerned with the victims, and his sympathy to some extent counteracted the effects of his theories. In *The Pit* it was the exploiter who occupied him, and he was strongly tempted, because of his admiration for the daring exploits of the captains of industry, to make Curtis Jadwin a romantic hero. His theory, however, required him to portray Jadwin as simply an instrument of benevolent natural forces. And his growing concern with the people showed Norris the cost of Jadwin's exploits: while such men were gambling, "the farmer—he who raised the wheat—was ruined upon one hand; the working man—he who consumed it—was ruined on the other." Unable to decide whether to regard Jadwin as hero, automaton, or villain, he avoided the problem by making the corner in wheat a subordinate theme in the story. The novel is principally concerned with the relations between Jadwin and his wife, and this involves Laura's affair with Sheldon Corthell, an artist whose wide range of interests attracts her when she is weary of her husband's preoccupation with business. But Corthell is as weak and aimless as Jadwin is determined and powerful, and it was easy enough to end the book with Laura in the arms of her defeated and penitent husband. For the reader who is chiefly interested in the love story there is this romantic and presumably satisfying ending. For the reader who accepts Norris' philosophy there is a purple passage about the wheat, which "had passed on, resistless, along its ordered and predetermined courses from West to East, like a vast Titanic flood, had passed, leaving Death and Ruin in its wake, but bearing Life and Prosperity to the crowded cities and centres of Europe." But for the reader who wants to understand the mind of the business man, and wants to see how speculative operations actually affect human lives, for the reader who asks that this novel should help him to understand the forces it deals with and to realize their expression in credible characters and events, for such a reader there is little but disappointment—some stirring descriptions of the Pit, some insight into the lust of the gambler, a few pictures of Chicago society, and not much more.

It is easy to see what Norris planned to do with the third volume of the series, and one fears that, neatly as it would have fitted his plan, it must still further have revealed the inadequacies of his philosophy. Whether he would in time have outgrown that philosophy is, of course, an insoluble problem. Other faults he was slowly overcoming: his prudishness, his fondness for melodrama, his reliance on the cliches of the Victorians. When one remembers his youth, one forgives all his faults—even his theories, which may well have been part of his relative immaturity—and thinks only of his virtues: the ambitiousness of his themes, the seriousness of his method, his mastery of a large canvass, the power of his descriptions. If clarity had been added, what might he not have accomplished?

* * *

One reason for thinking that Norris might have changed his views, might have come to pay more attention to the immediate evil and to be less certain of the ultimate good, is that, despite his theorizing, he was so opposed to passivity. He was not one to look calmly on at oppression, and even his confidence that right would triumph did not wholly assuage his indignation at cruelty and greed. It seems probable that a campaign of exposure, trying to bring the truth to the plain people, would have enlisted his pen. Such a movement began in the year of his death, and several novelists were affected by it. If we cannot tell how muckraking would have influenced Norris, we can examine its effect upon such writers as David Graham Phillips, Winston Churchill, and Robert Herrick.

Progressivism was fortunate, as the rise of muckraking shows, because it was so articulate. It had developed writers, and it had a vehicle of expression in the popular magazines that had sprung up in the nineties. S. S. McClure, for example, had built up a large circulation by aggressively seeking out the most popular authors and the most popular subjects. And when, by accident he has · maintained, his magazine turned to muckraking, there was a large audience for Lincoln Steffens' accounts of municipal corruption, Ida Tarbell's history of the Standard Oil Company, and Ray Stannard Baker's analysis of labor unions. The success of McClure's "accident" inspired other magazines: the *Cosmopolitan, Everybody's, Collier's, Hampton's, Pearson's,* the *American.* One by one, during the next decade, the popular magazines took up the task of muckraking, and even the more dignified monthlies occasionally engaged in the work of exposure.

It is chiefly by way of the muckrakers that we trace the connection between the progressive movement and the literature of the period. It is not merely that certain of the novelists—Sinclair, Phillips, White, Lewis—also wrote muckraking articles; the connection is more fundamental. In the first place, the muckrakers, by arousing a widespread interest in the operations of politicians and business men, created an audience for the novel of politics and business. In the second place, they revealed to the novelist the dramatic value in the lives of the great financiers and big bosses and in the struggles for supremacy. And finally, they helped to define the various attitudes the novelist might take towards this material.

The muckraking movement, as Lincoln Steffens has insisted, was journalistic in spirit. The muckrakers were not indifferent to reform, but, regarding their exposures as a sufficient contribution to the cause, they left the formulation of a remedy to their readers. Very few of them tried to evolve a theory of government or sought to discover the way in which the various forms of corruption were related. Even Steffens, keenest of them all, came very slowly to the realization that there was something more involved than the difference between virtuous men and dishonest ones. Ida Tarbell and Ray Stannard Baker never made that discovery. The latter could see nothing inconsistent in his having been both a muckraker and the author of *Adventures in Contentment*. The former, when it was charged that her eulogy of Judge Gary was treason to the principles underlying her attack on Rockefeller, replied quite simply that there were good trusts and bad trusts. Most of the muckrakers, when muckraking no longer paid, quickly found other fields of action: one as a movie director, another as author of sensational novels, another as writer of detective stories, another as philosopher, another as editor of a success magazine. They were journalists, giving the public what it wanted.

Most of the writers who swelled the volume of political and social novels took the same attitude. It would be difficult to list all the authors who, having achieved success as regionalists or romanticists or both, adopted the new fashion: Mary Wilkins Freeman wrote *The Portion of Labor;* Octave Thanet wrote *The Man of the Hour* and *The Lion's Share;* Alfred Henry Lewis turned from his Wolfville stories to write of Tammany in *The Boss*. Most conspicuous of all the converts, Winston Churchill followed his three popular historical romances with three novels of politics—*Coniston, Mr. Crewe's Career,* and *A Modern Chronicle*. Other men, hitherto inexperienced in the field of fiction, tried their hands at muckraking stories. Brand Whitlock wrote *The Thirteenth District,* and Joseph Medill Patterson wrote *A Little*

Brother of the Rich. Leroy Scott, who subsequently turned to detective stories, wrote *The Walking Delegate* and *To Him That Hath.* William Allen White interrupted his editorial duties to write *A Certain Rich Man.*

Among the young men who rode to popularity with the muckraking movement was David Graham Phillips. Since the movement was primarily journalistic, it was bound to have its sensational fringe, and by such articles as Tom Lawson's *Frenzied Finance* and Harold Bolce's "Blasting at the Rock of Ages" readers were entertained rather than edified. In view of his career in fiction, it is appropriate that Phillips' chief muckraking venture should have been as sensational a series of articles as the decade produced, "The Treason of the Senate." Calling the series sensational does not mean that the author wrote purely for popular consumption and with no moral fervor. The articles, on the contrary, vibrate with indignation; Phillips wrote in a fit of passion, recklessly mixing fact and gossip, and pouring over all a molten coat of vituperation. But the indignation is curiously unfocussed; Phillips could tell a good news story, but he could not draw up an indictment.

That was David Graham Phillips—an expert newspaperman, with an instinct for immediate effect and a hot-tempered zeal against fraud and oppression, but with little understanding of politics or economics. His career as a novelist began in 1901 with *The Great God Success,* based on his own experience with Cincinnati and New York newspapers, and, as muckraking got under way, he made himself its most prolific representative in fiction. *The Master Rogue* and *The Cost* took the reader into the world of finance. *The Plum Tree* described the operations of a political boss. *The Deluge* followed Lawson's exposures of Wall Street, and *Light-Fingered Gentry* followed the insurance scandals. *The Sec-*

ond Generation summed up Phillips' conclusions, contrasting the virtues of hard-working poverty with the evils of inherited wealth. Then, suddenly, as if sensing the decline of the popular interest in muckraking, he wrote *Old Wives for New* (1908) and *The Hungry Heart* (1909), both dealing with the new woman and her attitude towards love and marriage. This theme occupied him until, in his last and best novel, *Susan Lenox,* he combined his favorite themes, exposing the evils of Cincinnati slums and factories and the methods of New York gangsters and politicians, at the same time that he described the adventures of a country girl who reached success on the stage by way of poverty and prostitution.

The thing that Phillips did was to bring to fiction the equipment of a highly trained reporter. Nothing could be easier than to belittle him, to ridicule his Sunday supplement style, his incredible happy endings, his frequent introduction of melodrama. Nor is it possible to maintain that his social theories are anything but superficial. But *The Cost* and *The Deluge* describe some of the actual operations by which fortunes are made and lost, and *The Plum Tree* and *George Helm* indicate some of the steps by which political power is created. As any one who has read *Susan Lenox* can testify, Phillips had the kind of knowledge that the novelist must have if he is to write about American life.

However, necessary as such knowledge is, it clearly is not enough. When one asks how these various details are bound together, one finds that Phillips has no answer. In politics he was a liberal and a reasonably sincere one. His books all point out that America needs honest business men and upright politicians, and there is a reformer, Scarborough, figuring in several novels, who apparently exemplifies Phillips' ideals. And it is on this vague hope of improvement that he has to rely for the unifying theme of his novels. Obviously such a philosophy could not lead to the kind of understanding he needed. Indeed, it encouraged him to remain a journalist, merely pointing out abuses here and praiseworthy acts there. His criterion, in the choice of events to be portrayed in his novels, was the newspaperman's criterion—immediate interest—and liberalism could not show him that there were other ways of estimating the importance of what was happening. Liberalism could not even extirpate the typical American admiration for success, of which Phillips had his share, and the confusion of values affects the characterization of every one of his heroes. So far as journalistic talent could make him so Phillips was a good novelist, but he could not go beyond that point.

Other and less openly opportunistic liberals than Phillips exhibited not dissimilar faults. Winston Churchill, a supporter of Roosevelt and a moderate reformer, brought to the political novel the leisurely Thackerayan method he had developed in his historical romances and the knowledge he had acquired in New Hampshire politics. *Coniston* is a more or less accurate study of a rural boss; *A Modern Chronicle* depicts the political maneuvers of a railroad. In both the experienced hand of the romancer offers a pleasant love story as bait for the reader who might be bored by details of political strategy. And in both an implausible conversion solves problems Mr. Churchill does not care to face. So far as they have a serious purpose—and Churchill was in earnest, though he was careful not to let his earnestness diminish his market value—it is summed up in the afterword to *Coniston:* we are drifting away from the principles of the founding fathers and we should return to them. It is no wonder that in the end Churchill's shrewdness went for nought; like the good progressive he was, he would not follow his analysis when it was likely to expose the baselessness of his hopes.

William Allen White won his first fame as the author of a widely-read attack on the Populists; but it made a difference to him whose ox was gored, and he adopted many of the Populists' ideas when they were advanced by Theodore Roosevelt in the interests of the middle class. Although he had written several volumes of short stories, *A Certain Rich Man* (1909) was his first novel. It is the story of John Barclay, whose ruthless conduct of business in the decades after the Civil War brings him wealth and nation-wide power but in the end leads to ruin and unhappiness. The moral of the book is repeatedly made plain: the uncontrolled lust for wealth is punished by God, who in his wisdom has ordained the principles of honest business on which the nation is established. White's other novel, *In the Heart of a Fool* (1918), similarly points out that God is punishing the crude materialists in order to bring the country to its senses. There is a stirring peroration: "Here lay a continent—rich, crass, material. . . . And, on the other hand, here stood the American spirit—the eternal love of freedom. . . . This spirit met the god of things as they are, and for a generation they grappled in a mighty struggle. And men said: The old America is dead; America is money mad. . . . Then the new epoch dawned. . . . And the old spirit of America rose and responded. . . . To have lived in the generation now passing, to have seen the glory of the coming of the Lord in the hearts of the people, to have watched the steady triumph in our American life of the spirit of justice, of fellowship over the spirit of greed, to have seen the Holy Ghost rise in the life of a whole nation, was a blessed privilege." It may be necessary to point out that the pentecostal experience to which this passage refers was the entrance of the United States into the World War.

Though they documented their novels more adequately, the liberals had little more to say than had been said by such men as Boyesen in the nineties, and they were rather more confused than he. At the same time that they condemned greed and materialism, they gloried in the material progress of the country, and they praised the sturdy self-reliance of the small man. If ethical standards were to have any pertinence, they had to be consistent. There is nothing inherently absurd in demanding righteous conduct; the absurdity arises when the causes of dishonesty are ignored or the cost of honesty disregarded. To stand for integrity above all else, to search out the forces in American life that menace integrity, to discover how integrity may be maintained, that is neither absurd nor ignoble.

Robert Herrick rescued the ethical standards of the reformers from the confusions and contradictions of middle-class progressivism. A New Englander by birth and an English teacher by profession, he stood a little apart from the wild struggle of conflicting interests. Yet he was attracted by that struggle, and from the first realized that it must provide him with the themes of his novels. In *The Gospel of Freedom* (1898) he told the story of a young woman's search for independence and happiness, showing how Adela Anthon's demands upon her husband increased his eagerness for wealth, and how his devotion to money-making in turn increased her dissatisfaction and self-absorption. Side by side with Wilbur's selfish materialism he placed the equally selfish dilettantism of Simeon Erard, an artist, and over against Adela, Wilbur, and Simeon he set Molly Parker, who found happiness for herself by seeking happiness for others, and Thornton Jennings, a young lawyer with an interest in reform, who abandoned his career in order to be faithful to his ideals.

Thus Herrick, at the very beginning of his career, announced the two subjects that have been his principal concern: the conflict in our competitive society between the desire for success and the maintenance of personal integrity, and the place of women in American life. In almost every book he has treated both themes, sometimes emphasizing one and sometimes the other. In *The Memoirs of an American Citizen,* one of the earliest portraits of a millionaire in our fiction, the loss of integrity is the major theme. Van Harrington, telling his own story, presents, fully and not unintelligently, the opinions of a man whose expansive desires recognize no ethical bounds. In *Together* it is the question of the American wife that concerns Herrick as he describes half a dozen marriages and shows how, in our industrial system, the woman of the middle class is no longer a companion and helpmeet but a pampered queen, ruining both herself and her husband.

Again and again Herrick showed the disintegrating effect of contemporary life on both men and women. He pictured the corruption of architects, engineers, doctors, lawyers, educators. He described the dissolution of character as a result of the sudden acquisition of wealth. In a dozen books, written between 1898 and 1914, he set down a vivid record of the spiritual cost of the tremendous material progress America was making. And looking back on the whole process in 1924, he attempted to put the essence of his experience into a single novel, a panorama of American life from the Chicago Fair to the end of the World War. In calling this novel *Waste* he summed up the conclusions of thirty years of painstaking observation. In novel after novel he had shown that the result of lust for material gain is tragedy: Adela Anthon is forced to confess defeat; Jackson Hart becomes a murderer; Van Harrington is painfully conscious of the emptiness of his life; John Lane flees to Mexico. In *Waste* he not only stated the familiar themes once more; he explicitly indicted an era. All this effort, he says in effect, all this amassing of wealth and seizing of power, and what is there to show for it? All waste!

It was obviously impossible for Herrick to believe that such a situation could be remedied by the passing of a few laws. From the first he saw that more fundamental changes were necessary, and he had little confidence in the progressive movement. One of the characters in *Waste* says, "You think it's the old crusade of right against might. Nothing of the kind; it's the ancient revolt of the little hogs against the big hogs, the petite bourgeoisie against the big bourgeoisie of the country. Presently the big fellers will give up a little more, let the little fellers in on a few good things, and you won't be able to find the progressives." Herrick may have been less cynical, but he was quite as certain that the reformers were doomed to failure. Only the complete repudiation of the selfish materialism of the era could save the country. Towards such renunciation most of his heroes strive— Thornton Jennings, Hugh Grant, Steve Johnston, Jarvis Thornton. But Herrick was much too honest not to see that for a man of such ideals to live in the world involved constant compromise. Withdrawal from the world, a life completely free from every taint of commercialism, such a life as he describes in *The Master of the Inn,* that was the only way for the man who prized his integrity.

What this amounts to, of course, is the complete repudiation of industrial civilization. Herrick is a paradox, a man who has devoted his life to the portrayal of a social order that he ultimately rejects. We have seen many writers so distraught by the spectacle of industrialism that they refused to concern themselves with it, and we have seen writers who criticized this aspect and that of the machine age; but we have not found a writer who painstakingly studied that age and yet condemned it. In his manner of writing Herrick reminds us of both Howells and Fuller, and his attitude is, in a sense, a development of theirs. Howells' bewilderment resulted in large measure from his inability to decide what to accept and what to reject in contemporary civilization. Fuller made an effort to understand and to portray life in a commercial society, and then calmly turned his back on the whole problem. Herrick, moved by the same interests and faced by the same questions, carefully observed and honestly recorded the life about him, and then deliberately passed judgment upon it.

The connection between this attitude and the weaknesses of Herrick as a novelist can at least be indicated. Only rarely does the reader feel that he fully enters into the minds of Herrick's characters; he seldom participates in their lives, feels their struggles with them, and rejoices in their successes. Keen as Herrick's ethical judgments are, he has little sense for purely dramatic values. He is more successful in stating Van Harrington's self-justification than he is in making us share the satisfactions of the packer's victories. The reformers' aims and methods are clearly stated, but their motives, the forces that drive them, do not become real to us. Even the mystics—Holden, Renault, the Master of the Inn —seem almost purely products of the author's theorizing, vaguely admirable but far from substantial.

The reader is merely a spectator because Herrick is merely a spectator. Herrick cannot enter into this life because he cannot sympathetically assume the point of view of any active participant. To him the choice lies between greed, corruption, and grossness, on the one hand, and ascetic isolation on the other. To the men of his time the choice has lain between mastery of the industrial processes and overwhelming disaster. Herrick cannot ally himself with the business man, the reformer, or the worker. His analysis of contemporary civilization is accurate as far as it goes, but it leaves out of account elements in the situation that are of the greatest importance. They are important because one must understand the forces that can transform industrialism if one is to understand industrialism itself and appreciate its potentialities.

If Herrick has thus been barred from the front rank of American novelists, he nevertheless has helped to clarify both the nature of liberalism and the problem of industrialism. His attitude is a not illogical outgrowth of the liberal tradition in America. In its origins American liberalism was opposed to commercialism and to the whole industrial movement. As time went on and industrialism developed, liberalism compromised. By the time Herrick began to write, the issues were fairly clear: either liberals were men who merely wanted their share of the spoils, or they were men who stood for integrity at any price. Of course the majority of liberals refused to accept this statement of the case, arguing that this reform or that would sufficiently alter the structure of the industrial system to permit honest men to take part in it. Novelists such as Churchill, Phillips, and White adopted this attitude, with disastrous results. Herrick refused to deceive himself: individual integrity was more important than wealth and power, than industrialism itself. No Puritan in the narrow sense, he voiced what was probably Puritanism's last protest against a social order that, modern historians tell us, it did much to make possible.

*   *   *

As the issue defined itself, some men began to see more

clearly than Herrick and to make distinctions he had failed
to make. It was quite true, the socialists agreed, that no individual could maintain his integrity in a competitive industrial society; and it would do no good, they went on, either
to put virtuous men into office or to pass laws for the regulation of competition. They were willing to accept the dictum
of Shelgrim in *The Octopus*, "Blame conditions, not men,"
but they did not propose, on that account, to put their faith
in the blind operation of natural forces. Nor did they conclude that the individual should repudiate civilization and
find the path of virtue in the eremitic life; on the contrary,
they demonstrated the futility of such a course, for the individual concerned and for the society he deserted. There was,
they insisted, nothing intrinsically bad in industrialism or in
the amassing of goods it made possible. Industrialism was,
indeed, the hope of mankind, to whom it promised, for the
first time in history, an adequate supply of the necessities of
life. If industrialism failed to fulfil its promise, if its fruits
fell into the hands of a very few persons and the masses of
men were relatively, if not absolutely, poorer than they had
been in pre-industrial times, the problem was simply one of
reorganizing society so that its potential benefits might become real. It was, in short, a problem of control: if the in-
struments of production could be organized in the interests
of society as a whole, the evils of the machine age would
disappear. Not only would inequalities in the distribution of
wealth be eliminated; the efficiency of the productive system
would be tremendously increased. Not only would politics
be freed from corruption; the whole festering sore of greed
would be eradicated from the social body.

From this one would expect that a socialist, writing about
American life, would have an attitude towards that life different from any we have examined. He should, for one thing,

be able to avoid Herrick's sterile negations. For another, recognizing the influence of social conditions on men and women, he should be less concerned than the reformers with moral judgments and more concerned with the actual springs of conduct. Yet, realizing that social forces express themselves in men, and insisting on the necessity for action, he could escape the fatalism of Frank Norris. Most important of all, his socialism would point the way to an interpretation of the American scene, suggesting the significance of apparently unrelated events, and sharpening his perception of the essential pattern in the apparent chaos. Socialism, in those years of its enthusiastic growth, did find expression in novels, poems, and plays; and two American novelists, both with international reputations, belonged to the Socialist Party. Their work, unfortunately, shows that official allegiance to a theory and the development of a way of looking at life are two different things.

Jack London and Upton Sinclair had much in common. Both came from middle-class families, and from middle-class families that were descending in the social scale. The Sinclairs were southerners, with a long tradition of service in the navy, but the Civil War brought them so low that the novelist's father was a liquor salesman. The elder John London crossed the continent in the search for wealth, missed many opportunities for enrichment, went from venture to venture in Jack's boyhood, and finally became an Oakland policeman. He was, Jack once said, "too intrinsically good to get ahead in the soulless scramble for a living that a man must cope with if he would survive in our anarchical capitalist system."

Both knew hardships in their youth: London was early forced out into the world to earn his living as oyster pirate, member of the fish patrol, sailor, and factory hand; Sinclair earned his way through Columbia by manufacturing jokes and writing nickel novels at the rate of eight thousand words a day. Both came, in time, to look upon literary success as the way of deliverance, and the high hopes and hard struggles of one are recorded in *Martin Eden,* those of the other in *The Journal of Arthur Stirling.* Neither achieved great reputation with his early work, but *The Call of the Wild* brought fame to London, and *The Jungle* established the name of Upton Sinclair. Both, once success was achieved, availed themselves of the opportunity to escape from poverty. A friend advised Sinclair to learn to charge: "So I doubled my price to the next paper," he writes, "and might just as well have quadrupled it." "If cash comes with fame, come fame," said London; "if cash comes without fame, come cash." And both lived to accumulate and to spend more than one moderate fortune, though London spent his on yachts, farms, and expeditions, whereas Sinclair's went for colonies, propaganda, and moving pictures.

The joy of handling money, the satisfaction of having recouped dissipated family fortunes, is not the only mark of middle-class backgrounds. Neither, for example, quite eradicated the results of early religious training. London, it is true, flatly declared, "I am a materialistic monist," whereas Sinclair was a mild agnostic, capable of saying, "My quarrel with the churches is a lover's quarrel." Yet the latter's statement that "the world needs a Jesus more than it needs anything else" is paralleled by the former's "I have two heroes— one is Jesus Christ, the other Abraham Lincoln." It may also be noted that Nietzsche's doctrines, which so strongly influenced London, had at least a transient appeal for Sinclair, who maintains that he is largely responsible for Nietzsche's American vogue. Finally, both London and Sinclair, together with most of the intellectuals in the Socialist Party, supported American participation in the World War on the ground that the war was a crusade against evil rather than a struggle of imperialistic robbers.

However, the differences between London and Sinclair are more apparent than the resemblances, and they are especially clear in their choice of subjects for their novels. London, after his experiences as a manual laborer and his observations as a tramp, determined to lift himself from the working class. To train himself for success he entered the University of California, engaging, during his preparation and his brief period at the university, in labors as phenomenal as those of Sinclair at Columbia. His opportunity came, however, not as a direct result of his university labors, but as an incidental result of a trip to the Yukon in search of gold. His first published short stories, which appeared in the *Overland Monthly* in 1899 and in book form in 1900, were the fruit of that venture. Two other collections of short stories and a novel came out of that Yukon goldmine, and then *The Call of the Wild* established London in the eyes of the world as the Rudyard Kipling of Alaska.

Although he was converted to socialism at the time he was preparing to enter the university, socialist doctrine plays no part in these first five books. There are fine, vigorous pictures of the Alaskan scenery: the limitless expanses of snow, the intolerable cold, the bewildering brilliance of the aurora, the unfathomable blackness of long nights. Against this background heroic men and beasts perform magnificent exploits of strength and daring. If London gave little indication of having read Marx, he showed again and again how well he had mastered Spencer. The doctrine of the survival of the fittest and the theory of atavism influenced most of the Alaskan stories. Nothing attracted London more than the idea of the primitive man, the man of the Stone Age, strong, brutal, simple, seizing what he wanted, winning admiration even from those he conquered, marching in fearless independence to magnificent triumph or glorious death. For this man there is the ideal woman, sometimes one of lowly birth, more often nobly born, in either case fine and sensitive but with a strength that responds to her lover's strength, simple and pure but with a passion that responds to her lover's passion. Opposed to these are the weaklings, usually chosen from those supposed to be the very flower of civilization, but, as the event proves, not only weaker than their primitive antagonists but also less noble, less generous, and less admirable.

Since we know how eager London was for money, we might assume that his constant reiteration was merely a bid to hold his audience by the retention of a successful formula, and, especially insofar as the choice of the Alaskan background is concerned, there is truth in the assumption. But deeper forces than the conscious desire for success were dictating London's choice of theme. Never was he to abandon it. We find the primitive man, who is also the superman of Nietzsche's dreams, in the guise of Wolf Larsen, Martin Eden, Burning Daylight, Billy Roberts, and Darrell Standing. Even Ernest Everhard, the self-educated blacksmith and invincible propagandist of *The Iron Heel,* is merely the superman in red. For the most part London went where he could find his superman—to the South Seas, to prize-fights, to wars. But, whatever the setting he chose, the character appeared. The superman is Jack London, as he felt himself to be, Jack London fighting his way to success at sea, outdistancing all rivals in Alaska, battling against jealous critics and blind publishers as a novelist, subduing his bourgeois opponents as a socialist, surpassing his neighbors as a farmer. The force that had driven his father on from frontier to frontier drove him, both in fact and in imagination, from adventure to adventure, from conquest to conquest.

But all this seems strange doctrine from a socialist. London believed that he was a socialist and that his work showed the influence of his creed. *The Sea-Wolf,* he said, was to prove that "the superman cannot be successful in modern life. The superman is antisocial in his tendencies, and in these days of our complex society and sociology he cannot be successful in his hostile aloofness." Who, reading the book, can fail to see that Larsen's defeat is not due to "our complex society and sociology," and that the wolf of the sea has London's sympathies and is intended to win ours. *Martin Eden,* he declared, was a protest against the philosophy of Nietzsche, and Martin was deliberately made a thoroughgoing individualist for the greater glory of socialism. What reader, one wonders, would ever guess it? Even *The Iron Heel* can scarcely be called a socialistic novel: it contains, in Everhard's speeches, many arguments for socialism, and it deals with the revolution, but Everhard, far from being a typical socialist, is a typical London superman, and the revolution, which is unsuccessful, is the occasion for description of the typical red-blooded variety. *The Valley of the Moon* uses London's own experiences as a manual laborer, and the first third gives a fine authentic account of the life of the proletariat in such a city as Oakland. Yet if one had never heard of London's devotion to the revolution, one might easily suppose that the book was written by an opponent of socialism: the only socialist in the book is a weak dreamer, ineffectual, hen-pecked, and unhappy; the hero, on the other hand, deserts the working class in the midst of a crucial strike, goes back to the land like a good pioneer, and achieves success as a scientific farmer, exploiting the labor of others.

No, London might study socialist books, might give money

to the party, might lecture on socialism, might become president of the Intercollegiate Socialist Society, might sign his letters "Yours for the Revolution," but he remained very little of a socialist. He was sincere, of course; the proof is in the fact that he engaged in active agitation at a time when he knew he was losing popularity and therefore money. But his socialism never affected his way of looking at life, never touched the basic qualities of his personality, out of which his fiction came. Although he lectured on the incentives that would move men in a socialist state, he was personally driven by the desire for wealth, ease, and power. "It's money I want," he wrote, "or rather, the things money will buy." "Money will give me all things, or at least more of all things than I could otherwise possess." "I am in pursuit of dollars, dollars, dollars." "I flatter myself that I am one of the rare socialists who have ever succeeded in making money out of their socialism." No socialist, needless to say, scorns the value of material well-being, but no true socialist regards personal aggrandizement as a fundamental solution of his problems or ignores the implications of his own profits. In his attitude towards money London was indistinguishable from any middle-class man on the make.

And there are more important inconsistencies. London believed in the mission of the Anglo-Saxon race and preached it year in and year out: "I do not believe in the universal brotherhood of man. . . . I believe my race is the salt of the earth." His reading taught him that the industrial proletariat would bring about the revolution and that the struggle must be waged in the great cities; but his own interest was in the uncivilized portions of the earth, in Alaska and the South Seas, and he preached a return to the soil as a solution of the world's economic problems. Whatever his professed admiration for the proletariat ("So I went back to the workingclass, in which I had been born and where I belonged."), his experience as an employer on his farm convinced him that "most men are fools": "The reason a man works for me, is because he cannot work for himself. Stupid boobs, most of them." He resigned from the Socialist Party in 1916 because it was not active and belligerent enough on behalf of the working class, and the same year found him saying, "My choice for President is Theodore Roosevelt, whom nobody in this fat land will vote for because he exalts honor and manhood over the cowardice and peace lovingness of the worshippers of fat." Throughout most of his life he preached the yellow peril, and he was one of the foremost Hun-haters at the time of the World War. Finally, he was a pessimist, despite all his enthusiastic activity: his private opinions as expressed in his letters are strikingly like the views of Martin Eden, and many of his friends believe that his death, like Eden's, was at his own hands.

Jack London was never a thinker, and inconsistencies seldom bothered him. He was curiously juvenile and surprisingly sentimental. He read widely, but his reading only served to re-enforce his prejudices. His widow has said that he was at first an individualist and then, after achieving success, a socialist. The record, however, shows that individualism and socialism grew side by side: individualism became a conscious creed during his high school and college years, when he was studying socialism most avidly and advocating it most enthusiastically. He became a socialist because he felt himself one of the proletariat, and was eager to ally himself with his fellow-workers in their fight for emancipation. At the same time he was determined to achieve his own salvation. Individual success and the revolution were alike ways of escaping from poverty and oppression, and, characteristically, he accepted the philosophical implications of both methods. Later, when he no longer belonged to the working class, he continued to advocate socialism, but his individualism was as strong as it had ever been, and he could sympathize with Martin Eden as easily as with Ernest Everhard. Even when he resigned from the party, he defended his resignation on socialistic grounds, but it is to be observed that he resigned, not to build some better organization for the revolutionary cause, but to devote himself to his farm, his books, and his attacks on Germany.

If Jack London had had a disciplined mind, if he had understood all the implications of socialist theory, his outlook on life would have changed, and, if he had written at all, he would have written very different books. As it was, his mind could function on two levels and he could both be a socialist and cultivate what his widow calls a princely ego. It was on the egotistic level that his books were conceived, and in each of them that princely ego is projected in the creation of the hero. The discussion of his socialism indicates that we are not to expect in his work the virtues we had hoped to discover in the novels of a socialist, for his socialism scarcely entered into the conception of his fiction. The discussion still further defines the nature of his writing. We must not expect fine character portrayal, for there is only one character London could depict, and that one character is so much a product of his dreams, so nearly a personal myth, that we cannot find it convincing. We must not expect sound and beautiful structure: London, thanks to the lack of discipline, thought in episodes and, thanks to his impulsiveness and his eagerness for money, wrote in haste. We must not expect a subtle and dignified style; he had neither the sensitiveness nor the patience to create it. We can expect to feel vigor, the driving energy of Jack London, surging through the action, the characterization, the movement of the words. We can expect to find descriptions that, however much they may be over-written, do evoke their scenes. And we can expect to respond, with whatever atavistic qualities we may have, to tales of brutal men and their heroic adventures.

The ferment of the early years of the century was the direct economic result of the passing of the frontier. Perhaps it was also to some extent a psychological result; perhaps the energy that had gone into pioneering expressed itself, in part, in this way. Theodore Roosevelt, it will be remembered, was not only the leader of the reformers; he was also the preacher of the strenuous life, the friend of cowboys, the Colonel of the Rough Riders, the authority on animal life, and the author of *The Winning of the West.* The joy of open spaces and heroic adventure is one of the perennial themes of literature, but it was a theme that seems to have had special appeal in the first decade of the century when men were forced to realize that the era of pioneering had come to an unmistakable close. For millions of men whose lives industrial society has made dull and ugly and narrow, London provided the relief of vicarious adventure. He could take these people into a dreamland of heroic opportunity. He could not give them a sharp awareness of the kind of world in which they live, an understanding of the minds of their masters and their fellows, a sense of the power and destiny of their class, those things that we might expect to be the gifts of a socialist novelist.

* * *

Upton Sinclair began his career as a serious novelist with a love story, long since out of print, which he followed with *The Journal of Arthur Stirling,* a record of his own frantic struggles as a writer. Almost immediately after the publication of *The Journal,* he was converted to socialism, but his next novel was a story of the Civil War, *Manassas*. In 1904, however, he investigated labor conditions in the Chicago stockyards, and out of that investigation came *The Jungle*. This first venture in muckraking not only brought Sinclair success; it pointed out to him a path he could follow. He had always believed his books should serve humanity; after his conversion to socialism he knew what form that service should take. With *The Jungle* he became the novelist of the American scene, the recorder of great industrial movements, the fearless enemy of corruption and injustice. He wrote of millionaires, miners, socialists, labor spies. He dramatized the great struggles of his period: the Colorado coal strike, the war, the Mooney case, the Teapot Dome scandals, the murder of Sacco and Vanzetti. No such division of interests as deflected Jack London's purpose came between Sinclair and his career: what interested him as a socialist interested him as a novelist.

The Journal of Arthur Stirling reveals its author as an extremely sensitive young man, burdened down with the cares of the world but buoyed up by a sense of his mission and high destiny. Early in life, sharing his mother's fears for her irresponsible husband, Sinclair learned to take upon his own shoulders the obligations of others. The charity of rich relatives taught him something of the unequal distribution of wealth. His own struggles as an author showed him how little encouragement the callous world would give to noble purposes. All this ripened him for socialism: "It was like the falling down of prison walls about my mind; the most amazing discovery, after all these years—that I did not have to carry the whole burden of humanity's future upon my two frail shoulders." And his sensitiveness not only prepared the way for socialism; it became not the least of his literary gifts.

The great obstacle to Sinclair's development as a recorder

and interpreter of the struggles between capital and labor was his lack of experience. Having lived in middle-class boarding houses, supported himself as a hack-writer, and frequently retreated to the Canadian wilds or the New Jersey countryside, he knew nothing at first hand of mines or factories or financiers' offices. But even before he began his career as a muckraker he showed his ability to accumulate the material he needed. To prepare for the writing of *Manassas* he read some five hundred books and examined at least five hundred more. As a result the novel is solidly convincing in its account of the growth of hostility between North and South, and the characters have a firm basis in the events of history. And, as *The Jungle* showed, books were not the only sources of information on which Sinclair could draw: in investigating the stockyards he visited workers' homes, wandered about the plants, and talked with doctors, lawyers, politicians, and policemen.

The importance of this gift, this ability to accumulate the necessary material, cannot be exaggerated. The novelist who wishes to write about the complex structure of modern society cannot possibly have had all the different kinds of experience he finds it necessary to describe: he can scarcely have been both employer and employee, both union member and scab, both ward boss and reformer. We remember what Lafcadio Hearn said: "Fancy a good romance about Wall Street. . . . There is, of course, a tremendous romance there. . . . But what can the mere *littérateur* do, walled up to heaven in a world of mathematical mystery and machinery!" If a novelist is to write about the great social movements of his day, he must get some of his material at secondhand, and he is fortunate if he can accumulate it as accurately and as easily as Upton Sinclair has done. Consider his use of the inside story of the panic of 1907 in *The Moneychangers,* his treatment of the Colorado strike in *King Coal,* his portrayal of the activities of a labor spy in *100%,* his introduction of the details of drilling, piping, and selling in *Oil,* his handling of the Sacco-Vanzetti records in *Boston.*

Sinclair knows what facts he needs and how to get them, but unfortunately he is not so successful in assimilating them. Perhaps no writer can subject the data of research to exactly the same processes as he does the half-conscious perceptions that are the basis of creation, and thus achieve a perfect integration. Sinclair is far from perfection. In *Manassas,* for example, there is a long passage, between Allan's departure from the plantation after his father's death and his return just before the outbreak of hostilities, in which the method is simply that of historical exposition; and the same eagerness to describe the action of social forces, to present the facts as facts, is responsible for the mechanical manipulation of the hero's movements that makes him a witness of John Brown's raid, the firing on Sumter, and the Baltimore riots. In *The Jungle* the reader is less conscious of the documentation because, by virtue of his own suffering at the time, Sinclair entered directly into Jurgis' experiences, but there are nevertheless too many passages in which the author, clumsily trying to cover his tracks with some phrase about the tales of "an old fellow whom Jonas had introduced," lays before us, in the manner of a magazine article, the facts his investigation had uncovered. In *The Moneychangers* we settle down to read an exposure of the causes of the 1907 panic and the ways of the idle rich, and the adventures of the colorless hero seem merely an irritating interruption. *King Coal* limits itself, for the most part, to aspects of the strike that could have been present to Hal's experience, and *Oil* also concentrates on the hero's rather than the reader's education, but both books bear the stamp of the outside investigator, and in *Boston* we again find long passages of documentation. When critics complain that Sinclair is a propagandist, they suggest that he is given to direct argumentation. By and large the charge is not true, but he is guilty—and this may be an even greater sin against the art of the novel—of failure to assimilate the material he so wisely accumulates.

All this would suggest that Sinclair is primarily a pamphleteer. His pamphlets are undeniably effective. *The Brass Check,* despite its excessive preoccupation with the author's own sufferings at the hands of the press, banishes forever any lingering faith in the integrity of journalism, and *The Goose-Step* reveals not merely the plutocratic control of the universities but also the actual result of that control in the timidity and dulness of most college teaching and the consequent indifference and ignorance of most students. Even *The Profits of Religion,* with all its superficiality, builds a powerful case against the churches, and *Mammonart,* however weak as criticism, does attack the illusion that literature has no relation to life.

But, though Sinclair is a good pamphleteer, and though the pamphleteer in him sometimes triumphs over the novelist, his novels deserve to be examined as novels. When we examine them, we find that they are not weak because they are sugar-coated pamphlets; their weaknesses are both less reprehensible and more fundamental. Perhaps the easiest way to understand his failure is to analyze his choice of heroes and his treatment of them. In two of his books his heroes belong to the working class, *The Jungle* and *Jimmie Higgins.* The reason for his relative success with Jurgis is suggested in *American Outpost:* "Externally the story had to do with a family of stockyard workers, but internally it was the story of my own family." And the superiority of the first part of *Jimmie Higgins* to the second may be explained by Sinclair's knowledge of the affairs of a socialist local, on the one hand, and his ignorance, to say nothing of his false conception, of the war, on the other. He could write effectively about workers when he could draw directly on experience. But for the most part the heroes of Sinclair's novels are chosen from the middle class. Allan Montague in *The Metropolis* and *The Moneychangers* is so feeble a character that we may dismiss him at once. Hal in *King Coal,* however, is both likable and comprehensible, the Bunny of *Oil* is real enough to make us understand why millionaires' sons do sometimes flirt with radicalism, and Cornelia belongs with the not inconsiderable group of well-born Boston women who have espoused unpopular causes. There is no doubt that Upton Sinclair understands the mind of the convert and all the processes of conversion. Why should he not? He is himself a convert and, however active he has been in propaganda and agitation, he has remained outside the working-class movement. Hal's attitude towards the coal strike was easy enough for Sinclair to understand, for he had himself been an outside investigator, surprised and shocked by what he saw. Bunny's boyhood may have been very little like Upton Sinclair's, but his attitude towards the exploitation of labor was precisely that of his creator. The Boston blueblood may not be easy for a Californian of southern ancestry to understand, but obviously it is easier to understand her than it is to understand an Italian anarchist, an I.W.W. lawyer, or a communist agitator.

Sinclair's reasons for writing so often from the point of view of the middle-class convert to radicalism are quite clear, but it is also apparent that this convenient method has its disadvantages. In *Boston* he had the greatest theme of his career, but he could not master it. The significance of the Sacco-Vanzetti tragedy was twofold: to enlightened mem-

bers of the bourgeoisie it was evidence that the ideals of
their class were being betrayed by the rulers of America;
to class-conscious workers it was a symbol of their lifelong
struggle and a call to battle. Sinclair, though a socialist, devoted to the triumph of the proletariat, chose to emphasize
the significance of the death of these two Italians for the
bourgeoisie. Hence he chose Cornelia as his central character. She is skillfully presented, and, indeed, the whole account of life in Boston's ruling class is shrewdly perceptive.
But Cornelia, with all that can be said for her and her kind,
is a sentimentalist, and sentimentality pervades the entire
book. We follow the adventures of the runaway grand-
mother, we see Vanzetti through her eyes, we read about
the intrigues of the bankers and lawyers, we come upon
long expository accounts of the conduct of the defense, and
at the end we find the stark tragedy of the anarchists' death
smothered in a description of Cornelia's mystic experience.
The book is informing and at times moving, but the power,
the significance, the dignity, that we have a right to expect,
are missing.

What is true of *Boston* is true in some degree of all Sinclair's books. He is a socialist; he ardently desires the abolition of private property, and his loyalties are not divided as
Jack London's were. But the conception of the class struggle,
so fundamental in Marx's philosophy, the idea that the proletariat and only the proletariat will create the socialist state,
has remained alien to him. His socialism has always been of
the emotional sort, a direct response to his own environment,
and, as a result of his failure to undergo an intense intellectual discipline, he has never eradicated the effects of his
bourgeois upbringing. Though his aim has been socialistic,
his psychology has remained that of the liberal. Therefore,
whether he realizes it or not, he is always writing for the

middle class, trying to persuade his fellows to take their share of the burden of humanity's future, to pity the poor worker and strive for his betterment. Even the pamphlets are aimed at the middle class: *The Brass Check* proposes a weekly newspaper under liberal auspices; *The Profits of Religion* calls on the devout to put the churches on a rational basis; *The Goose-Step* demands the reform of the colleges by means of a teachers' strike.

Sinclair has always been in too much of a hurry. To every good cause he has given his time and energy in abundance. But he has never taken the pains to prepare himself adequately for his task as socialist and novelist. He has remained essentially what he was in the days when he wrote *The Journal of Arthur Stirling,* a sensitive man, full of sympathy for the woes of the world and eager to alleviate them. He has not looked on life as a member of the class with which, by his conversion to socialism, he allied himself. He has not written as a member of that class; except on rare occasions he has not written convincingly about that class; and, whatever his conscious intentions, he has not written for that class. Socialism could have given him a definite point of view, a clear attitude towards life, and, thus equipped, he could have assimilated the material he accumulated. As it is, though he knows a great deal about the life contemporary Americans lead, he has very imperfectly related this information to his own beliefs and purposes. This material is not part of him, any more than he is part of the working-class movement to which he has, within the limits of his nature, been so loyally devoted.

* * *

When all is said, the results of the enthusiastic literary activity of the first ten or a dozen years of the century are disappointingly meager. How many books written in those years deserve to survive? *The Octopus,* perhaps *The Jungle,* perhaps—for rather special reasons and for a special audience—*The Call of the Wild.* The novels of Churchill, White, and Phillips are already forgotten; O. Henry's vogue is a thing of the past; Herrick has few readers. Two-thirds of London's books are ignored, and most of the others slip towards oblivion. Upton Sinclair finds readers for each new book, but few of the earlier ones, except *The Jungle,* seem to be widely read in America. One or two other noteworthy books of those years—*Sister Carrie,* for example, and *Ethan Frome*—belong essentially to a later period. And aside from the work of these various novelists, there is almost nothing —a few poems by Edwin Markham and William Vaughan Moody, mildly testifying to the ubiquitousness of the social ferment; a half dozen plays, also concerned with social questions, that are read only by historians of the drama. Nothing more.

This is disappointing because, if all that has been said about the need for American literature to concern itself with the basic forces of American life is sound, this should have been the most fruitful decade since the Civil War. The novelists did strike at the very center of our national existence. They wrote of the great industries, the political movements, the struggles of labor. Whereas that characteristic phenomenon of the post-Civil War years, the multimillionaire, had scarcely been sketched before 1900, he sat for his portrait a dozen times before the decade was over. The novelists wrote of railroad owners, land speculators, stock brokers, meat packers, ward bosses, governors, and presidents. They showed how men made great fortunes and how they achieved high office. They wrote, too, of humble workmen in factories, on farms, in offices. They showed the influence of industrialism on women and children. They traced the course of commercialism in the professions. And they were not drawing on their imaginations; they knew how things were done. They were newspapermen, many of them, and had seen for themselves; and what further information they needed they knew how to get from books and investigations. Nor were they complacently recording the surfaces of life; it was dissatisfaction with the existing order that inspired them to write, and what they wanted to do was to understand how the abuses they described had come into existence and how they could be abolished.

They treated serious themes, and for the most part treated them seriously. That is their importance, and on the whole it is their only importance. Their millionaires and miners are seldom recognizable human beings, fully realized and comprehensibly presented. The movements they describe are not made real to us as movements of men and women like ourselves. These novels do not sharpen the reader's perceptions, quicken his mind, awaken his emotions, enhance his whole awareness of life. A dozen reasons could be given for this failure, all more or less relevant. It is true, for example, that none of the writers was able to develop a fresh colloquial style suited to his themes; so far as diction is concerned, every one of them is closer to the Victorians than to the writers of the twenties. It is true, too, that the muckraking generation had by no means emancipated itself from the sentimentality and prudery of the nineteenth century. Norris, for example, declared that morality—in the prevailing sense—was essential to literary greatness. London boasted that he had not written a word his little daughters could not read. Sinclair struggled constantly, and not with complete success, against the gentility of the Confederate tradition.

But such considerations are obviously secondary. If any

one of these writers had reached the level of true greatness, he would either have eliminated these weaknesses or succeeded in spite of them. The failure of each of these writers is the failure to find a satisfactory point of view. It is a little like a scout standing upon a mountain and seeking to discover the route the army can follow through the valley; he stands here and sees a forest, he stands there and sees a swamp, he moves again and sees a river; at last he finds a point from which he can look upon forest, swamp, and river, discover their proportions and relations, and map a course for the army. It is a little like a scientist, evolving hypothesis after hypothesis, finding that each fits some of the facts but will not fit others, until at last he finds the hypothesis that brings all his facts into order. The task of the novelist is to do justice to all the elements in his experience, weaving out of those elements a unified and patterned whole. It is far more difficult than the task of either scientist or scout, and if the novelists of the muckraking generation taught more by their failures than by their successes, we still have reason to be grateful to them. Their books may be forgotten, but their spirit lives in the works of their followers, and all that was sound in their attitudes and their methods has been perpetuated.

Chapter VII

TWO ROADS

THE years from 1912 to 1920 were years of disillusionment for the liberals. Though the election of 1912 seemed to many progressives a millennial dawn, they soon observed that Wilson, despite his diligence and apparent honesty in carrying out campaign promises, did not break decisively with big business. The younger liberals began to doubt if such a break was possible. Such men as Lippmann and Croly had already found the aims and methods of progressivism a little naïve, and they tried to formulate a philosophy of politics that would be, to use one of their favorite phrases, more realistic. But before the situation could be clearly defined, war had begun in Europe and liberalism was subjected to a new and decisive test. In the first months of the war it became apparent that few liberals had a consistent philosophy, and in 1917 their impotence was made altogether clear. The entrance of the United States into the war, to protect American investments, marked the end of progressivism. Not only were the liberals powerless to prevent the creation of militaristic sentiment and the ruthless suppression of dissent; they themselves, with few exceptions, fell victim to the hysteria of the moment. In the grip of wartime emotion, their consciences lulled by the Wilsonian phrases about a war to end war and making the world safe for democracy, they failed to see what was happening, and it took the Treaty of Versailles, the failure of the United States to enter the League of Nations, the election of Harding, and the return to normalcy to make them realize how their hopes had been blighted.

But if progressivism collapsed, broader and more important tendencies, which had begun before the end of the nineteenth century, continued and had a profound influence on art and literature. Enough has been said to indicate the bases and the character of American culture in the decades after the Civil War. To a great extent culture was in the hands of a relatively small group of prosperous middle-class people. These people accepted the narrow moral standards of the lower middle class, out of which many of them had recently risen, and they added to intolerance the timidity of the moderately well-off. They showed an interest in literature because to do so was a mark of social standing, and they demanded of books only that they should be respectable and entertaining. In the midst of the great economic movements that were sweeping the nation, this group consolidated its position and dominated the magazines and publishing houses. Most authors in the East were fully in sympathy with the genteel tradition, and the others, the few writers of originality, were forced to yield, in one way or another, to its power. Its influence extended to the West, where it weakened the expression of the frontier spirit. Indeed, as the century progressed, and the West and South entered the stages of economic development through which the East had been passing, those regions became the bulwark of the evangelistic morality and the prosperous respectability on which the genteel tradition rested.

Changes, however, came rapidly. The growth of large-scale industry brought moderate prosperity to a section of the middle class that was not rooted in any particular region. The whole tendency towards urbanization created what might almost be called a new class: a considerable group of persons who could afford to pay very little attention to what their neighbors thought, for at work they were part of great impersonal entities, and at home they enjoyed the anonymity of the apartment house dweller. And side by side with the growth of urbanism went a tendency towards cosmopolitanism: immigration brought many Americans into contact with other ways of life; the increase in travel and the reading of European books educated others. Nor could the growth of new standards be limited to the cities. By 1900 provincialism had little basis in economic fact. Not only was the interdependence of the various sections obvious; the development of nationwide news services, syndicates, and even chains of papers, and the growth of popular magazines with a national circulation meant that the attitudes and ideas of the cities would eventually reach the smallest village.

As the early years of the twentieth century accelerated earlier tendencies—as agriculture gave way to industry, as cities grew with enormous rapidity, as new inventions improved transportation and communication—the conditions that had created the peculiar culture of Victorian America disappeared. Attitudes based on those conditions did not yield at once, but the possibility of destroying them at last existed. Moreover, the emergence of the United States as a world power made colonial subservience an anachronism. And there were forces at work for the stimulation of creative activity as well as forces operating to eliminate the obstacles in its way. Again and again in world history a cultural renaissance has accompanied a marked development of national strength and prestige. In America, in 1911 or 1912, no artist could be unaware of the vastness of the country's resources, nor could he ignore the evidences of its great destiny in the affairs of the world. Artists did feel—we have the testimony of many of them—that all over the United States a new force was at work, an inexplicable force, it seemed, but an irresistible one.

To refer to the period from 1912 to 1925 as an American renaissance seems hyperbolical, and yet it has been so described, and not without some justice. The beginnings are found, of course, in the nineties, in the work of such men as Crane, Bierce, and Norris. The muckraking decade, though its results were in many ways disappointing, did much to prepare the way for the greater realism and greater technical skill of the middle generation. But the new forces in American life bore their real fruit in the novels of Theodore Dreiser, Edith Wharton, Sinclair Lewis, Sherwood Anderson, Willa Cather, and Joseph Hergesheimer; in the poetry of Edwin Arlington Robinson, Amy Lowell, Carl Sandburg, Vachel Lindsay, and Robert Frost; in the criticism of James Huneker, Joel Spingarn, H. L. Mencken, Van Wyck Brooks, and Randolph Bourne. Such a list of names suggests as nothing else could the vitality of literature in the modern period. And when one remembers that a list of artists, architects, and composers could be given to parallel this list of authors, one realizes that to speak of the rebirth of American culture is not wholly an exaggeration.

But we are not to suppose that the writers in whom this creative surge expressed itself acquiesced in the tendencies of American life. From the first the literature of the new forces was an intensely critical literature, as we have seen in examining the various forms of revolt in the nineties and the different types of protest in the muckraking decade. The middle generation continued the critical tradition, though the line of attack was shifted. Political evils were largely ignored, for there was a growing conviction that the cause of political reform was hopeless; but the critical spirit was, if anything, stronger. And these writers were not merely attacking the standards and attitudes that had survived from the past, though much time was and had to be spent in such onslaughts; they were also attacking certain of the tendencies that had made their own existence possible. Most of them were, for example, bitterly opposed to, or at the least intensely scornful of, the nationalistic sentiment that attended the growth of American imperialism. Most of them condemned, as harshly as any muckraker, the success ideal, though it was the ruthless quest for profit that had brought about the prosperity on which their welfare depended. Most of them denounced the standardization of life in the United States, though that was part of the process that had freed them from provincialism and gentility. They had even less respect than their predecessors for the rulers of the nation, and they sharply questioned the political and economic theories that had guided the country's growth.

To some extent the middle generation's criticisms were part of a general process of revaluation, which, outside the field of literature, was being carried on by such men as Veblen in economics, Dewey in philosophy, and Beard in history. But there was more involved than the necessary adjustment to new conditions. Most of the writers of the middle generation were pessimists. Robinson preached a gloomy philosophy; Amy Lowell and Carl Sandburg lapsed into pessimism; Conrad Aiken, Robinson Jeffers, and T. S. Eliot, all of whom began writing before 1920, frankly adopted a gospel of despair. For the novelists Dreiser, Anderson, and Cabell added their testimony, and Mencken, most widely read of the critics, constantly scoffed at any doctrine that offered a grain of hope for mankind. And more important than the overt profession of pessimism was the evidence, everywhere to be found, of a sense of frustration. Dreiser and

Anderson, in their clumsy but always moving books, conveyed a tacit recognition of defeat. Cabell and Hergesheimer romanticized their uneasiness. Mencken and Lewis spoke out of petulant disgust with American life. Scott Fitzgerald's *This Side of Paradise,* Floyd Dell's *Moon-Calf,* and Stephen Benét's *The Beginning of Wisdom* expressed the bewilderment and hopelessness of youth. Zona Gale in *Miss Lulu Bett* and Evelyn Scott in *The Narrow House* underscored what Dreiser, Anderson, and Lewis were saying about the stupidity of middle-class life in town and country. E. E. Cummings' *The Enormous Room* and John Dos Passos' *Three Soldiers* shattered the official glorification of the war. Poet after poet bore witness to his unhappiness; not one had the calm confidence of a Wordsworth or the impassioned hope of a Shelley. And it appeared that the younger the writer, the more emphatic his despair. For a time articulate society seemed to be entirely made up of youths who had nothing to say except that life in general was not worth living and that life in America was peculiarly and irremediably hopeless. The definitive statement of this attitude came in 1922 in Harold Stearns's symposium, called with deliberate irony *Civilization in the United States: An Inquiry by Thirty Americans.* Many of these critical thirty were so bereft of hope that they sailed at once for Europe. Others remained to tell each other, in the pages of Mr. Mencken's *Mercury,* how uproariously funny they found the whole farce of American life.

At first glance it seems almost impossible to reconcile this attitude with the facts of American life. The United States, a young nation just assuming the dominant rôle in the world drama, seemed to have before it a magnificent destiny. The middle class, to which most authors belonged and for which they chiefly wrote, was more prosperous than it had ever been before. Writers shared in that prosperity, and were able to take advantage of the new opportunities, created by the machine, for the expression of individual desires. So far as literature was concerned, the barriers were tumbling down, and the American author enjoyed an amazing new freedom. But on the other hand, the economic and political power of the middle class was steadily declining. As many events but especially the collapse of progressivism had shown, the heterogeneous group we call the middle class—composed of small business men, well-to-do farmers, white collar workers, intellectuals, and professional men—could no longer check the power of the major industrialists and financiers. Finance capitalism controlled not only the government but also the means of education and the organs of expression. Before this force the middle class was helpless; it could not prevent war; it could not abolish corruption; it could not eliminate cyclical depressions. However satisfactory its situation might be at the moment, it was at the mercy of forces it could not control.

Most authors belonged to a class that was caught in an iron contradiction. They were, moreover, peculiarly conscious of that contradiction, because they were in a position to realize the status of the middle class at the imperialist stage of capitalist development. However ignorant they might be of the economic theories involved, they could see the debasement of the middle class. They knew that it measured value only in pecuniary terms. They knew that its much-vaunted self-reliance went hand in hand with standardization. They knew that, though it had partly overcome its timidity with regard to morals, it had neither courage nor originality in dealing with political, economic, or cultural problems. Just as the muckrakers had protested, in the name of American individualism, against the abuses of power in business and government, so the writers of the middle generation protested, also in the name of American individualism, against the moral and intellectual stultification of the American people.

We can now understand why we find a sense of frustration everywhere in the work of the middle generation: their class was on the wane, and with that class, as it was and as it had to be at that particular stage of capitalistic development, they had no sympathy. We can also understand why optimism and pessimism are so inextricably mingled in the attitudes of these writers. Though there was an impulse towards creation and though opportunities for expression had multiplied, it was impossible either to be satisfied with the cultural level of the American people or to view the future with any confidence. Strange paradoxes resulted: philosophical pessimists wrote with enthusiasm and hope about the rebirth of poetry; such critics as Mencken spoke of man as a dizzy fly and yet fought furiously for man's right to say whatever he wanted to say; sardonic youths wrote poems to prove that life was not worth living and other poems to advocate the living of a full life. Whatever woes the writer might feel, he was in fact rather well-off. "How are we to write the Russian novel in America," Robert Frost ironically inquired, "as long as life goes so unterribly?" Life had been terrible for hundreds of thousands of soldiers in the World War; it was terrible at the moment Frost wrote, at the beginning of the era of Coolidge prosperity, for millions of underpaid laborers and their families; it would be terrible for more millions before a decade had passed. For a time, however, successful writers of the middle class were reasonably comfortable, and their complacency was, as Frost suggested, incompatible with the tragic attitude. But if tragedy was impossible, so was affirmation.

It is now apparent why the renaissance was so short-lived. It was based upon a condition that could endure but briefly. But before the collapse came, much had been accomplished. As we shall see, there is not a single writer of the middle generation whose work is not vitiated by faults that may be more or less directly traced to the instability of the basic economic situation. On the other hand, the vitality of the impulses, however brief in duration, that lay behind the literature of the period from 1912 to 1925 must not be underestimated. There had been better work in America, but there had never been so much good work, so many talented authors, such widespread interest in literature. And in particular we must remember that the middle generation emancipated American literature. Though the social foundations of Victorian prudery had already been undermined, prejudices lingered, and courage was necessary to topple over the towering structure of hypocrisy and repression. Courage most of the writers of the middle generation had, and it was only one, as will appear, of their real and important virtues.

* * *

A series of questions were posed to the author of the middle generation, and, whether he was conscious of the questions or not, his books were his answers. Should he or should he not use his new freedom in a more comprehensive portrayal of American life than had previously been possible? Should he allow his material well-being and that of his class to isolate him from the masses of the American people, or should he use his new-found resources for a more cogent examination of the contemporary scene? Should he yield to his pessimism and seek some haven from his doubts, or should he resolutely probe the sources of his discontent?

The issues were never, of course, so clearly stated, but two roads were there before the American writer, and much depended on which he chose.

Superficially it appeared that a great deal could be gained by following the road along which Edith Wharton, Willa Cather, Joseph Hergesheimer, and James Branch Cabell traveled. The authors of the muckraking period had dealt with most of the representative phenomena of an industrial civilization, and yet they had written singularly few important books. Their successors might well ask themselves if there was any hope for a writer who devoted himself to so complicated, so mysterious, and so genuinely distasteful a theme as the conduct of business operations. No one cares to commit suicide by attempting the impossible, and there is every temptation for an artist to seek perfection in small things rather than to risk failure in great.

In any case Edith Wharton could scarcely have chosen the other road. She did not belong to a family that had recently emerged from the lower middle class; her family was wealthy, she was educated abroad, and she associated with persons who thought of themselves as constituting the American aristocracy. Her background was a little like that of her adviser and friend, Henry James, and she felt as he did, and for somewhat the same reasons, that the novelist's proper field of study was that "in which initial forces had traveled furthest from their prime." Although in her early novel, *The Valley of Decision* (1902), she wrote of eighteenth century Italy, the problems she chose to deal with were of the sort that would have interested James; and when she turned to contemporary life, she tried, as he had done, to portray the delicate and subtle kinds of conflict that can develop only in an organized social group. She did not, however, turn to foreign lands for her themes, except in *Madame de Treymes* and portions of one or two other novels; she took James's advice and did what she could with America. She knew intimately the old, monied families of New York and Boston, and she had reason to think that she had there what James would have called a sufficient field for her imagination.

That she wanted to be honest *The House of Mirth* (1905) indicated. For her, being honest meant recognizing the weaknesses of the group she portrayed. The muckraking in which so many of her contemporaries were engaged must have seemed to her rather vulgar, and she had no intention of following their example, but she did refuse to abandon her own aristocratic ideals. The tragedy of Lily Bart is, she shows, a tragedy of false values, false values created by the "high society" in which Lily has been born and wants to remain. Similarly *The Custom of the Country* (1913) involves a criticism not only of the ambitious *nouveau riche* but also of the theories and practice of the group to which the indomitable Undine Spragg aspires. In these two novels, and in most of the books that came between them, Mrs. Wharton was saying quite frankly that the would-be aristocrats of the United States fell far short of true aristocratic standards.

She once said, writing of Henry James, "For him every great novel must first of all be based on a profound sense of moral values . . . and then constructed with a classical unity and economy of means," and in these words she defined her own intentions. On the one hand, the application of her sense of moral values to her chosen material forced her to become a critic and something of a satirist, and on the other, her concern with unity and economy helped her to "do" her subjects with a thoroughness James justly applauded. By contrast with other writers who were active between 1900 and 1912 she seemed not only remarkably skillful but also unusually certain of her aims. She was, however, obviously limited to a very narrow field. *The Fruit of the Tree* had shown that she was not only too ignorant of industrialism to write about it; all her structural and stylistic virtues disappeared when she faced a situation more complicated than the situations that might arise in good society. The success of *Ethan Frome* had suggested the possibility of her writing about country people, but the novelette, though dramatically effective, is somehow cold and mechanical, and, as *Summer* was to show, its peculiar virtues could not be reproduced. Moreover, even in *The House of Mirth* and *The Custom of the Country,* and certainly in *The Reef* and *Madame de Treymes,* there was evidence that her concern with the socially elect might easily force her in the direction of triviality.

At the time when most of the writers of the middle generation were beginning their careers, Mrs. Wharton was already an established author, but her greatest popular success came in 1920 with *The Age of Innocence.* This novel indicated her solution of her problems. She had apparently decided that she could not desert good society, and she had discovered that it was more and more difficult to apply her sense of moral values to the contemporary scene. Therefore she turned to the good society of the past, describing a time before the rapid amassing of great fortune had destroyed such stability as New York society had ever had; and she achieved in *The Age of Innocence* a finely ordered novel, in which the artful and faintly nostalgic treatment of the seventies throws a pleasant glamor over familiar themes. She repeated her success in the four novelettes that compose *Old New York.* But that success was a confession of defeat, as the books that came in the late twenties and early thirties showed.

From the first Mrs. Wharton, as has been said, had adopted a critical attitude towards the life she portrayed, and that attitude might have led her to a complete break with good society. That is, if she had tried resolutely enough to discover why the monied families of New York and Boston failed to conform to her aristocratic ideals, she might have questioned the whole conception of an American aristocracy. But this would have meant alienation from her friends and from the whole way of life to which she was accustomed, and it might have shattered the neat symmetry that she achieved in the construction of her novels. She was forced to compromise, and the results of that concession are apparent in all her later novels. Why are such books as *Hudson River Bracketed* and *The Gods Arrive* so dishearteningly trivial and cheap? It is because Mrs. Wharton has lost her sense of moral values—which was never quite so profound as she believed. And her sensitiveness to character, her lucidity of style, and her economy of structure have gone with the moral values.

Instead of moving from her rather circumscribed type of realism to a broader and more genuine realism, Mrs. Wharton has ended in romantic trivialities. Joseph Hergesheimer, another American who has written much about the idle rich, traveled more rapidly along a parallel path. Unlike Mrs. Wharton he had a rather austere childhood, and this bred in him, not loyalty to an aristocratic ideal, but an ambition for beauty and luxury. At first his longing for beauty partly redeemed his work, despite the turgidity of his style. In *The Lay Anthony* he succeeded in suggesting the irrational but by no means unappealing idealism of a young boy, just as a little later in *Linda Condon* he gave some substance to his vision of the desirable but unattainable woman. This work was romantic, but frankly and freshly and not unpleasantly so. But even such mild magic could not keep long its potency. Hergesheimer's love of luxury overcame his love of beauty, and his aspirations reduced themselves to a formula. In *The Three Black Pennys* and *Java Head* he had projected his romantic visions into the past, and in portions of these novels, as in some of his short stories, he suggested a kind of life in which beauty played a conspicuous part. But even here he frequently yielded to the temptation to find his beauty in mere ornamentation, in the houses, the furnishings, the clothes. This zeal for decoration dominated *The Bright Shawl* and *Balisand* and had become an obsession by the time he wrote *Quiet Cities.* In the novels of contemporary life, such as *Cytherea* and *The Party Dress,* his passion for physical luxury nakedly revealed itself as simply the vulgar longing of the idle rich for conspicuous waste. His stories, many of which were printed in *The Saturday Evening Post,* might almost have appeared as part and parcel of the magazine's advertising. To this, then, his romantic dreams reduced themselves—to a gross satisfaction in expensive dresses, rare wines, and ornate furniture. His pessimism, which at first remotely recalled the dignity of Conrad's philosophy, became an obvious pose, an attempt to mask his porky complacence.

Healthy romanticism, the youthful expression of hope and confidence such as we find in the heroic tales of Cooper and Melville, was impossible for the writers of the middle generation. Their unwillingness to look at the life about them was a symptom of disease, and the disease did its work swiftly. James Branch Cabell, whose name is so often coupled with Hergesheimer's, stated in *Beyond Life* the philosophy, if it may be called that, to which both subscribe.

This Virginia gentleman and genealogist could hardly be expected either to approve of life in the United States or to feel that he was under any obligation to improve it. Instead he has converted his petulant disgust into a melodramatic pessimism. If a man could soberly regard his lot for five minutes, he has flamboyantly stated, he would become a gibbering idiot. The fact that his despair does not deter him from constant activity as a writer he has explained at some length in several books. The artist has a function in this mad world, Mr. Cabell argues; it is to create beautiful illusions, which alone make life endurable. But, far from occupying himself with the dissemination of dynamic lies, Mr. Cabell has devoted all his talents to attacking men's illusions. He is, then, a fraud; in fact, he is doubly a fraud, for neither his romanticism nor his pessimism is genuine. He is a sleek, smug egoist, whose desire to be a gentleman of the old school breeds dissatisfaction with the existing order, but who has not enough imaginative vigor to create a robust world in which deeds of chivalry and gallantry are performed. Instead, he has written mild little fantasies, carefully baited with delicate obscenities. His whole work is a structure of lies, from his tinselled style to his theorizings on life and literature. His reliance on sophomoric artifices—his footnotes, his authorities, his last appearances, his reincarnations—so underscores his fundamental venality that one marvels at the success with which, for a time, he practiced his petty deceptions.

Fortunately few writers have followed the example of Cabell and Hergesheimer, but there have been other and perhaps more legitimate ways of avoiding industrialism and its consequences. The life of the countryside is, after all, as much a part of the American scene as the life of the cities, and the fact that so talented a writer as Willa Cather has

tried to continue the tradition of sectionalism is in itself of
some importance. Certainly the middle generation has given
us few books that can be reread with more pleasure than
O Pioneers! and *My Ántonia.* Picture after picture is unfor-
gettable: the death of Mr. Bergson, the visit to Old Ivar,
Emil at the fair, Frank Shabata in prison, Christmas at the
Shimerdas, harvesting on the farm, the home of the Cuzaks.
The two women are truly heroic—noble Alexandra and impulsive Ántonia. And how impressively Miss Cather sets
before us the passage of the seasons, desperate winters and
hard-working summers, with poverty gradually yielding to
prosperity for the Bergsons in the one book, with Ántonia
unchanged through toil and sorrow in the other!

Yet we cannot deny that much of the pleasure we take in
Willa Cather's books is the result of her elegiac tone: she
makes us look wistfully back at a life that, in her accounts
of it, seems nobler and richer than our own. The very basis
of *O Pioneers!* is a kind of mysticism—the sacredness of the
soil, the religious aspirations of the frontiersman. "A pioneer should have imagination, should be able to enjoy the
idea of things more than the things themselves," she writes.
She speaks of "The Genius of the Divide, the great, free
spirit which breathes across it," and she says of Alexandra:
"It fortified her to reflect upon the great operations of nature,
and when she thought of the law that lay behind them, she
felt a sense of personal security." At the end Alexandra says,
"The land belongs to the future. . . . I might as well try to
will the sunset over there to my brother's children. We come
and go, but the land is always here. And the people who
love it and understand it are the people who own it—for a
little while."

Carl Linstrum, who leaves Nebraska, not only laments the
heartlessness and emptiness of city life; he regrets the pass-

ing of the old frontier and the coming of prosperity: "I even think I liked the old country better," he says. "This is all very splendid in its way, but there was something about this country when it was a wild old beast that has haunted me all these years." When Lou Bergson talks of blowing up Wall Street, Carl makes fun of his radicalism: "The same business would go on in another street. The street doesn't matter. But what have you fellows out here got to kick about? You have the only safe place there is. Morgan himself couldn't touch you." Once, Miss Cather says, an idyllic life was led on the frontier; that life is vanishing, but its spirit is expressed in such persons as Alexandra and Ántonia, and in admiring them we pay tribute to the values they embodied. "Fortunate country," she says in the last sentence of the book, "that is one day to receive hearts like Alexandra's into its bosom, to give them out again in the yellow wheat, in the rustling corn, in the shining eyes of youth!"

What makes Miss Cather's elegiacism—in *O Pioneers!*, *My Ántonia,* parts of *The Song of the Lark,* and *A Lost Lady*—more than a weak romanticizing of the past is her closeness to the life she describes. Her childhood had been spent in the Nebraska of the eighties and nineties, and she had seen for herself the valiance of humble immigrants in their struggle with the elements. She selected carefully the incidents she depicted, and omitted much that was important in the experience of the pioneers; but there were heroic elements in the life of that time and place, and she both loved and understood them. Her stories were not merely the expressions of her dreams; they were, to some extent, the faithful reflection of a noble episode in the conquest of the American continent.

But even if dignified heroism had been so common on the Nebraskan frontier as Miss Cather seemed to believe, the fact remained that the situation that created it could endure but briefly, and she was forced to recognize its passing. "Optima dies," we read on the title page of *My Ántonia,* "prima fugit." The realization that the happiest experiences she had ever known belonged to a vanished world saddened Miss Cather, and gave to her sense of frustration, which she shared with most of her contemporaries, a peculiar wistfulness. As she turned from the portrayal of the heroic frontier, she was forced to deal with baffled hopes and empty lives. In *One of Ours* she wrote of the unhappiness of a sensitive, idealistic Nebraskan boy, and she escaped from the devastating drabness of the first portion of the book only by ignoring the problems she had raised and giving a romantic account of American participation in the World War. The sterile dulness of the life led by the St. Peters was so heartbreaking for her that she had to introduce the colorful tale of Tom Outland into *The Professor's House* in order to comfort herself and her readers. Her two novelettes, *A Lost Lady* and *My Mortal Enemy,* are studies of defeated women, just as *O Pioneers!* and *My Ántonia* are studies of triumphant women, and in *A Lost Lady* she seems to say that compromise is the price of survival and corruption the inevitable outcome of the love of life.

The Professor's House (1925) and *My Mortal Enemy* (1926) made it clear that Miss Cather was rapidly sinking into an unfathomable morass of personal pessimism and artistic sterility. But suddenly she found what seemed to her a way of salvation. In *Death Comes for the Archbishop* (1927) she returned to an earlier frontier, New Mexico in the fifties, and described a series of episodes in the lives of two Catholic priests, and in *Shadows on the Rock* she wrote of seventeenth century Quebec. In both books she was able to concern herself with the heroic qualities and colorful setting

that had appealed to her so strongly as she looked back on
her Nebraskan childhood, and in both books she showed
how her characters were fortified by the ancient traditions
and long-suffering piety of Catholicism. Thus her problems
were solved: a theme to match her interests and talents, and
a faith to serve as bulwark against her own sense of futility.
But what a price she paid! Instead of the vivid re-creation
of frontier realities we find poetic fantasies. Instead of vigorous narrative we find delicately embroidered little episodes. Instead of heroes and heroines we find paragons of
piety. Miss Cather's sins have overtaken her. Her method
of building novels out of colorful episodes has led to the creation of a series of elaborate tapestries. Her recourse to the
charm of reminiscence has become dependence on sweet
sentiment and vague nostalgia. With her mastery of rhythm
and her gift for imagery at their peak, she has become dull
and empty except for those who can find religiosity a satisfactory substitute for imaginative power.

Though she has spent a certain part of her life in great
cities, surrounded by the phenomena of an industrial civilization, Miss Cather has preferred to write about the frontier and to describe the simple conflict of man with the
forces of nature. In her earlier work, catching the spirit of
pioneer life, she wrote with much beauty and some power.
When, however, her childhood reminiscences were exhausted
and she was forced into a larger world, she was confronted
by all sorts of problems that she could not solve. At last,
harassed by her conviction of the sterility of contemporary
life, she chose a time and place that, because of its remoteness, would permit her to order events according to her own
ideals. Having turned to the past as a refuge and not because of some perception of the relation of the past to the

central issues of the present, she could do nothing but paint pretty pictures.

Sectionalism has always had its dangers, and those dangers have grown constantly greater. Ellen Glasgow began her career in 1897 with the determination to portray faithfully the life of Virginia. She was preoccupied with the problems of the individual's adjustment to the barren ground that the Civil War had made of that state, and her work, though inevitably provincial, was for the most part solid and convincing. But she had to struggle constantly against the sentimentality that was part of her tradition, and that struggle robbed her of much of her creative force. In the twenties she won the reputation that had previously eluded her with *The Romantic Comedians* and *They Stooped to Folly,* in which she mocked Virginian sentimentality. But sympathy was mingled with her mockery, and she showed the pathos as well as the ridiculousness in the lives of the romantic comedians. In *The Sheltered Life* she further showed that this pathos might border on tragedy, and her book became virtually a defense of Virginian values. "I find my sympathy shifting," she has written, "to that outcast from the machine civilization, the well-bred person." But her sympathies are with the well-bred person because he is well-bred, and she makes no attempt to discover why he is an outcast. Thus she tumbles into the pitfall she had previously so scrupulously avoided, and becomes one more apologist for a way of life that is rapidly vanishing.

* * *

We have seen where one of the roads led. We have seen that the fugitive of the middle generation was exposed to greater perils than the fugitive of the seventies and eighties. It was even more difficult for Mrs. Wharton to write of aris-

tocratic life than it was for Henry James, and her collapse
was far more complete than his. Miss Cather and Miss Glasgow found the limitations of sectionalism much more
promptly than Miss Jewett and Mrs. Freeman did, and their
subterfuges were consequently much more desperate. The
romanticism of Cabell and Hergesheimer sank to an infan-
tile level that Hearn and Bierce, to say nothing of the earlier
romanticists, had never reached. Despite, then, the failures
of the muckrakers, experience clearly showed the novelist
that he must face the central issues of American life.

Out of a poverty-stricken home, his boyhood overshadowed by the bigotry of his father and the misfortunes of
his sisters, Theodore Dreiser emerged, looking for success,
at first in business and then in journalism. In Pittsburgh, at
the age of twenty-three, he read Tyndall, Huxley, and
Spencer. They liberated him from superstition, and, unpre-
dictably, they weakened his desire for success. What could
success mean, he began to ask himself, in a trivial little world
where man was a wisp in the wind? He would never, of
course, quite kill the longing for gilt and tinsel born of his
drab boyhood and fostered by the almost universal acceptance in America of pecuniary standards. But he had been
led to question the values preached by his contemporaries,
and other interests began to influence his decisions. Even as
a boy he had had a certain sensibility, vaguely poetic, that
his shrewder associates recognized as a literary gift. In
Pittsburgh he read novels as well as books of science, Balzac
as well as Spencer, and the desire grew in him to express
what he saw and felt. Four years of poverty and hack-work
in New York intensified his sense of the mystery and terror
of life, and at last he sat down to write *Sister Carrie*. He had
none of the faith in social reform that was hesitant in Norris, intermittent in London, and ineradicable in Upton Sin-

clair. He had studied the materialists too well to be able to
justify any hope for mankind. But their honest contemplation
of facts, however unpleasant, inspired in him a determination to be equally honest in recording the life about him.

Sister Carrie is the work of a bewildered man, willing to
admit he is bewildered. One feels the man in the book, asking questions he cannot answer, recording his confusion,
shaking his head with weary resignation over the course of
his tale. One feels his effort, as he laboriously amasses detail,
as he clumsily probes into motives, as he ponderously gropes
for words. And one feels his honesty, his determination to
present life exactly as he sees it. He may not approve of the
deeds he describes; often he expresses his disapproval in
ways that show how imperfectly he has conquered the prejudices of his boyhood; but the desire to understand triumphs
over conventional morality, and the story of Carrie, Drouet,
and Hurstwood is inexorably unfolded. One cries out against
the author's clumsiness, his sheer stupidity, and yet one surrenders to his honesty and acknowledges in the end that he
is a master. In *Sister Carrie* Dreiser not only shattered, in a
single aimless gesture, a score of sacred conventions; he
created living men and women in a world we recognize as
ours.

It is a passion for truth, lodged in the deepest stratum of
Dreiser's mind, operating in spite of conflicting interests,
that gives his work its importance. *Sister Carrie* and *Jennie
Gerhardt* came out of his observations, and in them he
showed what happened to lower middle-class American families such as the Dreisers. For *The Financier* and *The Titan*
he had to rely largely on research, but he succeeded in creating such a figure as had not previously appeared in our literature, a man of lusts so fierce that the ruthlessness of Van
Harrington or John Barclay or Burning Daylight seems al-

most amiable by comparison, a man worthy of the exploits attributed to him. In each of his six novels Dreiser has touched the fundamental forces that shape American life. Whether he deals with poor girls who stray from the path of conventional virtue or with millionaires who dominate cities, whether he portrays the struggles of an artist or the tragedy of a factory-hand, he makes us feel the importance of his people because he shows us the forces that work through them. Despite innumerable faults, his six massive novels, built on the rocks of honesty and pity, stand while the works of shrewder architects crumble.

Like Dreiser, Sherwood Anderson came from a mid-western family with many children and little money. Like Dreiser, he at first worshipped the bitch goddess, achieving moderate prosperity as a business executive and as a writer of advertisements, and he too discovered the emptiness of material success. But if their early experiences are somewhat similar, their literary gifts are utterly different. Incapable of sustained, exact description, Anderson relies upon the lightning flash. Surfaces, deeds, even words scarcely concern him; everything is bent to the task of revelation. When he succeeds, there is the character of Elmer Cowley or Dr. Reefy or Louise Hardy, about whom we need to be told nothing more. If one were to judge Anderson only by his best work, one could scarcely avoid the conclusion that his talent was of the first order. Here, one would note, was a prose-writer with the courage to create his own idiom and his own rhythms. One would marvel at the man's penetration, his understanding of the strangeness and terror that life holds even for the humblest. And one would find, in such a book as *Winesburg, Ohio,* an authentic picture of the small town, and, in *Poor White,* the record of the small town's transformation. Except in *Poor White,* one would find little about industrialism, and yet one could never be unaware that the civilization portrayed was in travail. Others have described more fully how the common people live; no one has shown so authoritatively what they feel.

In Sinclair Lewis we have to reckon with a different kind of talent, neither Dreiser's massiveness nor Anderson's penetration. Lewis is the shrewd reporter, armed with the skepticism and frankness of his generation, the shrewd reporter with a chip on his shoulder. For six years he wrote books in which he gave free play neither to his powers of observation nor to his acute exasperation with his complacent contemporaries. *Main Street* (1920) he wrote deliberately, as a foreword shows, to expose "our comfortable tradition and sure faith," to "betray himself as an alien cynic," and to "distress the citizens by speculating whether there may not be other faiths." Its success pointed to the existence of other persons not quite convinced that "Main Street is the climax of civilization."

Once he had abandoned himself to his temperament and his talents, Lewis took his place among the recorders of the contemporary scene. With systematic zeal he has described the small town, the prosperous mid-western city, and the great metropolis, and he has written of business, medicine, the church, and social work. If what one wants is the detailed, accurate record of the way people live, Lewis is the most satisfying of our authors. What Carol Kennicott saw in Gopher Prairie might be seen in thousands of American communities; the day in Babbitt's life that Lewis so minutely records has been duplicated in the lives of tens of thousands of small business men; it is to the keeping of such doctors as Martin Arrowsmith met in Wheatsylvania, Nautilus, and the McGurk Institute that our lives are entrusted. About the middle stratum of the population, the moderately

prosperous professional and business men, Lewis has written with a keenness of eye and an alertness of ear that any
novelist might envy him.

In the books of these three authors we have the best that
the middle generation has contributed to the study of the
contemporary scene. They have brought our literature
closer to the center of American life, and we can rejoice in
Dreiser's strength, Lewis's shrewdness, and Anderson's sensitivity. But can we be satisfied with their work? We are
grieved, of course, by such things as Dreiser's clumsiness, Anderson's frequent obscurity, Lewis's reliance on mimicry;
but these are superficial faults, lamentable but chiefly significant as symptoms of more serious failures. Dreiser seems always to be heavily stalking some secret that constantly eludes
him. The brilliant flash of Anderson's imagination illuminates a tiny spot in a black night of mystery. Lewis's amusing chatter fails to conceal his blind helplessness.

What have these men to say about life? Only five years
ago Dreiser wrote, "I can make no comment on my work
or my life that holds either interest or import for me. Nor
can I imagine any explanation or interpretation of any life,
my own included, that would be either true—or important,
if true. . . . In short I catch no meaning from all I have seen,
and pass quite as I came, confused and dismayed." This
honest confession of bewilderment helps us to interpret
Dreiser's career in fiction. He has not, of course, been completely consistent: even the most chaotic kind of novel involves the assumption of some sort of continuity, and talk
of chemisms and reflexes indicates a belief that there are at
least partial explanations of life. But his confusion is genuine,
and it is never more apparent than when he is trying hardest
to formulate a philosophy. Not only is he crude and uninformed in his statement of materialistic monism and his at-

tempts to apply its principles; he is capable of holding opinions that flatly contradict it. And this confusion is found in all his judgments. He has never, for example, quite emancipated himself from his boyhood longing for crass material success, and, though he has remained loyal to his standards of literary integrity, he betrays again and again a desire for the ostentatious luxuries of the successful business man.

In a way, of course, Dreiser's confusion is responsible for some of his virtues. He is usually on the side of the oppressed, even though he can find no satisfying theories of right and wrong, and, despite his insistence that strength is its own justification, he has more than once recorded his determination not to exploit his less fortunate fellows. It is by his sympathy for the downtrodden that in recent years he has been led, in the face of all his theories, to support the proletariat in its struggle against the ruling class. But this alliance, which might once have been so fruitful for him, has probably come too late to influence his writings. It seems likely that he will pass, not quite so dismayed as he came, but quite as confused.

The mystery of life, so distressing to Dreiser, has been scarcely less terrifying to Sherwood Anderson. Though *Winesburg, Ohio,* gave the impression that he was principally concerned with the blighting effects of small town life, it soon became apparent that he regarded industrialism as the real enemy. In *Poor White* he traced the transition in the Middle West from agriculture and the handicrafts to machine industry, and showed that Hugh McVey's inventions not only failed to bring happiness but destroyed values that had previously existed. The real hero of the story is Joe Wainsworth, the harness maker who takes pride in his work. "What has mankind, in America, not missed," Anderson asked in *A Story-Teller's Story,* "because men do not know, or are forgetting, what the old workman knew." "Aha, you Stephenson, Franklin, Fulton, Bell, Edison," he exclaimed, "you heroes of my Industrial Age, you men who have been the gods of the men of my day . . . all of your triumphs come to the dull and the meaningless absurdity, of say a clothespin factory. There have been sweeter men in old times, half forgotten now, who will be remembered after you are forgotten." It is little wonder that in the later twenties, when he felt his creative powers flagging, Anderson went back to the small town. The small town newspaper, he said, might help in the struggle against industrialism and standardization, and he advised young men and women to use such papers to start a backfire in favor of individualism.

But Anderson can never be satisfied with an easy solution. He continued to worry about the machine, and to wonder if it could not somehow be made to serve the ideals in which he believed. He wondered if poets could not take a different attitude towards machines, and he wrote poems himself in which he made tentative affirmations. He went even farther: he began to realize that all the problems that troubled him were bound up in one problem, and like Dreiser he took his stand with the party of revolution. These two men, both of them intimately acquainted with poverty and hardship, both of them very close to the common people, have both discovered that their hopes are inextricably linked with the hopes of the working class. Since he made this discovery Anderson has written one book, *Beyond Desire*. It has most of the virtues of his earlier work, and most of the faults. It shows that his approach to communism is almost purely personal; it attracts him because it seems to answer some of the questions that have long troubled him. The economic and philosophical implications of communism mean little to him, and certainly he is not yet filled with the spirit of the fighting vanguard of the proletariat. Therefore he is still a long way from overcoming the effects of years of bewilderment and frustration, and *Beyond Desire* is as lacking in unity and as chaotic in its analyses as any of its predecessors. But the book is significant because a change in Anderson may signify a change in the American people, to whom he has always been extremely close. And when one compares the characterization of Red and the description of the mill girls with the work Anderson did in *Many Marriages* and *Dark Laughter,* there is reason to believe that he may have found a basis for further development.

Sinclair Lewis, though he became interested in socialism many years ago, has not joined Dreiser and Anderson in endorsing the Communist Party. In *Ann Vickers* the heroine recognizes a certain validity in the communist position, but she is irritated by the fanaticism of a party member she knows, and in any case her life is too full for her to limit herself to a particular program. Lewis is rather like her. In his own way he perfectly illustrates the middle-class contradiction. Since the success of *Main Street*—and probably before as well—he has got a good deal of enjoyment out of life. As has often been pointed out, he, like H. L. Mencken, is not far removed from the people he satirizes, and he enjoys many of the things they enjoy—cocktails, for example, travel, boisterous fellowship, country estates, and the like. So long as he can have such things, he can be reasonably happy. But on the other hand, he is subject to fits of exasperation. He is exasperated with small-town bigots, complacent realtors, quack doctors, and ecclesiastical hypocrites, and he has a gift for satire that enables him to give his exasperation the kind of expression that relieves his own irritation and that of his readers. The side of him that secretly sympathizes with Will Kennicott and George Babbitt lends authority to his portraits, and the side of him that damns them gives his books their salt.

Criticism and satire imply the conception of a better way of life. Lewis knows what he would like to destroy—provincialism, complacency, hypocrisy, intellectual timidity, and similar faults—but he has only the vaguest idea of what kind of society he would like to see in existence. Carol Kennicott's attempts to reform Gopher Prairie are not only futile; they reveal standards almost as inadequate as those of the villagers. George Babbitt's only guides, as he goes along the path of revolt, are the old-fashioned liberalism of Seneca Doane and the dull bohemianism of the Bunch. Beside Elmer Gantry's foul hypocrisy Lewis can place only the weak modernism of Frank Shallard and the sentimental piety of Father Pengilly; he is as incapable of revealing the strength of the church as he is of expounding the nature of honest, intelligent atheism. Dodsworth returns from Europe, freed from subservience to both the narrow American idea of success and the narrow European idea of culture; and he returns to build better houses—an experiment in constructive capitalism in which Jack London's Elam Harnish had already anticipated him. Ann Vickers, who wants a career and has one, finds happiness in a man and a baby. The man, Judge Dolphin, seems to be Lewis's ideal, a straight-shooting he-man who plays the game; and he is one of the few characters in Lewis's books that are completely unconvincing. Only once, in all his novels, has Lewis succeeded in creating a worthy antagonist to the myriad of petty-minded men he has described: in *Arrowsmith* Max Gottlieb's devotion to pure science is both convincing and admirable.

Arrowsmith is Lewis's strongest and most unified novel. In *Main Street* and *Babbitt* he showed his keenness of eye and ear and his sharpness of tongue; but the very effectiveness of his satire compelled him to speak in positive as well as negative terms, and in *Arrowsmith* he succeeded in doing so. Lewis's discovery of the scientific method as a possible alternative to the confusion of the age was, as has been noted, characteristic of the middle generation. And for the moment his assumptions worked. But pure science operates in too narrow a field to provide a theory and an attitude for a social critic, and Lewis could not establish the relevance of science to his own interests. He was thus forced back into his old confusion, and his superficiality became increasingly apparent. *Elmer Gantry, Dodsworth,* and *Ann Vickers* are inferior to *Main Street, Babbitt,* and *Arrowsmith. Ann Vickers* not only is less unified than *Arrowsmith,* which in its general outlines it resembles; it shows less interest in the characteristic details of American life and is less convincing in the handling of detail; its satire is diffused, and Lewis's old power of indignation is felt only in the description of Copperhead Gap Penitentiary; the ending is a peculiarly painful confession of surrender to standards the satirist has pretended to scorn. Lewis's virtues were never enough, and he is losing those virtues.

Not only is the absence of adequate comprehension itself a weakness in the work of Dreiser, Anderson, and Lewis; it accounts for many of their other faults. It is inevitable that Dreiser, with his sense of chaos, should amass details with no discrimination and little logic. Anderson, though he can build effectively enough in the short story, where he can make his flash of revelation the climax, cannot achieve proportion and order in the longer narrative, and it is little wonder that in the novels of his middle period, such as *Many Marriages* and *Dark Laughter,* he lost all sense of form in the foggy subjectivity of his psychological analyses. Lewis, acute as he is in noting revealing mannerisms and tricks of speech, has only created two or three rounded personalities.

However, with all their faults, these three writers are far more important than Mrs. Wharton, Miss Cather, Hergesheimer, and Cabell. Not only have they achieved more; their failures have more significance for the future of American literature than the successes of the others. Their work was a natural development of the tendencies of the muckrakers. Less concerned with specific reforms, they had the same interest in the dominant tendencies of American life. And they made real advances over the muckrakers: they ended the tyranny of boarding school standards; they substituted the fresh, natural speech of the people for the language of books; they created a certain number of convincing and representative men and women. The novel grew in their hands, but the great central problem—emphasized by the failures of all the realists from Howells on—was left unsolved.

*   *   *

The appearance of volume after volume of original and effective poetry in the years from 1912 to the end of the war was the most dramatic evidence of the emergence of new forces in American literature. Poetry had been peculiarly under the influence of the genteel tradition, and the weakening of that tradition was essential to its emancipation. The poets who wished to take advantage of the new freedom were less fortunate than the novelists, for poetry had been weaker than fiction, and there was little in the American past that they could use. Whitman they made the most of, and they rescued Emily Dickinson from something like oblivion; otherwise they could find few predecessors worthy of anything but contempt. The progress of economic forces, however, had narrowed the gulf between Europe and America, and many of the new poets turned to France for inspiration. In particular the imagists—Ezra Pound, Hilda Doolittle, John Gould Fletcher, and Amy Lowell—studied the experiments that had been undertaken on the French Parnassus. Imagism met the needs of the times, in the United States as in France. For several decades French poets—as well as critics and painters —had insisted that, in the eternal flux, only the immediate impression was certain, and this was consoling doctrine to poets who had nothing else to write about. Moreover, concentration on the concrete image permitted poetry to ignore problems that the poets could not solve.

Not because she was the greatest of the American imagists, but because she remained closest to her native land and propagandized most vigorously for her faith, Amy Lowell, frankly relying on the publicity value of her personality, succeeded in establishing herself, at least in the popular mind, as queen of the new-found realms of poetry. In her manners she violated the conventions of the prosperous and conservative society into which she was born, and in her poems she shattered the traditions of generations of respectable versifiers. She was openly and even noisily a poet in revolt. Emphatically an individualist, she insisted on the supreme value of the immediate impression, and for her a poem was either a single image or a succession of images—and often no more than that.

The complete subjectivism Miss Lowell advocated had, without doubt, a tonic effect on her own poetry and that of her contemporaries. It was one way of breaking down the old traditions of the literary poets, with their stock themes and their threadbare phrases, and of restoring the poet to the rank of creator. But her absolute individualism, her utter rootlessness, destroyed the possibility of growth. She wrote in twenty different manners, and yielded to this influence and that. This woman, who was so belligerently determined to be herself and to express only herself, left no body of work that we can point to as purely her own, the complete and distinct record of a unique vision of life. She seems gradually to have realized her fate, for the enthusiasm of her early work gave place to the melancholy of the posthumous volumes.

Vachel Lindsay was wiser than Amy Lowell. Whether he realized or not that the weakness of the respectable poets was the weakness of their class and its shoddy, superficial culture, he turned for his inspiration to the common people. He wrote of their heroes: Lincoln, Booth, Jackson, Bryan, John L. Sullivan, and P. T. Barnum. He used their language and often the simple verse forms their spokesmen employed. He espoused their causes—prohibition, evangelistic Christianity, populism, and socialism. He borrowed many of his devices from their preachers and their actors. And he went out among them, preaching the gospel of beauty. This contact with people uncontaminated by the small talk of display-counter culture gave Lindsay the vigor and the firm, unsullied language of "The Congo," "The Broncho That Would Not Be Broken," "General William Booth Enters Heaven," and "In Praise of Johnny Appleseed." It set his imagination moving along the paths that the makers of myths have trodden.

But merely to accept the common people was not enough, as Lindsay knew; he had to create for them a vision of the future. And in his vision he could find no place for the machines. He hated industrialism and all its fruits:

> *Factory windows are always broken.*
> *Other windows are let alone.*
> *No one throws through the chapel-window*
> *The bitter, snarling, derisive stone.*

He could think of the future only in terms of the farms and small towns:

> *O you who lose the art of hope,*
> *Whose temples seem to shrine a lie,*
> *Whose sidewalks are but stones of fear,*
> *Who weep that Liberty must die,*
> *Turn to the little prairie towns,*
> *Your higher hope shall yet begin.*
> *On every side awaits you there*
> *Some gate where glory enters in.*

His heroes were men like Altgeld and Bryan, who fought "against the towns of Tubal Cain . . . against the ways of Tubal Cain, too cunning for the young." He vituperated the whole race of money-getters and dreamt of their extirpation:

> *You,*
> *Short-legged, short-armed, short-minded men,*
> *Your short-sighted days are over,*
> *Your habits of strutting through clover,*
> *Your movie-thugs, killing off souls and dreams,*
> *Your magazines drying up healing streams,*
> *Your newspapers, blasting truth and splendor,*
> *Your shysters, ruining progress and glory,*
> *Babbitt, your story is passing away.*
> *The Virginians are coming again.*

But Lindsay was obviously no prophet, leading his people to deliverance. He preached the gospel of beauty, which for him was the beauty of rural life. He sang of the days that were past, and refused to face the problems that the common people were being forced to face. Unable to accept the rôle of leader, he was compelled to accept the rôle of entertainer. He became more interested in the art of recitation and the playing of games than in writing poetry. His weaknesses became fixed mannerisms, and in a kind of second childhood he spun his poems out of endless repetitions of commonplaces.

Carl Sandburg did not feel Lindsay's fear of the machines. He sang out the praises of Chicago, wicked, dishonest, brutal, but strong, courageous, laughing——

Laughing the stormy, husky, brawling laughter of Youth, half-naked, sweating, proud to be Hog Butcher, Tool Maker, Stacker of Wheat, Player with Railroads and Freight Handler to the Nation.

In his little sketches of lake boats, docks, street cars, skyscrapers, and parks, of teamsters, ditch diggers, miners, shop-girls, and soldiers, of Dagoes, Niggers, and Bohunks, the tenderness of a rich imagination touched a world that hitherto had been unknown to poetry. His seeing eye, finding beauty on the drab prairie and in the smoky factory, not merely extended the province of the poet; it began the difficult but essential task of humanizing the waste places of American life:

A bar of steel—it is only
Smoke at the heart of it, smoke and the blood of a man.
A runner of fire ran in it, ran out, ran somewhere else,
And left—smoke and the blood of a man
And the finished steel, chilled and blue.
So fire runs in, runs out, runs somewhere else again,
And the bar of steel is a gun, a wheel, a nail, a shovel,
A rudder under the sea, a steering-gear in the sky;
And always dark in the heart and through it,
Smoke and the blood of a man.
Pittsburg, Youngstown, Gary—they make their steel with men.

Like Lindsay he came from the common people—porter, scene-shifter, dish-washer—and he writes about them. His literary methods are not, as Lindsay's were, akin to those of the newspaper versifiers; like Whitman he has written for the common people, not as they are, but as they may become. But he is close to them as they are, and he is never unaware of their lot. If he has seen the beauty of the machines, he has never ignored their cost in human suffering. The strange loveliness of skyscrapers does not blind him to the tragedies of poverty, nor does the tender grace of corn-flowers obscure for him the bitter, unrewarded toil of the farmers.

It is these two qualities—the quick perception of unsuspected beauty and a deep sympathy with the oppressed—that makes it so easy to forgive the faults in *Chicago Poems, Cornhuskers,* and *Smoke and Steel*. But it is true that Sandburg seems always to be dealing with unrelated entities. In his world everything is disparate; each object, each person, each event stands by itself. Perhaps that is why, in *Good Morning, America* (1928), he seems to have yielded, like so many of his contemporaries, to despair. The title poem of that volume is not merely an attempt to depict contemporary life; it is a series of questions for which Sandburg has no answers. Like the man from Chillicothe, whose self-examination he describes, he is always seeking for explanations that always elude him. It is no wonder that, unable to see how beauty and goodness can triumph over evil and squalor, he finds his kind of poetry rather futile. That may be why he has spent most of his time, of late, writing stories for children, collecting old songs, and writing a romantic biography of a national hero.

Long before Amy Lowell announced her credo, before Lindsay began preaching the gospel of beauty, before Sandburg discovered Chicago, Edwin Arlington Robinson was

quietly studying the people of his Maine town. The enthusiasms of the renaissance and the consequent growth of his
own popularity did not make an evangelist of him; he
calmly continued on his solitary way. Neither Amy Lowell's
theories of prosody nor Sandburg's zeal for the precise accents of modern life moved him. He had his own world, un-
defined in either space or time, made up of the kind of persons that interested him, and to this he devoted himself.
Whether this world was called Tilbury Town, London, or
Camelot, whether its inhabitants were named Captain Craig,
Shakespeare, or Merlin, it was one world, a unit in the poet's
imagination; and nothing outside it existed for him.

One should not underestimate the advantages to a poet of
having a world of his own. There have been ages in which
a poet could feel the underlying unity of all the forms of life
he observed, and could move freely and confidently through
all the provinces of experience; but in our day the complica-
tion of the social structure, the extension of the bounds of
knowledge, and the multiplication of human contacts have
broken the world into apparently unrelated atoms. If a poet
draws indiscriminately on his experience, as Sandburg has
done, his work is very likely to be as fragmentary and im-
perfect as Sandburg's work. If, on the other hand, he concerns himself only with the elements of his experience whose
relations he can understand, as Robinson does, he may
achieve order and proportion.

Robinson's world is, obviously, an abstraction. He is primarily interested in problems of personality, especially in
the problem of success and failure. To see this problem
clearly he deliberately isolates his characters from many of
the complexities of modern life. In any of his poems the men
and women stand, like the Man Against the Sky, at a certain distance from the routine difficulties of daily existence.

He permits himself to concentrate on Avon's passion for revenge or Bartholow's jealousy or Cavender's remorse. His
world includes many historical personages—Crabbe, Shakespeare, Rembrandt, Paul—and it extends into the realm of
mythology, to embrace Merlin, Lancelot, and Tristram.
Robinson's method of treating these men from the past is
no different from his method of treating his contemporaries:
Merlin and Captain Craig are the same sort of bewildered
sages, Lancelot and Penn-Raven the same sort of disloyal
lovers, Rembrandt and Fernando Nash are the same sort of
inspired artists. Only such kinds of experience as are apparently unaffected by changes in politics and economics, developments in science and technology, and fashions in art
and morality, exist for his poetry.

Robinson's admirers defend this method of abstraction by
saying that he concerns himself with the eternal problems.
But the only problems we really know are those that are
posed by our own age. There are no eternal problems; each
age has its own dilemmas, and, though some of these recur,
they take their character from a particular situation. Robinson's fine dignity, the nobility of much of his blank verse,
the subtlety of such poems as "A Poor Relation" and "Eros
Turannos," the wisdom of some passages in *Captain Craig,*
the interpretation of history in "Ben Jonson Entertains a
Man from Stratford" and "Rembrandt to Rembrandt," and
the lyric beauty of the beginning of *Tristram* have enriched
American literature. At times, in other words, he speaks directly to us, and we listen. But we cannot forget the interminable dialogues in *Merlin* and *Lancelot,* the triviality of
Roman Bartholow and *The Glory of the Nightingales,* the
tenuous arguments in *Tristram,* and the utter emptiness of
at least half the poems in *Nicodemus.* Is it possible for the
poet to touch the enduring strands of humanity's thought

and emotion and endeavor, unless he finds them, as in daily experience we ourselves do, inextricably part of the warp and woof of man's concrete struggle with a particular environment in a particular age? Whence came Robinson's skepticism if not from the intellectual currents of his day? Could he have been so interested in failure if he had not seen real defeats and been conscious of specific frustrations? By taking attitudes that are the product of a particular situation and projecting them into a world of his own design, he has gained poise of a sort that was impossible for Sandburg and Lindsay: his poems are precisely planned and firmly molded. But much of his poetry is cold and remote, and some of it has no significance at all for Robinson's America.

Robert Frost also has a world of his own, and his great advantage over Robinson lies in the fact that his world is, to some extent, identified with a particular area as it has existed at a particular time. Though his world is as compact and as nearly self-sufficient as the less tangible realm over which Robinson rules, any one who has traveled north of Boston can recognize the language he speaks, the scenery he describes, and the people he presents. Yet it cannot be denied that Frost has achieved unity by a definite process of exclusion. One not only realizes that life in New Hampshire is not altogether representative of life in the United States as a whole; one has to admit that Frost disregards many elements in New Hampshire life, and especially the elements that link that state with the rest of the country. For example, northern New England has been greatly affected by the growth of industrialism, and yet one would never suspect this from Frost's poetry. Can one believe that it is by accident that he has never written of the factory towns, now so abjectly in decay, or of the exodus to the cities and its failure, now so apparent, to bring deliverance? Has he never heard of the

railroads and their influence on the state's politics, touching
the smallest hamlet? Do not automobiles and radios exist in
New Hampshire? No, Frost is too shrewd not to be well
aware that he is excluding from his poems whatever might
destroy their unity. He knows the full value of his self-
imposed limitations, and he is even willing to boast of his
good fortune in the parable of the star in the stone boat:

> *Such as it is, it promises the prize*
> *Of the one world complete in any size*
> *That I am like to compass, fool or wise.*

Much of Frost's experience is close to ours, and we can
share his appreciations and his insights. His strong narratives, his clear and unpretentious lyrics, and his thoughtful,
sensible allegories are more satisfying than most poetry of
our day. But, to the extent that his imagination concerns itself only with what is personally congenial and poetically
available, he too leaves us discontented. For all his common
sense and his originality, he has chosen to identify himself
with a moribund tradition. Many poets, these hundred and
fifty years, have written of mountains, fields, and brooks, and
of farmers at their humble tasks; these things have become
part of our imaginative inheritance, and one must be insensitive indeed not to be conscious of the beauty in them. But
there are other objects now more frequently before our eyes
—factories, skyscrapers, machines. We see mechanics, shop-
girls, truck-drivers, more often than we do farmers, and we
see the farmer not as a romantic figure but as the victim of
cruel economic forces. There is new territory that we beg the
poet to conquer for us. Perhaps to-day no poet is capable of
that conquest, but, if the task is ever to be accomplished,
some one with the talent of a Robert Frost must make a beginning.

The careers of five representative and important poets have indicated the principal patterns of the period of activity sometimes called the poetic renaissance, and the study of such writers as Edgar Lee Masters, Edna St. Vincent Millay, Conrad Aiken, and Ezra Pound would add little to the lessons we have already learned. It was a period that produced many fine poems but no mature and satisfying poet, and a decade after it began a younger generation was rebelliously repudiating the methods and achievements of its representatives. Even the most sympathetic observer was forced, by 1925, to recognize that the good tidings so enthusiastically borne to the world by Amy Lowell and Louis Untermeyer had been premature. The enthusiast could still boast of the poetry that had been written, and look hopefully to the future; the more somber critic might wonder if he had not witnessed an ending rather than a beginning.

* * *

Perhaps the most pitiful aspect of the whole dilemma of the middle generation was the desperate inadequacy of the critics. It is not that they were insensitive to talent, hostile to experiment, or prejudiced against unconventionality; there were plenty of critics to celebrate the virtues of each new novelist or poet, however daring and unprecedented his work. But there was no one to perform the essential task of clarification. Sensitivity and courage—important virtues in the days when the new writers were fighting their battle— were no longer enough. American life was a jungle whose tangled fastnesses no explorer had charted. Artists had started hopefully on this path and that, only to find themselves plunged into some dismal morass. Almost more than anything else America needed a map-maker.

Nothing, it soon appeared, was to be expected of the impressionists, for they denied that the making of maps was part of the critic's function. James Huneker had been a useful pioneer, but he left no body of ideas over which a later generation could fruitfully ponder. Once his taste, which was good but not impeccable, and his enthusiasm, which was genuine and often contagious, had done their work, once his erudition had been absorbed and the objects of his admiration had won a following, there was nothing to preserve his books from oblivion. J. E. Spingarn, on the other hand, at least tried to evolve the rationale of impressionism. The critic, he said, should ask himself what the author was trying to express and how far he succeeded in expressing it, and should answer these questions by "becoming (if only for a moment of supreme power) at one with the creator." But the great advocate of creative criticism thus placed the critic in a secondary position, and he saved himself from admitting the critic's complete passivity only by his hocus-pocus about identification with the artist. H. L. Mencken, though his "Criticism of Criticism of Criticism" pokes fun at Spingarn, had nothing more fundamental to suggest than the substitution of the modest "catalytic" for the pretentious "creative." The critic, he said, is the middleman of the arts: "It is his business to provide the reaction between the work of art and the spectator."

In order to avoid problems they did not care to examine, the impressionists consistently misrepresented the character and minimized the importance of literature. Spingarn's theories were vitiated both by his conception of what the artist expresses and by his failure to see that, if art is expression, it is also something else. In the first place, he refused to admit that the artist expresses more or less completely the civilization of which he is part, the civilization that has made him what he is. And in the second place, he would not see

that art not only expresses something but also does something, has consequences as well as causes. Mencken went
further and declared that the arts, like religion, "are only
second-rate means of achieving man's chief purpose in the
world"; their denial of "the pains of reality" is "a poor substitute, perhaps, for the actual conquest of the harsh facts,
but it is nevertheless a substitute." The impressionists wanted
to free American writers from the dogmas of the conservatives, and yet they were unable to dispose of these dogmas by
analysis and argument. Mencken, indeed, has attacked the
conservatives in many of their citadels, taking politics and religion as well as literature as his province. But the same faults
are found in all his thinking. His praise of aristocracy is a convenient club in the fight against the Babbitry, but the elabora-
tion of the aristocratic theory in *Notes on Democracy* is
superficial and uninformed. His views on religion are well
suited to shock the Bible Belt, and his *Treatise on the Gods*
is an excellent polemic against the church, but he has nothing
to offer the hosts of bewildered agnostics except a blind nihil-
ism. He has not been timid, and a list of the heads he has hit
would include a notable number of obscurantists, reaction-
aries, and cowards. He has written with great vigor and unusual skill, and his sympathies have often been sounder than
his intellect. He and the other impressionists encouraged the
writers of the middle generation, and up to a point their encouragement was valuable; but beyond that point they could
do nothing for the bewildered poets and novelists.

The expansive development in American life between 1912
and 1925 enabled the impressionists to weaken the influence
of the conservative critics without answering their arguments. But the arguments remained. "It is not enough," Irving Babbitt wrote, commenting on Spingarn's "The New
Criticism," "that the critic should ask what the creator aimed

to do and whether he has fulfilled his aim; he must also ask whether the aim is intrinsically worth while." As a matter of fact, no critic, unless he had resolutely put common sense behind him, could avoid asking himself this further question. But the answers the impressionists gave were personal, arbitrary, and often indefensible, for they were quite unwilling to examine the sociological and philosophical implications of their scale of values. The humanists, however, had evolved a definite conception of the function of literature, based upon a definite conception of the nature of man. These conceptions were, of course, by no means invulnerable. The humanistic dualism of nature and man could find no support in anthropology and psychology; the humanists were forced back, despite all their talk of positive philosophy, on religion. Their selection of self-restraint as the distinctively human virtue had no basis in science or ethics, and in practice it meant a defense of private property, the existing order, and Puritan morality. With their reliance on ancient precedents and their insistence on self-restraint, they had little that was pertinent to say about the literature of their own period, and they dealt intelligently neither with the virtues nor with the faults of that literature. Yet, for all their weaknesses, they occupied themselves with fundamental problems, and the impressionists were unable to overthrow their doctrines.

In the perspective of history the issues of the critical battle become clear. The progress of the nation had created a situation to which the old Victorian standards had no relevance. The humanists proposed to salvage all that was valid in the old standards and, taking advantage of changed conditions, to consolidate the position of the privileged class. Their philosophy fitted the needs of the rulers of a society that was beginning to crystallize. The doctrine of the inner check, for example, not only would serve, if the masses accepted it, to stifle protest and prevent revolution; it was also good doctrine for the fortunate few who were more anxious to keep what they had than to make more. Moreover, the humanists' insistence that the only way to alter society is to alter the individual made it possible for them to oppose all humanitarian and radical proposals without specifically defending capitalism. Although they usually relied on vague generalities, the more heated passages of Babbitt's *Democracy and Leadership* and More's *Aristocracy and Justice,* denouncing labor unions and factory laws, for example, betray the animus of their arguments.

The impressionists, on the other hand, felt in the changed situation a great opportunity. The forward surge of literature filled them with rejoicing, and they devoted themselves to the task of sweeping the conservatives out of its way. Like many members of the middle class, they were more troubled by the narrow morality of the late nineteenth century synthesis than they were by the economic injustice on which that synthesis was based. And in every other way they mistook the symptom for the disease. By making articulate a social pressure in the direction of new standards, they served their purpose. But the humanists were to have their revenge before the decade was over.

Neither the humanists nor the impressionists were willing to examine the social order and analyze the relations of literature to it. Both groups glibly affirmed that the world in which the author lived had no necessary effect on his work, asserting the inviolate isolation of either the ethical imagination or the pure creative spirit. It remained for other and, at the moment, less influential critics to attempt the study of the artist in his environment. Van Wyck Brooks, in *America's Coming-of-Age* (1915) and *Letters and Leadership*

(1918), analyzed the literature of the preceding century and found failure after failure. These failures, he realized, could not all be tragic accidents, and he found the explanation of them in the absence of any real appreciation of literature in money-mad America. The literary man, he pointed out, had no sense of engaging in an important task, no sense of belonging to a worthy fellowship, no sense of sharing in a great tradition.

One would have expected Brooks to proceed to the formulation of some sort of social program, on the theory that a new social order would bring into existence a new set of values to protect the integrity of the artist. This seemingly inevitable next step he refused to take. He even deprecated the proposal made by his friend, Randolph Bourne, to ally the intelligentsia and the workers. He could never do more than demonstrate the unhappy effects of our cultural attitudes on our writers. His one remedy was for artists to ignore everything in their environment that militated against their artistic integrity and to act with full consciousness of their worth. This advice, salutary though its vigor might temporarily be, was, as Brooks might have known and apparently did sometimes suspect, easier to give than to follow. Brooks himself, if one can judge from his *Life of Emerson* (1932), eventually found limp, lifeless description easier than vigorous analysis. Perhaps he had grown tired of challenging the artists of America to lift themselves by their bootstraps.

The period is rich in critics, able men most of them, shrewd in their appraisals, quick to praise, fearless in condemnation, better critics by far than recent generations had produced. But the need for clarification was desperate. The impressionists were absorbed in other tasks; Babbitt and More had their own interests to protect; Brooks was restrained by a strange sort of timidity. If there had been someone to say, "This is the situation of society to-day; these are the forces that have shaped that situation; here is the power that can bring change," novelists might not have stumbled quite so blindly or taken quite such precipitate flight. If some one had said, "Though this civilization is dying, a new civilization is in the process of building," poets might not so quickly have lost their hope. If some one had said, "You need not stand alone in your fight against the corruption in and about you, for here are your allies," artists of every kind might have faced with new confidence the tasks of creation. Not every artist could have responded to such words, but some would have. The words, alas, were not spoken!

*   *   *

So pessimism grew. Though it lurks in almost every poem and novel of the period, it is most completely stated in the plays of Eugene O'Neill. He it is who has made the most exhaustive studies of frustration in its various manifestations. Beginning with studies of simple defeat in *Beyond the Horizon* (1920), and *The Straw,* he went on to examine the disintegrating effect of the lust for wealth in *Gold* and *Marco Millions,* of maladjustment to environment in *The Hairy Ape* and *All God's Chillun Got Wings,* of sexual passion in *Diff'rent, Welded,* and *Strange Interlude,* of metaphysical bewilderment in *Dynamo.* In dramatizing these themes he has shown the utmost ingenuity, employing all his knowledge of theatrical resources to contrive forms suited to the expression of the subtleties that engage his attention. The seriousness of his purpose, coupled with his mastery of the theater and his sympathetic comprehension of all the stages of disintegration, have made him our principal dramatist.

In O'Neill, as in the novelists and poets, some vague hope struggles against the prevailing gloom, and he is not content to leave that hope inarticulate. Side by side with his study of disintegrating forces he carries on a quest for some principle of redemption. The longings of Robert in *Beyond the Horizon,* of Jason in *The First Man,* and of Ponce de Leon in *The Fountain* express O'Neill's own aspiration. And the desire to justify these hopes has dominated more than one of his plays. In *The First Man* Jason breaks away from the tyranny of his petty-minded relatives, typically conventional, prosperous people; he plans to educate his son to feel a confidence he has nearly lost: "When he's old enough, I'll teach him to know and love a big free life." In *Anna Christie* and *Welded* humble women find courage enough to accept whatever ills life may bring. Says the prostitute in *Welded,* "Sure. You got to laugh, ain't you? You got to loin to like it." *The Fountain* is the elaborate poetization of these simple affirmations; at the end Juan cries, "I see! Fountain Everlasting, time without end! Soaring flame of the spirit transfiguring death. All is within. All things dissolve, flow on eternally. ... O God, Fountain of Eternity, Thou art the All in One, the One in All—the Eternal Becoming which is Beauty." And in *Lazarus Laughed* the protagonist, having faced and triumphed over the ultimate evil, death, is supposed to fear nothing life can offer.

In *Lazarus Laughed* other persons share the hero's courage so long as they are with him; when they can no longer draw on this source of confidence, their old cowardice triumphs. So with the play itself: we feel its power as we read it, but later contemplation can discover little significance in its emphatic affirmations. What does the affirmation of life mean? We cannot affirm the value of life in the abstract; we can only affirm the value of those forces in life that work for ideal ends. His inability to discover those forces, and show them to us, robs O'Neill's affirmations of all vitality. Indiscriminate hope is as pointless as indiscriminate despair, as his manner of turning from one to the other shows. In *Mourning Becomes Electra* the gloom lightens only when Orin speaks of his enchanted isles, and O'Neill is too conscientious a Freudian not to make quite plain the significance of this dream of escape. Have his hopes, he seems to ask, no more significance than the longings of a maladjusted person to return to the womb?

O'Neill's restless preoccupation with one type of frustration after another suggests that he is not satisfied with his own analyses and has no assurance that he has found the poison responsible for the destruction he sees. Nor has his search for an antidote been more successful: though the right mood can inspire vigorous and momentarily effective affirmations, despair promptly follows hope. Few writers are less predictable than O'Neill, but it is significant for the future that in *Mourning Becomes Electra* he seems to be concerned with suffering for its own sake. The theme that in the hands of the Greeks touched the most fundamental problems of human destiny offers O'Neill only an opportunity to portray futile lives and to ask himself questions that he cannot answer.

It cannot be denied that most of O'Neill's plays affect the emotions of the spectator, in whom they arouse a distress like that by which the author is agitated. But one has a curious sense, as one watches these plays unfold, that they are somehow beside the point. One is even a little irritated because one feels that some profound truth has just eluded one. In *Dynamo* O'Neill creates a symbol of the new forces that have been released in the world. It seems an apt symbol, lending itself to the dramatic statement of a fundamental problem. But at the end of the play one feels that the real problem of the dynamo has never emerged at all. To most people the dynamo is neither god nor devil; it is an instrument by which a few are given wealth and power and a multitude are enslaved. O'Neill may be quite justified in using the dynamo as a symbol of a metaphysical dilemma, but why should he ignore the much simpler and, at least for millions of people, much more important dilemma created by the dynamo and by every other machine?

Enough has been said to suggest an answer to this question. We can see now why O'Neill's problems never seem quite fundamental, and why his study of frustration is so inconclusive. O'Neill's pessimism, though he has dealt with it more fully, does not differ from that of contemporary poets and novelists. Having begun to understand it, we can understand one reason—the most important reason—why a generation rich in promise, and to a point rich in achievement, has met a dismal fate.

Chapter VIII

TRUMPET CALL

In 1925 the middle generation seemed secure. Stuart Sherman had deserted the humanists, and they were apparently silenced forever. H. L. Mencken and George Jean Nathan were finding a larger and larger public for their *Mercury*. Theodore Dreiser's *An American Tragedy* was hailed the country over as a masterpiece. Louis Untermeyer still talked of the poetry renaissance. The reputations that had been made in the preceding ten or twelve years were, so far as anyone could tell, intact.

Suddenly revaluation began. The death of Amy Lowell brought a series of attacks on her work. A biographer denounced Anderson; Ernest Hemingway, an erstwhile disciple, satirized him. The opinion grew that Mencken was rather cheap and distinctly *vieux jeu*. Within three or four years practically every writer of the middle generation had been severely criticized, and, as the decade ended, observers agreed that another chapter in American literature had been brought to a close.

The middle generation did not fall before a counterattack by the old moralists; its overthrow was brought about by the emerging group of younger writers. These younger writers, it soon appeared, had different interests, made different demands on literature, and held different views of society. They classed almost all their predecessors as reformers, Mencken and Lewis as well as Sinclair and Herrick. To be concerned with sexual emancipation or the low intellectual level of the small town was, they maintained, as stupidly naïve as to be concerned with pure food laws and the direct election of senators. One real prophet, they said, would have accomplished more than all the sociological novelists. For themselves, they were interested in literature as an art. Writing, said one of them, is "a craft in which the most exquisite pleasure is received by the novelist in the posing and solution of esthetic problems."

This attitude, obviously, did not spring into existence overnight, nor did it develop in a vacuum. While the writers of the middle generation were establishing their reputations, the men and women who were to be their successors were receiving their preparation. It appears that most of them, even in their extreme youth, felt none of that zeal for reform that had created the Intercollegiate Socialist Society and set undergraduates to debating the respective merits of the new freedom and the new nationalism. At Harvard the place of such men as Walter Lippmann and John Reed had been taken by the esthetes—E. E. Cummings, John Dos Passos, Robert Hillyer, Foster Damon, and Malcolm Cowley. According to one of them, they had no interest whatever in social problems; they read Casanova in French and Petronius in Latin, discussed Pater's prose, and argued about the voluptuousness of the church and the virtue of prostitution. They believed "that the cultivation and expression of his own sensibility are the only justifiable ends for a poet; that originality is his principal virtue; that society is hostile, stupid, and unmanageable." They held that the poet "triumphs over the world, at moments, by mysteriously including it within himself," and they maintained that "art, the undying expression of such moments, ... is the poet's revenge on society."

A not dissimilar attitude must have existed in Edmund

Wilson's Princeton and Thornton Wilder's Yale and at the University of Chicago where Elizabeth Roberts and Glenway Wescott were students. Probably it was embodied in a little group of students at every college that attracted the young men and women of well-to-do families. For most of these youths came from homes that had prospered with the advance of American business. They had not known the hardships that London, Sinclair, Dreiser, and Anderson had known. They had not, moreover, felt either the fear or the hope that had created the progressive movement. In their own way, without bothering to formulate the problem, they had reached a decision: if the general organization of society did not conform to their desires, they would ignore society and make the most of the advantages with which they were blessed. Thus they cut the knot that was puzzling their elders. It was the natural response of members of a privileged group.

So far as most of them were concerned, the war did not destroy this attitude; rather, it intensified it. Many of them took part in the war, and they realized afresh that society, since it was capable of such cruelty and stupidity, was their enemy. Once the war was ended, each devoted himself to cultivating his own garden. Many of them stayed for a time in European countries, watching and often participating in movements based on impulses like their own. In Europe or at home they founded magazines—*Broom, Secession, Contact, S4N*. Many of them wrote for the *Dial*. They believed passionately in the importance of art, so passionately that they fought with each other as well as with their elders. Some of them hoped at first that they could impress their views on the people of America; despite their theories they were evangelists, preaching the gospel of estheticism. But ambition soon waned, and they came to feel, as one of them has said, "not the wish to change society as a whole, or even literary society, but merely to write a poem, an essay, a story worth the trouble of reading to one's friends."

The America of the early twenties may not have favored the broad ambitions of the new esthetes, but in certain ways it encouraged their attitudes and their more modest activities. Their indifference to politics was no longer an uncommon attitude. A new gospel was being preached, a comforting gospel: under the new dispensation of mass production and high wages all problems were to be solved. Without benefit of socialism, without benefit of political action, without benefit of humanitarianism, indeed without benefit of either good will or good sense, industrialism was creating an era of boundless prosperity in which everyone could share. European countries sent experts to study the American miracle, and the good tidings were spread abroad. If any poet or novelist had perchance stopped to wonder what was happening in the world, he could, after hearing the good news, pick up his hoe and return to his garden.

Not everyone succumbed to the siren song of the new capitalism, but many minds and consciences were lulled to rest by its refrain. The few skeptics who kept up the fight found almost no one to listen to them. Even young men who in their college days had not been utterly indifferent to political questions, who perhaps had called themselves socialists, gradually ceased their labors, if they did not formally abandon their convictions, and turned their attention to literary tasks. And as young writers came out of the colleges, youths who could scarcely remember the war and certainly could not remember Roosevelt and Wilson at Armageddon, the new attitude became more and more common and seemed to indicate the beginning of a new literary era.

If a privileged group feels in no danger of losing its privileges, it comes in time to take them for granted. The artists of the younger generation quickly adjusted themselves to the situation that had bewildered their predecessors. They accepted what pleased them in their environment and ignored the rest. So far as they found it necessary to justify their indifference to the problems of their day—poverty, injustice, war—they could easily offer a defense. They could say, as many statesmen and industrialists were saying, that these problems were being solved, and there was no need for artists to worry about them. They could argue, as privileged classes have argued in the past, that the achievements of the minority are more important, *sub specie aeternitatis,* than the sufferings of the majority. Or they could pessimistically maintain that, since there was no salvation for the human race, the individual had best avail himself of his transient opportunities. Whatever their defense, and even if they made no defense, they were determined to let nothing interfere with their cultivation of their interests.

The basis for both the arguments and the actions that spoke louder than arguments was a faith in the stability of the existing order. If that assumption had been sound, the younger writers might have gone their way for many years. But almost before the new attitude could be defined, the beginning of the depression had demonstrated the unsoundness of the assumption on which it rested. At first, of course, few persons realized what had happened, but as month after month of the depression passed, even the most aloof young dilettante was forced to open his eyes. In the first place, many of these complacent youths were directly affected by the depression, as their incomes or their fathers' incomes declined. In the second place, the surface prosperity of the Coolidge era vanished, and misery walked, ragged and hungry, upon the streets. And in the third place, even the most privileged, even the most calloused individual became aware that his good fortune might be short-lived. Talk of revolution ran through Greenwich Village speakeasies and Park Avenue apartments, and the joking and drinking could not banish the reflection that perhaps there was something in this talk, perhaps the end was at hand.

At last the issue was becoming clear, not perfectly clear of course, not clear for everyone; but many saw that a choice was forced upon them. Either they accepted the existing system or they whole-heartedly opposed it. If they opposed it, they must work to overthrow it; if they accepted it, they must work to defend it. Some writers realized that the lines were being drawn, and others did not; but, consciously or unconsciously, they took their sides. Those who had decided against the existing order were, because of the effort involved in that decision, more sharply aware than the others of where they stood and why. The defenders of the system were, like apologists in every age, more likely to conceal, from themselves as well as from others, the reasons for their choice and its significance. But the course of the depression made concealment less and less easy, and it needed little insight to see what their principles were and why they clung to them.

* * *

As we turn back to the era of prosperity to examine the literature of the past ten years, we note that pessimism has by no means disappeared. Indeed, what we might call the definitive statement of contemporary pessimism is found in Joseph Wood Krutch's *The Modern Temper,* published in the spring of 1929. Krutch reviews the familiar argument: medieval man lived in a static, anthropocentric world with recognized values and an unquestioned way of salvation; modern man has been robbed by the physical sciences of faith in the beneficence of the universe and by psychology of belief in his own dignity. It is his thesis that this change has undermined the arts, and he maintains that great literature is impossible in the present era. It may be, he admits, that power will some day fall into the hands of men who are undismayed by the bleakness of the science-revealed universe. But the possibility of such an occurrence cannot console us, since the new barbarians will have no regard for our values, and their triumph will destroy everything we hold dear.

The Modern Temper is an excellent statement of the philosophical theories of contemporary pessimism, but it would be less significant if it lacked this honest confession that there is but one alternative to pessimism, faith in the emergence of the masses, and that this alternative is unacceptable to Krutch and his kind. What we have already suspected is thus brought to the clear light of day. Beneath the complacence inspired by the new capitalism lay the haunting fear that the class to which most writers belonged, and therefore the culture that had nurtured them and that they hoped to enrich, were doomed. That fear could be momentarily banished, as artists went about their absorbing tasks, but even at the height of prosperity it could not be completely destroyed.

What Krutch states coldly and reasonably in *The Modern Temper,* Robinson Jeffers has been expressing for the past ten years with all the power of his passionate nature. Though he knows as well as Krutch that the universe is merely indifferent, he can only express his rage at its indifference by portraying it as a malicious demon. Though he knows that man is at worst only an animal, the bitter recognition that he is not a god makes him hate the race as if it were a race of fiends. Nothing in man's experience seems to him so significant as suffering, and no quality of man's nature seems to him admirable except the capacity to endure suffering. Our nature, he writes,

> *is rather ignoble in its quiet times, mean in its pleasures,*
> *Slavish in the mass; but at stricken moments it can shine terribly*
> *against the dark magnificence of things.*

We are not, of course, to take Jeffers with perfect literalness; we are not to suppose that the inhabitants of Carmel spend their time in bestiality and incest, torture and self-torture. Jeffers chooses his events not because they are representative in any statistical sense, but because they do symbolize what seem to him the significant and revealing moments of human life. But what explains his principle of selection? When, as sometimes happens in the shorter poems, he substitutes straightforward indictment for his customary symbolism, he denounces man's petty greeds, his brutal inhumanity, and his cowardly helplessness before the forces he has created. Does his conviction that the race of man ought to be extinguished rest, then, upon his realization that this particular civilization cannot and should not endure? It rests on other things, too, no doubt, but certainly it rests on that. Wiser than Krutch, he sees that his world not only will perish but deserves to; but he is too moved by his vision of destruction to see, as Krutch sees, that another world may take its place. Blindly he reaches out for symbols to express his sense of doom, and only violent horror will serve his purposes. But in piling horror upon horror to convey his conviction of human unworthiness, he moves farther and farther from ordinary experience. The real horrors of our world seldom figure in his poems, and the experiences he does describe therefore partake of unreality. Neither his terrible themes nor his desperately violent style can create in us an effect more enduring than the brief trembling that follows an evil dream.

William Faulkner also seeks for symbols of despair. His characters are meaner than Jeffers'; not even suffering can endow them with nobility. But they can be more easily recognized than Jeffers' characters, though one may have met them before only on the pages of textbooks of pathology. His themes are suffering and violence. Death is central in all but one of his seven novels: death and betrayal in *Soldiers' Pay* and *Sartoris;* madness and decay and death in *As I Lay Dying;* suicide, idiocy, and prostitution in *The Sound and the Fury;* madness and murder in *Light in August.* Even the attempt at satire in *Mosquitoes* ends in a description of useless suffering and meaningless disaster. Faulkner's men and women are, with few exceptions, twisted shapes in the chaotic wreckage of a world.

Faulkner himself could not tell why he is so concerned with death and abnormality; certainly we cannot. The decline of the Faulkner family has something to do with it; so has the war; so, perhaps, have many other things. But if Faulkner's mind must remain a mystery to us, we are not wholly ignorant of the forces that have made the world he writes about what it is. He himself gives us hints. He shows us families that have lost money and social position—the Sartorises, the Compsons, and the Hightowers. He shows us families that have no hopes of rising from squalor—the Bundrens, the Groves, the Hineses. He shows us all the meannesses of a Snopes on the make. It is easy for us to recognize such phenomena, for we know how and why the South has been transformed.

But Faulkner is not primarily interested in showing us how people live in the South, and why they live as they do. Passages in *As I Lay Dying* and *Light in August* reveal a fine talent for realistic description of contemporary life. Faulkner has not only watched the people of the South carefully; he is one of them and he knows them from the inside. But he will not write simply and realistically of southern life. He is not primarily interested in representative men and women; certainly he is not interested in the forces that have shaped them. In *As I Lay Dying* he picks a period of unusual tension in the lives of the Bundrens, and he chooses to tell his story in a way that brings out all their eccentricities. *Light in August* soon forsakes the rather amusing and wholly credible story of Lena Grove to portray murder and flight through the abnormal consciousness of Joe Christmas. The ordinary affairs of this life are not enough for Faulkner; even the misery and disease born of generations of poverty and ignorance are not adequate themes for the expression of his horror and disgust. Nothing but crime and insanity will satisfy him. If he tried to see why life is horrible, he might be willing to give a more representative description of life, might be willing to occupy himself with the kind of suffering that he can see on every hand, the kind of crime that is committed every day, and the kind of corruption that gnaws at every human being in this rotten society. As it is, he can only pile violence upon violence in order to convey a mood that he will not or cannot analyze.

There can be little doubt of the intensity of Faulkner's bitterness. Despite the silliness of his talk about writing his guts out, one has to recognize in his work the most vehement effort to express a burning hatred. But what it is he hates he scarcely knows, and because he fears that he is somehow missing the mark, he has to apply every possible device for heightening the effect upon the reader. Faulkner's novels are complex because he recognizes the necessity for this heightening of effect. He tries to hammer out, as if with brute force, fit symbols for his mood. There is nothing in the story of the Compsons that requires Faulkner to use the fleeting memories of the idiotic Benjy; but disgust is made almost palpable by that device. The wild meditations of Darl and the childish hallucinations of Vardaman do very little to help us understand the Bundren family, but they intensify, even more effectively than the introduction of loathsome physical details, the horror that Faulkner wishes to arouse in the reader of *As I Lay Dying*. An enormous ingenuity has gone into the construction of Faulkner's novels, but it has not been devoted, as James's ingenuity was devoted, to discovering "the way that most presents the subject and presents most of it"; but rather to discovering the way that creates in the reader the most violent loathing.

It is apparent that Faulkner's methods are not altogether illegitimate: if what he chiefly wants to express is his disgust, he must use whatever means are available. But it is also apparent that, if he understood more completely the reasons for his disgust, he would not have to resort to arbitrary devices. And there is the danger of his becoming a mere showman, mechanically manufacturing thrills in the Grand Guignol manner. How real this danger is *Sanctuary* shows. The method of presentation has no inherent relation to the theme: information is withheld from the reader merely to create as violent a climax as possible. There is nothing but cleverness to distinguish the book from any cheap shocker. And what is true of *Sanctuary* as a whole is true of parts of other novels. Faulkner's unwillingness to try to understand the world about him not only robs his novels of true importance but brings them dangerously close to triviality.

It is significant that *Sanctuary* has been much the most popular of Faulkner's books. Though it is the poorest of his later books, it is the one that comes closest to providing the kind of thrill beloved by readers of detective stories. The situation is a little ironic: Faulkner, who obviously wants to force his readers to recognize what he calls "the logical pattern to evil," helps them to forget, for a few hours, their petty cares. It is the price he has to pay for his particular kind of blindness. Certainly a novelist who gave a comprehensive account of life in the South, based not only on a disgust with misery and vileness but also on an understanding of why misery and vileness exist and how they can be eliminated, would be in no danger of becoming a Sax Rohmer for the sophisticated.

* * *

Jeffers and Faulkner seem definitely committed to their pessimism, and there is little reason to expect changes in either matter or manner. Krutch, however, has tried in *Experience and Art* to find some basis for hope, at least so far as literature is concerned, and other erstwhile apostles of gloom have gone far beyond his timid affirmations. For ten years T. S. Eliot was prince of the waste land. Sardonically he mocked his own weaknesses. He confessed his futility in "Gerontion":

> *Here I am, an old man in a dry month,*
> *Being read to by a boy, waiting for rain.*

He had accomplished nothing:

> *I was neither at the hot gates*
> *Nor fought in the warm rain*
> *Nor knee deep in the salt marsh, heaving a cutlass,*
> *Bitten by flies, fought.*

He lived in a world of corruption and obscenity:

My house is a decayed house,
And the jew squats on the window sill, the owner,
Spawned in some estaminet of Antwerp,
Blistered in Brussels, patched and peeled in London.
The goat coughs at night in the field overhead;
Rocks, moss, stonecrop, iron, merds.

"The Waste Land," puzzling when it first appeared, came to seem a lucid and effective revelation of the dilemmas of the modern man, and in "The Hollow Men" there sounded the death rattle of a civilization:

> *We are the hollow men*
> *We are the stuffed men*
> *Leaning together.*

When Eliot began writing the enthusiasms of the renaissance were reverberating about him, but the esthetes who followed him at Harvard quickly recognized that he was closer to them than were the poets of the middle generation, and both his mood and his method won him admirers. The method borrowed something from the imagists, but it relied largely on the device, practiced by Ezra Pound among others, of using quotation and allusion to suggest the contrast between the grandeur of the past and the meanness of the present. No one expressed better than Eliot the beliefs and attitudes of the esthetes: the mixture of rebellion and condescension in their relations with their contemporaries, their self-conscious modernity and their wistful admiration for the poets of bygone days, their strange self-contempt and their boundless egotism.

But Eliot was so bitterly aware of the emptiness of modern life, the sterility of its negations and the futility of its hopes, that he desperately sought for some abiding place of faith and peace. At first he found a kind of refuge in his art, even though that art celebrated uncertainty and unrest, but in time that refuge proved inadequate. Not long after he had feebly announced his prostrate helplessness in "The Hollow Men," he defined his general point of view as "classicist in literature, royalist in politics, and anglo-catholic in religion." He had turned for support to what were, for him, the only institutions that offered strength and permanence, the British Church and State. We need not ask how so melodramatic a skeptic can accept the dogmas of Anglicanism, or what so intelligent an observer can expect from the King of England, or why so resolute an experimenter should affirm his allegiance to the laws of ancient art. The need for security was too strong to pay any attention to common sense or logic.

But the poetry Eliot has written since his conversion suggests that he has gained little—and may have lost much. In his critical pronouncements he can dogmatically affirm his new faith, but the poems in *Ash Wednesday* are as weak and elegiac as any he wrote in his unregenerate state. In fact Mr. Eliot's principles seem to be strangling his poetic gifts: he can now speak neither as poet of faith nor as poet of doubt. The unity of tone that once made his poems memorable has disappeared, and nothing of comparable value has taken its place. "A Song for Simeon" and "The Journey of the Magi," for example, are full of the old despair, and yet, merely as statements of that despair, they are less moving than "The Waste Land" or "J. Alfred Prufrock."

Mr. Eliot continues, however, to have his following. Allen Tate, John Crowe Ransom, and John Brooks Wheelwright are among the defenders of the faith, and the interest in religion has spread, influencing many men who have not joined the Church. Catholicism, whether Roman or Anglican, provides the writer with a body of ideas that have the dignity of age and, for that reason, the appearance of stability. It offers him, moreover, the support of a thoroughly dignified tradition. Poets do not join the Baptist Church or the Methodist. The evangelical Protestant churches are strongholds of the lower middle class, against whose standards the poets are in rebellion. It is to Anglicanism that the writer usually turns, grateful for its traditional association with aristocracy, its historic friendliness to the arts, and its complacent assertion of a realm of values outside the comprehension of the average American business man.

And for the writer who is not quite ready for the Church there is the pleasant halfway house of humanism. Humanism, though from the first many of its adherents have been church members, and though even its less pious exponents have been emphatically friendly to religious traditions and ecclesiastical institutions, has professed to be a philosophical system that does not need the support of divine revelation. As a matter of fact, as T. S. Eliot and Allen Tate have pointed out, humanism is meaningless once its dogmas are separated from the sanctions of religious authority. The dualism of man and nature is a poor substitute for the dualism of matter and spirit; the guidance of the ethical imagination is a poor substitute for the guidance of the divinely ordained Church. But this has not prevented Irving Babbitt and the other secularists from insisting that humanism is positive and non-theological. In practice humanism, whatever its illogicalities, has many of the virtues of traditional faith: it provides its followers with a justification of the existing order and a bulwark against the importunities of humanitarian reformers; it holds out the hope of stability and certainty in a world of doubt and change; it sanctifies the cultivation of the individual garden. One can easily see why it had a brief vogue in the twenties and why that vogue ended almost as soon as the depression began.

One understands the appeal of both Catholicism and humanism when one examines the novels of Thornton Wilder. He is a Christian novelist; that is, his interpretation of life is guided by the teachings of the Church. No doubt he sincerely believes in those teachings and finds them confirmed by his observation. When, however, he wants to depict the operation of Christian principles, he chooses to describe the life of an aristocracy. *The Cabala* tells of a little group of noblemen in Rome, a strange survival of paganism, and of the surrender of this group to Christianity. *The Bridge of San Luis Rey,* with its doctrine of divine providence, is laid in eighteenth century Peru, and its principal character is the Marquesa de Montmayor. *The Woman of Andros,* which is supposed to teach that the highest nobility is impossible without the grace of Jesus Christ, portrays a little section of aristocratic Greece. Wilder does not show how providence functions in a steel strike or what grace means to the unemployed; for him the Christian virtues are apparently inseparable from the dignified ease of the Marquesa de Montmayor and the culture of Cardinal Vaini. In both *The Cabala* and *The Woman of Andros* he teaches that the aristocratic virtues can only be perfected by the acceptance of Christianity, but one observes that the aristocratic virtues are taken for granted. If these were absent, would Wilder be so much interested in the Christian tradition?

It is possible to regard Wilder's novels either as parables of the Anglo-Catholic faith or as pictures of aristocratic life. As parables they are scarcely convincing, for they are so remote from contemporary experience as to seem, at best, merely mythological. As pictures they completely fail to give us a robust and credible world of living, admirable aristocrats. Not only are Wilder's people lifeless and shadowy; his style is precious to the point of insipidity, and his romantic embellishments have a tawdriness that can only suggest charlatanism. His mild and timid spirit longs for freedom from the noise and dirt, the toil and worry, the confusion and complexity of contemporary civilization. He longs for the security, material and intellectual, of a Christian aristocracy. But, ardent as his desire is, it cannot create even romantic fiction that is vigorous and moving, and his work merely reflects the cowardice and dishonesty of his spirit.

The popularity of *The Bridge of San Luis Rey* suggests, since one cannot assume that all of its thousands of readers were attracted by the elaborate structure or the euphuistic style, that at the time it appeared—1927—there existed in America a certain class of persons intelligent enough to be dissatisfied with the cultural standards of their communities and prosperous enough not to be primarily concerned with the problem of earning a living. The vulgarity of Wilder's way of pandering to this class is unmistakable. The Anglican critics and poets do not seem so flagrantly guilty of this vulgarity, and yet one sometimes detects a certain cheapness in their ideas, their style, and their manner of dealing with their contemporaries, and it is not difficult to understand why they have failed to find either a basis for sound criticism or an inspiration for enduring poetry.

*   *   *

Eliot and Wilder are typical of the young men who have tried to find some sort of certainty in this world of disillusionment and despair; Ernest Hemingway presents himself frankly as a representative of the lost generation. From his two novels and his short stories there emerges a sort of composite character, the Hemingway hero, whose story is, in its broad outlines, the story not merely of Hemingway's life but of the lives of a not inconsiderable group of his contemporaries. This Hemingway hero, though born in America, was from the first a passive rebel, avoiding the familiar forms of American upbringing and associating with individuals outside the ranks of middle-class respectability. Never sure of any code of values, he let himself drift, and in time he drifted into the war. As a soldier he did his work competently, not through any sense of duty and certainly not because of patriotism, but because it was simpler to go straight ahead than to try to dodge. The war intensified his distrust of conventional values and impressed him afresh with the difficulty of preserving individuality. He came out of the war anxious to simplify life and willing, for the sake of simplification, to sacrifice much that other persons valued. He could not keep himself from feeling, but he could minimize the outward evidences of emotion; he could not keep himself from thinking, but he could refuse to attach much importance to the results of thought. As skeptical of esthetic standards as of moral, quite indifferent to philosophy, he sought no elaborate rationalization of his attitude, but he had his own conception of the good life. He found his chief satisfactions in bodily activity. To fish, to ski, to watch a boxing match or a bull fight not only made it possible to stop thinking but also gave life that momentary intensification that seemed the only reward for living.

Hemingway has, as a matter of fact, two heroes: the autobiographical hero, whose spiritual history we have traced, and the hero that Hemingway is not but thinks he would like to be. He has written often of simple, uncritical barbarians—the tramps in "The Battler," the gunmen in "The Killers," and the peasant in "An Alpine Idyll"—whose lives he finds free from hypocrisy and from the muddy swirl of thoughts and emotions that accompanies the acts of so-called civilized men. But recognizing the dulness of such existences, he prefers men who combine direct and unrationalized action with a capacity for intense response to the events of life. He admires, therefore, men of the sporting world and bull-fighters in particular. "Nobody," says one of his characters, "ever lives their life all the way up except bull-fighters." Thus Hemingway proposes a kind of remedy for the disease of his generation: if all else fails, if social obligations lose their force, if the desire for success is dead, if all philosophies seem equally meaningless and all philosophers equally futile, action remains, not action for a cause but action for its own sake, the unthinking, unhesitating, and if possible hazardous exercise of the body.

But no one with any awareness of the problems facing Hemingway's generation can doubt that this concern with physical activity is an evasion of responsibility. Moreover, it is not, even for Hemingway, an entirely satisfactory evasion. The whole problem of values, which he is trying to escape, rises up to haunt him. What gives significance to *The Sun Also Rises* is the character of Jake, who exercises self-control when it is most important and most difficult, and who fights against self-pity and the consolation of lying dreams. If he were merely a drifter, whining over his misfortune, one would have no sense of the tragedy of his life. Nor is Frederic in *A Farewell to Arms* merely a drifter; he has been drifting, it is true, but the book describes the establishment of a relationship, presumably the first in his life, that has value for him and that he wants to endure, and it is the interruption of that relationship that makes the story tragic. Even the short stories about the arena, the prize-ring, and the race track are less concerned with instinctive actions than with displays of courage and fortitude.

When it serves his purposes, Hemingway reveals the values he accepts, but he refuses to consider their implications. It is significant that he never attempts to defend his Catholicism, as Eliot and the others do; he gives no reasons for his conversion to the Church, and what lies behind his conversion is only hinted at in his books. The truth is that, if he once tried to state and justify his position, he would have to repudiate his novels and stories, for he would be forced to see, and so would his readers, that in his fiction he has created an artificial environment for his characters. In order to avoid problems that he is unwilling to face, he isolates his people from the forces that have made them what they are. The sense of futility he describes is not an accident; the values he accepts have a wider significance than he attributes to them or they have no significance at all. The effectiveness of Hemingway's work depends not so much on his accurate account of the actions and words of such people as Jake, Lady Brett, and Frederic as on his suggestion of the implications of what they say and do. But his refusal to examine those implications and to try to understand them limits the value and importance of his fiction.

It seems unlikely that he will ever transcend his limitations. "The great thing," he says at the end of *Death in the Afternoon,* "is to last and get your work done and see and hear and learn and understand; and write when there is something that you know; and not before; and not too damned much after. Let those who want to save the world [save it,] if you can get to see it clear and as a whole. Then any part you make will present the whole if it's made truly. The thing to do is work and learn to make it." This statement might be interpreted so that any author, whatever his convictions, could accept it; but saving the world and seeing it clear and as a whole are not so unrelated as Hemingway supposes. In fact the connection is so close that his contempt for those who would save the world betrays his unwillingness to see it for what it is. The artist makes his contribution to the salvation of the world by seeing it clearly himself and helping others to do the same. But certainly he does not see it clearly if he is constantly running away from whatever frightens or worries or bores him. Hemingway says, "After one comes, through contact with its administrators, no longer to cherish greatly the law as a remedy in abuses, then the bottle becomes a sovereign means of direct action. If you cannot throw it, at least you can always drink from it." If, in other words, you are troubled by the world, resort to personal violence, and if personal violence proves, as it usually does, to be ineffective, undignified, and even dangerous, console yourself with drink—or skiing, or sexual intercourse, or watching bull-fights. There is a point at which retreat becomes surrender and evasion becomes impotence. *Death in the Afternoon* suggests that Ernest Hemingway may not be far from that point.

* * *

The twenties have not, of course, failed to develop their particular form of that familiar phenomenon, regionalism. In a nation so large as the United States, with such marked geographical divisions and such a diversity of peoples, it is still easy to consider only sectional differences and to ignore the fundamental unity of the nation. Once that unity is ignored, regionalism offers, now as formerly, a convenient way of escaping certain of the basic problems of American life. As these problems have grown more intense and more complex, the desire to avoid them has naturally grown stronger.

Moreover, one result of our coming of age as a nation has been an increase of interest in the past, and in our past the section has played an important part.

Much of contemporary regionalism is merely antiquarian; much of it is the sentimental expression of sectional pride. But there have been writers who have written of life in a particular region simply because it was the material experience gave them. Foremost of these is Elizabeth Madox Roberts, and in her work we see once more that regionalism may have value at the beginning of a career. Her first novel, *The Time of Man,* is one of the books of the decade that deserve to survive. Though the life it describes is remote from the lives we lead, its people are real people, and we can sympathize with them and even be heartened by the courage they show in facing their difficulties. The author's close knowledge of these people and her long reflection on the significance of their history give the book firmness and beauty. It is the kind of book that can only grow out of a comprehensive understanding of a particular way of life.

But it was as true for Elizabeth Roberts as it was for Willa Cather that the memories of childhood could not be made the basis of a literary career. As if aware of the folly of trying to repeat her first success, she experimented with the Joycean method in *My Heart and My Flesh,* and hazarded with *Jingling in the Wind* a venture in fantasy. The complete failure of both books indicated that there was but one path to follow: the frankly poetic and elegiac romanticism of *The Great Meadow* and *A Buried Treasure.* Diffuse and over-written, these later novels offer no credible characters and no interpretation of life that is in any way relevant to us and our age. That Miss Roberts' collapse came more promptly than Willa Cather's suggests that even ten years have multiplied the obstacles in the regionalists' road.

The career of Glenway Wescott points to much the same conclusion. It began quite as encouragingly as Miss Roberts'. *The Apple of the Eye* is not, like *The Time of Man,* a simple poetic record of the joy and sorrow in pioneer lives. It concerns the spiritual aspects of pioneering, especially the bleak, sterile attitude towards life that frontier hardships sometimes foster. Fundamentally it is the story of the conflict between two religions and of the effect of that struggle on a boy who wavers between them. On the one hand we find the narrow, rigid, utilitarian Protestantism of the frontier; on the other, a pagan acceptance of life and all its pleasures. The orthodoxy of Mrs. Bier is not only destructive of beauty; it no longer has the function it once had as a disciplinary force in the struggle against the soil. Yet it has conquered her husband, Jule, who had once shared with Bad Han the joys of passion; it turns their daughter's encounter with Mike, a preacher of paganism, into tragedy; and it stands in the way of their nephew's acceptance in practice of Mike's creed, though he is convinced that the creed is sound. The book ends with the nephew leaving for college, still torn between the two principles, thinking with fondness and admiration of Mike, yet bearing with him the admonition "to form some church connection in Madison" and to "ask God to show you a way to use your talents for His kingdom."

In *The Grandmothers* Wescott continued as he had begun, describing the frustration of three generations of pioneers. The pioneers, he suggests, were from the first unhappy men, and it was the absence of happiness that sent them westward. They struggled with the land, always in poverty. "God was poverty, but He was poverty which would become wealth." So they identified piety and prosperity, and bent their necks before the divinely-imposed yoke. In due course the continent revealed its riches and many became

wealthy. "Nevertheless," Wescott goes on, "millions remained poor. Before their eyes lay the feast—they could not
eat; and though there were millions of them, each felt alone
in his poverty. They grieved, but stifled their grief, being
ashamed of it; for if they had worked harder, if they had
led purer lives, if they still worked harder. . . . Those who
did not give up hated life secretly; those who did, despised
themselves." Of the Towers, the family he is describing, he
writes: "They said little, but this conviction took possession
of all their minds: they were not born to be beasts of burden; they should not have to work as these others worked;
they were not menials, but deserved a sweeter fate; life was
unjust. This conviction was inherited by every Tower, from
father to son; and in that inheritance younger son shared
equally with elder. A grievance was their birthright."

Wescott himself, obviously, inherited this grievance, and
in his novels and most of his short stories, he made it articulate. It was, for a novelist, not a bad inheritance: it protected
him from the more obvious forms of sentimentality, and it
sharpened his eyes to see the actual results of life on the
much-romanticized frontier. He saw hardship and bitterness
and sterility rather than the beauty and heroism Willa Cather saw. Like Hamlin Garland thirty years before he knew
what the fruits of pioneering were because he had tasted
them. But he felt none of Garland's early desire to transform
the conditions he detested. Instead, he felt from the first
what Garland came soon enough to feel, the desire to escape.
And, with him as with Garland, departure from the scene
of his stories had an immediate effect upon his writing. For
a collection of his stories, one picture after another of dis-
torted lives, he wrote an introduction from which the volume
takes its title, *Good-Bye, Wisconsin*. We detect here, when he
speaks of "the former ardent, hungry, tongue-tied life with

its mingling of Greek tragedy and idyll," a note of romantic nostalgia that, if he had continued to write of Wisconsin from his French retreat, must have substituted itself for the critical austerity of the earlier work. But Wescott had no intention of concerning himself with Wisconsin's past and certainly not with its present. He could recognize the importance of dealing with the Middle West as it had become: "It is a grave situation; and I believe that in the near future descriptive writing about average American destinies must inevitably be that of a reporter, an analyst, a diagnostician. ... The more such an author has in common with his characters the better; typical trivialities surpass in significance the noblest feelings; an immediate report is more valuable than reminiscences." But he could not stoop to typical trivialities and immediate reports. "I should like to write a book about ideal people under ideal circumstances. No sort of undernourishment, no under-education, nothing partial or frustrated, no need of variety or luxury—in short, no lack of anything which, according to its children, Wisconsin denies. Only the inavertible troubles, all in the spirit, and only those characteristic of a period in which, here and there, certain bans have been lifted, certain jealousies appeased. The ease of nature and healthy plants in a well-kept garden, but an indoor book, in which human beings alone, not the weather or swamps or the beasts of the field, shall have parts to play."

It is an admirable statement of what is desired by more authors than Glenway Wescott. He wants to avoid the nostalgic diffuseness of Willa Cather and Elizabeth Roberts; he wants to escape the narrowness, the suffering, and the bewilderment of contemporary life in America. And so he bids farewell to his literary past. Since his book about "ideal people under ideal circumstances" has not yet appeared, the results of that abdication cannot be judged. That he has found it more difficult than he assumed to say good-bye to Wisconsin an allegorical short story, "The Babe's Bed," would suggest. He has also, one surmises from *Fear and Trembling,* found it not altogether simple to discover people "with the ease of mature and healthy plants in a well-kept garden." This most recent volume, revealing his sudden perception that grave situations are not confined to Wisconsin, betrays as well the completeness of his confusion. What does he want? Peace, stability, and recognized esthetic values. But he is no more willing to fight for them in this world of his later venturings than he was in Wisconsin. That farewell, one suspects, embraced more than Glenway Wescott knew.

Mr. Wescott and Miss Roberts have written of particular regions, but neither has proposed regionalism as a way of life. That proposal could, one imagines, come only from the South, where there is a strong tradition of agrarian culture, and where the rise of industrialism has had a peculiarly devastating effect. The proclamation of Messrs. Davidson, Ransom, Tate, and the others who have taken their stand for agriculture as opposed to industry, and for southern ideals as opposed to northern, may deserve whatever admiration one can accord to a quixotic gesture; but it is peculiarly futile. The young Confederates ignore the economic forces that are spreading industrialism; they ignore the political forces they would have to contend with in order to bring about the kind of agrarian section they believe in. Nevertheless, they usefully demonstrate that regionalism is meaningless as a literary program unless it can be founded on economic and political realities.

As Ruth Suckow, author of shrewd and clear-cut studies of mid-western life, has pointed out, it is a pity that there should be, at this time, so much talk of sectionalism in literature. Even if there were some self-sufficient section, with its own traditions and its own way of life, the mere necessity for comparison with other sections would promptly involve an author in the very difficulties he wants to avoid. The novelist begins, of course, with what he knows, and if he knows the manners and speech of a particular region, all well and good. But he cannot stop there; any honest attempt to understand the region quickly takes him outside its borders. And if he cannot or will not recognize the obligation, the penalty is plain.

* * *

As we have noticed, the young esthetes came in time to feel that it was sufficient "to write a poem, an essay, a story worth the trouble of reading to one's friends." Certainly much of the literature of the twenties is curiously esoteric. It is difficult, for example, to understand a poem of T. S. Eliot's unless one has read the books that Eliot has read; and not many people have. Much of the poetry of Eliot's followers is almost completely unintelligible if one has not lived a certain kind of life. And the criticism of such men as Yvor Winters, Dudley Fitts, and R. P. Blackmur resembles the impassioned quibbling of devotees of some game. Little groups of writers sprang up in Paris, New York, and Cambridge, each with its own symbols and allusions. On the basis of assumptions shared by a few friends the poet or critic could and did elaborate vastly ingenious structures.

Such a development was the not unpredictable result of the isolation of these writers from the activities and interests of the masses of the American people. They had, as we have seen, no functional relationship to any class in American society, and they quickly discovered that they could not impress their standards on others. So each went his private way, finding what consolation he could in the understanding and appreciation of his friends. Some of them, indeed, denied that even the understanding of friends was necessary. The little group of Americans associated with *transition* frankly proclaimed that the world of private meanings is the author's only true province. The revolution of the word accomplished the ultimate statement of individualism. Its adherents, accepting the logical consequences of the theory of self-expression, completely repudiated any idea of the author's responsibility to the reader and simply denied the existence of the problems that had been troubling American authors for generation after generation.

But there was another possibility. If the author found it rather tiresome to write only for the few friends who understood him, he might contemplate the creation of a whole class of responsive persons. It is easy enough to see what the existence of a true leisure class and a genuine leisure-class culture might mean to the young writers of the twenties and thirties. Since the World War there has been, within the framework of bourgeois society, no group that can command the loyalties of the writer. He seldom has much respect for the leaders of finance and industry, and he usually has only contempt for the complacent, standardized Babbitts. As for the insurgents, the reformers and liberals, the writer is quite likely to be out of sympathy with their aims and certainly he can have little confidence in their methods. But if there were a group of persons with "the ease and maturity of plants in a well-kept garden," how pleasant it would be to associate with them, how comforting to write about them, how stimulating to write for them!

Before the depression of 1929 the creation of a leisure class seemed altogether possible. For years, of course, there had been many wealthy people, and a certain number of people who lived in leisure. But during the period of rapid capitalist expansion fortunes were made and lost so rapidly that stratification could not take place. In time, however, the risks and opportunities diminished, and great fortunes could be more safely handed from generation to generation. As this happened, the number of persons who had no functional connection with the productive system inevitably grew. Even in the twenties, however, these leisured persons had not grown into a compact and orderly group, with a common body of ideals, ideas, and interests. But so great was the need of many of the younger writers that they could not wait; they had to force the growth of a leisure-class culture.

There were many signs of such an effort in the twenties. T. S. Eliot's acceptance of the British Church and State is the most obvious indication that certain sorts of writers were feeling the need of the support that a leisure class could give. But one can point also to the interest of other writers in ecclesiastical tradition and to the humanists' treatment of economic problems. Wilder, as has been noted, deals almost entirely with aristocrats. Wescott, describing the subject he would like to write on, gives an idealized picture of a leisure class. Tate and his young Confederates dream of the revival of the plantation aristocracy. Most of the members of Hemingway's lost generation find time to devote to sports and drinking because they live on unearned incomes. In the work of the novelists and poets we can see the growth of the ideal of the leisure class and in the work of the critics we can see the attempt to forge the requisite intellectual bonds.

The depression demonstrated the prematureness of these efforts. At first it was regarded merely as an irritating interruption, but in time its implications became obvious even to the blindest and most isolated of the younger writers. Many of them have tried to adapt themselves to the new situation. Wescott, as we have seen, has become alarmed at the apparent disintegration of his world and the consequent shat-

tering of his hopes. In the *Hound & Horn,* once so esoteric
in its interests, articles appear on capitalism, Jeffersonianism,
and Russia. There is the case of Archibald MacLeish, whose
earlier poetry rivaled Eliot's in the communication of the
hopelessness and self-distrust of a generation. But MacLeish,
like Eliot, wanted to escape from the limbo of futility. Essentially a romantic, he desired values to affirm and heroes
to admire. After expressing for years his disillusionment, he
tried to create heroes in *Conquistador,* an elegiac account of
Cortes and his little army of veterans in Mexico. MacLeish
turned to the past for the heroes of his poem. But now he is
looking for heroes in the present, and looking for them in
Wall Street. America, he says in an article in the *Saturday
Review of Literature,* "requires of its governors a conception
of capitalism in which a man can believe—which a man can
oppose in his mind to other and no longer visionary conceptions." Thus he appeals to big business men to be his heroes
and to provide him with values.

There are many other signs that in the coming years the
effort of a certain number of writers will be devoted, not to
the creation of a leisure-class culture, but to the development
of a body of capitalist apologetics. After all, the writers of
whom we have been speaking do depend on the capitalist
system. A while ago, when all was going well, they could
ignore that fact, but now most of them realize it very keenly.
At present they content themselves with attacking the enemies of capitalism, the while they discuss plans for its modi-
fication and preservation. But if the situation grows worse
and capitalism is still further imperiled, it is reasonable to
suppose that a certain number of writers will take a more
definite stand in its defense. Most of them will not, presumably, defend capitalism as such, but they will defend a
set of doctrines that involve not merely the preservation but

the consolidation and extension of capitalist power. They will, in short, become fascists.

* * *

There is an alternative. John Dos Passos was one of the Harvard poets, but he seems to have been less completely drugged than his companions by Baudelaire, Petronius, and the Old Howard. He could write typical undergraduate poems and stories; he could make the usual Harvard jibes at "long-haired ultra-socialism"; but he could not blind himself to the fact that "millions of men perform labor narrowing and stultifying even under the best conditions." As was natural he blamed industrialism. "Are we not like men crouching on a runaway engine?" he asked in 1916. "And at the same time we insensately shovel in the fuel with no thought as to where we are being taken."

His experiences in the war intensified his distrust of an industrial civilization, and increased his longing for some sort of sanctuary. "God!" cries the autobiographical hero of *One Man's Initiation,* "if there were somewhere nowadays where you could flee from all this stupidity, from all this cant of governments, and this hideous reiteration of hatred, this strangling hatred." But the war also fostered a conflicting desire, the desire to understand and change the system that made such horror possible. The two desires lived, side by side, during his travels in Spain, as recorded in *Rosinante to the Road Again,* and in the East, as recorded in *Orient Express.* We shall have to know much more than we do now to be able to explain why the desire to flee was weaker in Dos Passos than in most of his contemporaries. But it was, and eventually the desire to understand and to affect the world in which he lived triumphed.

It was not, however, until 1925, when he wrote *Manhattan*

Transfer, that Dos Passos was quite willing to take a long look at the world he had hated and sometimes fled from. Since there was so much in American life that baffled and irritated and alarmed and interested him, he could not write a conventional novel, but built his book out of some two hundred episodes, dealing with fifty or sixty persons, recurring again and again to some and carrying them through several years, giving only the briefest glimpses of others. Uniting these many episodes, which tell of reporters, actresses, waiters, politicians, milkmen, lawyers, bootleggers, sailors, and housewives, there is a basic rhythm, an underlying movement—beginning, struggle, bewilderment, defeat. Dos Passos summoned all his powers of description, all his knowledge of character, and packed into one book a richness of life that pounds upon the reader's sense with all the irresistibility of the composite din that daily strikes the metropolitan ear. Yet, though he had achieved much, he had not achieved enough: the book suggests the complexity of city life, but it gives us few memorable characters; it leaves us with a sense of the drift of men and events, but it does not indicate the direction of the drift. What keeps the novel this side of greatness is the author's bewilderment, which is not unlike the bewilderment of Jimmy Herf, the character who comes closest to being Dos Passos' counterpart and spokesman. When Jimmy leaves New York, we feel with him a temporary sense of relief; but we know well enough that his departure is no real solution of his own problems and can have no bearing upon the problems of the other characters still struggling in the metropolitan wilderness. Based on a bitterness that finds no adequate expression, culminating in a retreat that is a confession of futility, *Manhattan Transfer* leaves us with only a recollection of isolated scenes and an impression that the author has seen but has not understood.

In the difference between Dos Passos' two plays, *The Garbage Man* and *Airways, Inc.,* we trace the change that makes *The 42nd Parallel,* his next novel, so superior to *Manhattan Transfer. The Garbage Man,* in its attempt to reproduce the chaos of modern life and to catch the glamorous spectacle that it makes, is close to the former novel and ends quite as unsatisfactorily. *Airways, Inc.,* bad as its overambitiousness makes it, is a fighting play, free from romanticism and doubt. At last Dos Passos is willing to face America because he has faith that out of the squalid chaos a decent civilization may come. When one believes that the horrible can be defeated, when one has good reasons for that belief, feels it deeply as a challenge, acts upon it as a philosophy of life, then one need no longer think of flight.

It is in the spirit of *Airways, Inc.,* that Dos Passos has written *The 42nd Parallel* and *1919.* In these novels he tells the stories of a number of representative Americans in the years before, during, and immediately after the World War: an I.W.W., a stenographer, a publicity agent, an interior decorator, and a garage hand; a sailor, a minister's daughter, a Harvard liberal, an impulsive Texan, and a Jewish radical. Some of these characters are involved with others; some, at the end of *1919,* still pursue their solitary courses. What holds these narratives together is not any web of intrigue or chain of circumstance. These persons belong together because they are being swept along by the same forces, a fact that Dos Passos indicates by interrupting the story of one to tell the story of another, and emphasizes by making his reader aware of broad social movements in the background. To portray this background, to give us the fullest possible sense of the mass emotions and actions that lie behind the comparatively few lives he has singled out to describe, he employs three devices: in the "Newsreels" we find the raw material of history, the actual and undigested stuff of experience, out of which the narrative sections have been fashioned; "The Camera's Eye," with its impressionistic bits of autobiography, strengthens the effect of reality by suggesting that the author, too, has been part of what he describes; the portraits, records of human heroism, meanness, bewilderment, victory, defeat, set before us the gods, demigods, and devils of our time, and give the novels an epic scope.

But the particular devices Dos Passos uses are relatively unimportant. It is what the devices express that matters. The ten narratives, the innumerable newspaper extracts, the autobiographical passages, and the tabloid biographies are held together by the author's realization that all of us, sailors and stenographers, interior decorators and publicity agents, J. P. Morgan and Wesley Everest, Charles Proteus Steinmetz and Woodrow Wilson, have been moving steadily towards a great crisis. That is why he can treat his characters both as individual entities and as parts of a larger whole, why he can let us see and sympathize with their hopes and sufferings at the same time that we are conscious of the larger drama in which they are merely supers. All his powers of observation and understanding have been intensified. As the scientist's hypothesis sharpens his perceptions by giving him a principle of selection, so the concept of the class struggle and the trend towards revolution, deeply realized in the emotions and translated into action, has given Dos Passos a greater sensitiveness to the world about him. But it has done something more important than that: it has shown him the relations between apparently isolated events and enabled him to see the fundamental unity beneath the seemingly chaotic complexity of American life. And it has banished, at last, all the dismay and doubt that, subtly insinuating themselves despite his efforts to dispel them, at one time sapped the vitality of his imagination.

Dos Passos has grown steadily during the last decade, and there is no apparent obstacle to his continued growth. For whom of his contemporaries can the same claim be made? Not for Elizabeth Madox Roberts with her pretty little elegies; not for Glenway Wescott, looking the world over for his ideal people; not for Thornton Wilder, playing with his dolls; not for William Faulkner, spinning complex melodramas out of his neuroses; not for Ernest Hemingway, with his twin opiates, drink and bull-fighting. There is the tragedy of Hart Crane, who longed, perhaps more deeply than anyone else in his generation, to reveal in enduring lines the innermost significance of all that America is and has been. Sharing the despair and bewilderment of his generation, he resolutely strove to put all that behind him, and in *The Bridge* wrote a powerful affirmation of the intrinsic worth and the majestic destiny of his country. The stark determination of the man speaks in the sonorous lines, the subtle rhythms, the bold metaphors. But what, fundamentally, was Crane seeking to affirm? He perceived the beauty of such structures as Brooklyn Bridge; he was aware of the poetic treasure concealed in our history and legends; he recognized in the courageous comprehensiveness and simple idealism of Walt Whitman a worthy inspiration. Intuitively he knew that there existed forces that could bring about the triumph of all that he cherished in American life; but what those forces were he could not tell, and in the end his affirmations rested only on a vague mysticism. Continued creation on such a foundation was for him, clear-sighted as he was, impossible. Worn out by his struggles, broken by his defeat, the prey of neuroses such as are often the product of extreme individualism, he refused to strive any longer in a world that for him held no possibility of success.

The tragedy of Hart Crane is more apparent than the tragedies of some of his contemporaries, but scarcely different in kind. If there are harsh words to be said about such men as Eliot, Hemingway, and Faulkner, it is not because one fails to understand the reasons for their failures, nor because one is loath to pay tribute to their virtues, but because the futility of the ways they have chosen to follow must be recognized. And since that is true, we have reason to feel and to show satisfaction in the achievements of John Dos Passos. What he has done is important, but what he has shown that it is possible to do is more important. He has his faults, faults that probably are the results of his early environment and training; his heritage was, after all, that of most of the members of his literary generation. Other writers, we trust, will overcome those faults; but it is Dos Passos that has shown the way.

*   *   *

It is not to be supposed that Dos Passos stands alone or that his career is in any sense an accident. He is one of a small but growing group of writers who have found an answer to the doubts and denials of their generation in an alliance with the proletariat in its struggle for revolutionary change. The revolutionary attitude is new in American literature, as it is relatively new in American life. Territorial expansion and industrial development long inspired in Americans of every class a confidence in the ability of the individual to achieve independence and even wealth. Factory workers and small farmers shared the attitudes of the middle class, not unnaturally since there was a real possibility that any given worker might raise himself above his associates. Only after the frontier had disappeared could self-reliant individualism begin to yield to a sense of class solidarity. And it yielded slowly: not only did old attitudes persist; the lack of racial unity and the existence of a group of privileged workers prevented the growth of a strong labor movement. The Socialist Party drew much of its support from the middle class, and its faith in gradual parliamentary reform showed the persistence of middle-class ideas. The rapid rise of the I.W.W. indicated a growing restlessness, but the development of this organization in the direction of syndicalism called attention once more to the political immaturity of American laborers. The most hopeful sign, as the leadership of the Socialist Party became more and more conservative, was the growing dissatisfaction of many of its members. American participation in the World War sharpened the differences, not merely revealing how little dependence could be placed in the socialism of many party members, but also suggesting the helplessness of the orthodox parliamentary socialists in the face of the tasks that confronted them. The Russian revolution, the establishment of the Union of Socialist Soviet Republics, and the founding of the Third International promptly brought the break between the more and less radical socialists and led to the founding of the Communist Party. This party, whatever its weaknesses, has raised the standard of revolution on American soil, and the revolutionary tradition is now a fact in American life.

That tradition has had a parallel development in our literature. The individualistic revolt of Emerson and Thoreau took on a socialistic hue in the later writings of Whitman and Howells. Utopian socialism became a force in the nineties, after the appearance of *Looking Backward*. Parliamentary socialism found expression in the novels and pamphlets of Upton Sinclair. The suggestion of a revolutionary zeal appeared in the confusion of Jack London's mind, but it was not until the founding of the *Masses* in 1911 that revolutionary ideas comparable to those long current in European nations found expression in American literature. And even in the *Masses* the revolutionary philosophy was inextricably involved with the notions of the muckrakers and the iconoclastic rebelliousness of the bohemians. It required the war to clarify the revolutionary tendency, and in the wartime development of John Reed, who threw himself into the fight for the world-wide overthrow of capitalism, who gave in *Ten Days That Shook the World* a stirring record of the Bolshevik triumph, and who died in the midst of his struggle for communism, one sees the clearest symbol of the change that was taking place. When some years after the war, the *New Masses* was founded under the editorship of Michael Gold, and aimed itself as directly as it could at the rousing of the proletariat, the tradition of John Reed became a living tradition in American art and literature.

The few radicals who, in the midst of Coolidge prosperity, continued to insist on the need for revolution must often have been irritated and discouraged by the blindness of their contemporaries. But what their arguments could not accomplish the depression brought about. For a considerable number of young writers that depression meant the end of an era. Some had taken part in the radical movement in the days of the *Masses* and the *Liberator,* and had gradually drifted away. Some had been liberals, progressively disillusioned by the war, the defeat of LaFollette, and the failure to save Sacco and Vanzetti from legal murder. Others had come of age without illusions, so to speak, in the strange atmosphere of prosperous estheticism. All of them shared the contemporary interest in technique, and all of them had succumbed, in one degree or another, to the current sense of futility. The depression stung into wakefulness their dormant humanitarian sympathies, bringing squarely before their eyes the hopeless suffering that the myth of prosperity had concealed. Furthermore, it made them realize that, without admitting it to themselves, they had been, as one of them said, betting on capitalism, and it forced them to recognize the implications of this position. The choice presented to them was the choice presented to all their contemporaries whose awareness of life had not been dulled by too prolonged an isolation from social realities, but, whereas one group merely made the greater haste in throwing together some sort of bulwark against the storm, this group clearly perceived that capitalism could not and did not deserve to survive.

The extent of the movement to the left became apparent when, early in 1931, Edmund Wilson published in the *New Republic,* of which he was at that time an editor, an article describing what he called the breakdown of liberalism and affirming his allegiance to communism. Theodore Dreiser took the same stand, followed in time by Sherwood Anderson. Steadily the list grew. These new advocates of revolution were eager to serve the cause in which they now believed: they organized committees for the defense of political prisoners and for the aid of striking miners; some of them investigated conditions in Harlan County and gave assistance to the strikers there; and in 1932 they formed the League of Professional Groups for Foster and Ford. Fifty-two American intellectuals signed a statement endorsing the candidates of the Communist Party.

A complicated situation has resulted. Some of these men and women, though they are convinced of the necessity of radical change and though they have given loyal support to radical causes, have gone on writing much as they did when they were voting for Coolidge or LaFollette or were not voting at all. Others have been affected in certain of their attitudes towards life. Still others have made a determined effort to study Marx and Lenin and to understand and assimilate the whole philosophy of the revolutionary movement. Undoubtedly a certain proportion of the recent converts will change their minds and will drift away, as radicals have drifted away in the past. But the revolutionary tradition in American literature is now too firmly entrenched to be affected by individual apostasies.

One has only to survey the present literary scene to appreciate the strength of the communist sympathizers. In criticism Joseph Freeman, though the diversification of his interests has prevented him from winning the reputation to which he is entitled, has for nearly a decade been demonstrating the effectiveness of the Marxist method. V. F. Calverton's *The Liberation of American Literature* is a valuable piece of pioneering, though it may well be superseded by subtler and sounder studies. Joshua Kunitz and Bernard Smith have written on Marxist theory, and more recently Newton Arvin, formerly a follower of Van Wyck Brooks, has written in Marxist terms on American authors. Edmund Wilson and Waldo Frank show the influence of Marx, and Malcolm Cowley, Matthew Josephson, Clifton P. Fadiman, and John Chamberlain have interpreted literature as a social force. Other reviewers are moving in the same direction, and there is a growing body of theoretical discussion.

In poetry it is less easy to point to satisfying work, though Horace Gregory has often reflected the decay of the social order and has sometimes caught the accents of revolt. The appearance of Langston Hughes and Countee Cullen, the two principal Negro poets of our time, in the list of intellectuals supporting Foster and Ford is peculiarly significant. Negro writers have taken a more and more important place in the literature of the past two or three decades, but their preoccupation with a particular problem has resulted in ignorance of broader social movements, and too often they have been content to reflect the blind estheticism of their white contemporaries. As, however, the emotions of an oppressed race are merged with a passion for the liberation of all the oppressed everywhere, the Negro novelist and poet will be more likely to see the contemporary situation in its true proportions. Already Hughes is showing the way by his poems of protest, in which the bitterness of the Negro and his pathetic longing for deliverance take on the militant and confident note of a call to battle.

Ever since the founding of the Provincetown Players there has been a tradition of revolt in the drama, and in the midst of the era of prosperity this spirit expressed itself in the New Playwrights' Theater, which enlisted the support of a number of talented dramatists, among them Michael Gold, John Dos Passos, John Howard Lawson, Paul Sifton, Francis E. Faragoh, and Emjo Basshe. Basshe, in *The Centuries,* showed not only his sympathy with the people of the East Side but also his understanding of the economic causes of their misery. In *Processional,* and less successfully in *Loud Speaker,* Lawson drew on the popular arts to suggest the confusion and pathos of American life, but these plays, as well as the more recent *Success Story,* show how bewildered and cynical he is; he can create effective scenes but not a satisfying play. The Siftons' play, *1931—,* is a moving portrayal of the tragedy of unemployment, somewhat in the manner of the old morality plays. One can also point to two intense and powerful dramatizations of conspicuous examples of class injustice, *Precedent* by I. J. Golden and *Gods of the Lightning* by Harold Hickerson and Maxwell Anderson. Elmer Rice's *We, the People* tries to do for the theater what *42nd Parallel* and *1919* do for the novel, and in many of its scenes Rice does suggest the play of revolutionary forces in the lives of representative and credible people. The ending, however, is based on old-fashioned liberalism, and is consequently undramatic and unconvincing. There is a question whether revolutionary drama can ever be produced on the commercial stage, but the fact that a good proportion of our playwrights are in sympathy with the radical movement means that revolutionary ideas are certain to influence the drama. And at the same time the plays of Paul Peters and others, produced by workers' groups, are laying the foundation for a proletarian theater.

But it is the novel that reveals most completely the literary potentialities of the revolutionary movement. No one has succeeded so well as Dos Passos in showing the play of economic forces in all the various social strata and in all the different activities of life, but particular writers have equaled or surpassed him in portraying the life of particular classes. There is Michael Gold, for example, whose *Jews Without Money* is an authentic and moving picture of life on the East Side. The East Side figures, too, in Samuel Ornitz's *Haunch, Paunch, and Jowl,* an up-to-date version of the story told in *Memoirs of an American Citizen.* Another section of the city appears in Edward Dahlberg's *From Flushing to Calvary,* which, like his *Bottom Dogs,* depicts the lives of men and women who have been brought to physical and mental ruin. Erskine Caldwell, in *Tobacco Road* and *God's Little Acre,* shows the southern poor whites who have clung to the soil, and many of Moe Bragin's stories and sketches describe the fate of the farmer in the Middle West. Jack Conroy has written of coal miners and wandering workers, and in *Union Square* Albert Halper describes communists, peddlers, artists, and courtesans. The middle class also has been described: office workers in Edwin Seaver's *The Com-*

pany and a traveling salesman in John Herrmann's *The Big Short Trip.*

Few of these writers portray militant workers, and not all of them take a militant attitude. But they do show, often with great skill, the forces that lie behind the misery and destruction they describe. *Tobacco Road,* for example, describes the steps by which Jeeter has been reduced to shiftlessness, poverty, and disease. *Haunch, Paunch, and Jowl* records the process by which poor Jewish boys rise to wealth and political power. Seaver makes us understand why the employees of "The Company" live thwarted, miserable lives. Bragin not only portrays the economic forces that have ruined the farmer; he subtly suggests the ways in which the farmer himself is becoming conscious of the causes of his plight. In such work as this we see the conditions that make revolution inevitable.

And in other novels we are made to realize the fighting spirit of those workers who have begun to understand their position and their power. Louis Colman's *Lumber* describes the battles of the I.W.W.; James Steele's *Conveyor* portrays the growth of class-consciousness in a Detroit auto-worker; certain stories of Moe Bragin's and Whittaker Chambers' depict organized struggles of workers in city and country. It is the Gastonia strike, however, that has figured most in radical fiction. Mary Heaton Vorse's *Strike,* a description of events largely from the point of view of a young reporter, has been followed by Fielding Burke's *Call Home the Heart,* Grace Lumpkin's *To Make My Bread,* and Myra Page's *Gathering Storm.* Both *Call Home the Heart* and *To Make My Bread* describe the life in the mountains and the migration to the mill towns, as well as the strike itself. *Gathering Storm* traces the rise of class-consciousness in the workers, black and white, of the South.

No one supposes that the poems and plays and novels of the radical writers are flawless. One cannot ignore such faults as the argumentation in *Gathering Storm*, the naïveté and formlessness of *Union Square*, the lack of proportion in *God's Little Acre*. One is bound to be conscious of Dahlberg's constant straining for stylistic effect, the slowness of the narrative in *To Make My Bread*, the ridiculousness of the last scene of *We, the People*, the inconclusiveness of *Call Home the Heart*. For some of these weaknesses there is an evident explanation: all radical writers, even those born in the working class, have acquired many of the ideas and attitudes of the bourgeoisie, and, though there may be much of value for them in bourgeois traditions, there is also much that is incompatible with the philosophy to which they now subscribe, and the resulting conflict makes itself felt in their work. Even Michael Gold, who has been in the radical movement for years, interpreted East Side life largely in terms of his original attitude towards it, and as a result we are not prepared for the conversion to socialism with which *Jews Without Money* ends. These writers, it must be remembered, belong to an intermediary stage; their work will be superseded in time by a genuine proletarian literature and, eventually, by the literature of a classless society.

And yet the vigor of the revolutionary tradition is unmistakable. It is significant that almost all the younger writers who make any attempt to deal with contemporary life are allied with the radical movement. There are a few authors, such as Thomas Wolfe and Evelyn Scott, who do not realize the implications of their own work, but most of the writers who are not in sympathy with the revolutionary movement are writing about ancient Greece or eighteenth century Kentucky, about murder mysteries or bull fights. It is to the radicals we must turn to discover the kind of world in which we live. And how vividly we see the tenement described in *Jews Without Money,* the factories described in *Conveyor,* the office described in *The Company,* the orphanage described in *Bottom Dogs.* How many memorable characters we meet: Ishma in *Call Home the Heart,* Jeeter in *Tobacco Road,* Meyer in *Haunch, Paunch, and Jowl,* Leon Fisher and Mr. Boardman in *Union Square!* There is a reason why the work of the revolutionary writers is the most vigorous that the era is producing or can produce: it stands in the most vital relationship to the best in the American literature of the past, and it alone offers hope for the future.

* * *

We have attempted to view American life of the industrial age as the artist might view it. We have understood why some writers turned away in boredom, disgust, or fear, and we have walked along the paths they chose to follow. With other writers we have marched out upon the field of battle, sympathizing with their hopes and recording their defeats as well as their victories. The achievements of the first group have sometimes gratified us, but we have realized that their limitations were of the sort that must in the long run be fatal. After all, surveying the whole of literary history, one can scarcely think of any writer, commonly recognized as great, who did not immerse himself in the life of the times, who did not concern himself with the problems of his age— even when he chose some other time or place as the setting of his poem or his play. As we have seen, industrialism became more and more important in American life, the implications of capitalism grew clearer and clearer, the lines of the class struggle were drawn more and more sharply, and consequently the cost of evasion grew greater and greater. Comparing Edith Wharton with Henry James, or Willa

Cather with Sarah Orne Jewett, or Robert Frost with Emily Dickinson, we have realized that it has been increasingly difficult for those who ignore industrialism to create a vital literature.

On the other hand, as we looked at the writers who tried to understand American life, we have found a steady growth. William Dean Howells made a beginning in the early seventies. His first sketches were simple realistic descriptions, but his novels came to embrace more and more of American life, and in such books as *A Hazard of New Fortunes* he came closer than any of his contemporaries to portraying the complicated changes that were going on in America. He was, it is true, quite as prudish as any other Victorian American, and he could no more understand the changes he described than could the kind of persons he wrote about. Yet he succeeded, as Hawthorne and Melville had not done, as James and Mark Twain did not do, in founding a school, and it was the men who followed his example who dominated our fiction at the end of the century. These men—Crane, Fuller, Garland, Norris—did something towards the breaking down of taboos, and they brought literature closer to the main stream of American life. Their successors, the muckrakers, turned their attention directly to urgent problems of industrialism and politics. And the writers of the middle generation—Dreiser, Lewis, and Anderson—completed the liberation of literature from the stranglehold of prudishness and hypocrisy, and at the same time wrote out of a wider and deeper knowledge than their predecessors had possessed.

But the problem of intelligent mastery remained. Critics sometimes dwell on the failure of American writers to achieve order, form, significance. They do not realize that the question is not exclusively literary. One cannot achieve form by fiat; one has to understand the significance of the materials one uses, as Howells pointed out in *Criticism and Fiction,* if one is to make that significance felt in their literary organization. And that is what Dos Passos and some of the other radicals have done. They stand in the major tradition of our literature, for they deal with representative American men and women in representative situations; and in their work, moreover, the tradition moves towards its consummation. Equipped with a many-sided knowledge of contemporary life and unhampered by conventional reticence, so that their work is quite as honest and quite as comprehensive as the work of any of their predecessors, they are also feeling their way towards an interpretation of the American scene that enables them to bind together in satisfying forms its diverse phenomena.

The tradition of realistic fiction of contemporary life has been, of course, dominant in the literature of most nations in the last century, but it has been faced with peculiar obstacles in the United States, and has had a peculiar importance. We plunged into the maelstrom of industrialism before we had developed any indigenous culture. Life was not organized for the American artist. Industrialism was not sapping away an established order; it was boldly creating a new civilization. The artist could not rely, even temporarily, on pre-industrial traditions; struggle was the only alternative to abject flight. Moreover, such pressure as American culture could exert on the writer was all in this direction: men were crying out for an interpretation of the apparent chaos in which they lived. Slowly, as we have seen, our writers responded, and now comes the promise of success.

The writer, if he is accurately and intelligently to portray American life, if he is to express whatever is vital and hopeful in the American spirit, must ally himself with the working class. Again and again we have seen the question raised:

what is the relationship between the existing social order and the highest hopes and deepest desires of mankind? If a writer settled that problem, it scarcely mattered where he found his themes, for he could see them in true perspective. But if the problem remained unsolved, the failure to contemplate industrial development became a fundamental evasion. To that question Karl Marx long ago provided an answer: the machine is potentially a source of good; it is, however, in fact a source of evil so long as it is operated for private profit; its full benefits can be realized only when it is socialized, and that can be accomplished only when the exploited overthrow the exploiters. For decades that answer seemed inapplicable to America, where the existence of the frontier gave meaning to the doctrine of self-reliant individualism; but the passing of the years has shown that America is no exception, and that, here as elsewhere, the only clue to the tangled web of life in the last century is the Marxian analysis.

It has become increasingly clear, even to those who do not want to see, that the central fact in American life is the class struggle. The writer has a series of choices. If he ignores the class struggle, he surrenders all hope of arriving at a clear interpretation, out of which a significant formal pattern may be devised, and he commits himself to evasion after evasion. If he assumes the rôle of impartiality, he merely deceives and confuses himself, since impartiality is impossible. If he accepts the existing order and assumes that it operates for the best interests of mankind, he becomes an apologist, and dishonesty and misrepresentation follow. If he recognizes the existing order for what it is and nevertheless accepts it because he profits by it, he avoids the weakness of evasion, but he cuts himself off from a large part of the human race, and callousness is substituted for the sympathy which is so important an attribute. If however, the writer allies himself with the proletariat, there is no need of evasion or self-deception. He may be tempted to exaggerate the faults of capitalists or the virtues of workers, but if he is wise he will find in facts his all-sufficient bulwark. Moreover, as this way of looking at life becomes an integral part of his imaginative equipment, he can not only perceive the operation of underlying forces; he can also rejoice in their play because of his confidence in what they will eventually accomplish.

In John Dos Passos and in his like-minded colleagues we find the modern expression of the spirit that moves in the noblest creations of the past. What stirs us in Emerson is his confidence in the common man, his courageous appeal for action, his faith in the future. He and Thoreau were rebels against the shams and oppressions of their day. Their rebellion inevitably took an individualistic form, but they spoke for all the oppressed, and some of their words remain a call to arms. Whitman, though no less an individualist, felt more deeply his kinship with the workers and farmers, and in later years was not unaware of the wisdom of curbing the individual for the collective good. Howells, too, taught himself to think in terms of a new order, and he and Bellamy tried to create, in imagination and in fact, a better world. Garland and Norris denounced oppression; Herrick and Phillips worked for reform; Sinclair and London called themselves socialists.

This is the great tradition of American literature. Ours has been a critical literature, critical of greed, cowardice, and meanness. How can authors refuse to strike at the sources of the evils they have so constantly attacked? It has also been a hopeful literature, touched again and again with a passion for brotherhood, justice, and intellectual honesty. How can authors refuse to struggle against an order based upon falsehood, oppression, and the division of mankind into exploiters and exploited? The issue is now so clearly drawn that evasion is almost impossible: on the one hand lies repudiation of the best in the American literary past, on the other the fulfillment of all that was dreamed of and worked for in the past and the beginning of struggle for more than the past could ever have hoped. Not every writer can make the choice that his ideals demand, but many can and will break the ties that bind them to the bourgeoisie, and give their support to the class that is able to overthrow capitalism.

Let no one be deceived; difficult years loom before us and the very existence of art may seem to be imperiled. Revolutionary writers will have obstacles of their own to overcome and peculiar temptations to resist. But certainly we cannot despair of the eventual outcome, and even in the days of stress revolutionary writers will have a kind of courage that others cannot share. For they will know that what is struggling for utterance on their pages is the spirit, not of an isolated individual, not of some literary clique, not of some decadent tradition, but the spirit of that class with which the future rests and into whose hands the highest hopes of mankind are entrusted. They will know that, whatever destruction the future may bring, they are allied with the forces of construction. They will know they are participating in a battle that, in the long run, is for civilization itself, and they will have no doubt of the outcome.

BIBLIOGRAPHY

GENERAL

Historical. In the first four chapters I have made special use of Allan Nevins' *The Emergence of Modern America* (New York, 1927), A. M. Schlesinger's *The Rise of the City* (New York, 1933), and A. M. Simons' *Social Forces in American History* (New York, 1911). In the latter chapters I have used John Chamberlain's *Farewell to Reform* (New York, 1932) and Harold Faulkner's *The Quest for Social Justice* (New York, 1931). Throughout I have drawn on Charles and Mary Beard's *The Rise of American Civilization* (New York, 1933), Louis Hacker and Benjamin Kendrick's *The United States Since 1865* (New York, 1932), and Fred E. Haynes's *Social Politics in the United States* (Boston, 1924).

Literary. I am particularly indebted to V. F. Calverton's *The Liberation of American Literature* (New York, 1932) and V. L. Parrington's *Main Currents in American Thought,* especially Volume III, *The Beginnings of Critical Realism* (New York, 1930). Bibliographies of most of the writers mentioned in the first five chapters can be found in *The Cambridge History of American Literature,* Volumes II and IV (New York, 1918 and 1921) and in F. L. Pattee's *A History of American Literature Since 1870* (New York, 1917). Bibliographies of more recent writers are given in Manly and Rickert's *Contemporary American Literature* (New York, 1929). Among the other works I have consulted are: *Classic Americans,* by Henry S. Canby (New York, 1931); *Portrait of the Artist as American,* by Matthew Josephson (New York, 1930); *Our Singing Strength,* by Alfred Kreymborg (New York, 1929); *Expression in America,* by Ludwig Lewisohn (New York, 1932); *American Writers on*

American Literature, edited by John Macy (New York, 1931); *American Humor,* by Constance Rourke (New York, 1931); *The American Novel,* by Carl Van Doren (New York, 1921). I have made constant use of the ten available volumes of the *Dictionary of American Biography* (New York, 1928-1933).

CHAPTER I

For some of the material in the second section I am indebted to Lewis Mumford's *The Golden Day* (New York, 1926), to the same author's *Herman Melville* (New York, 1929), and to Newton Arvin's *Hawthorne* (Boston, 1929). Material on Lowell is drawn from Horace Elisha Scudder's *James Russell Lowell* (Boston, 1901) and from *Letters of James Russell Lowell,* edited by Charles Eliot Norton (New York, 1894). I have made much use of Emory Holloway's *Whitman* (New York, 1926) and some use of Horace Traubel's *With Walt Whitman in Camden* (New York, 1906, 1908, 1914).

CHAPTER II

The best sources for Bret Harte's life are George R. Stewart's *Bret Harte, Argonaut and Exile* (Boston, 1931) and *The Letters of Bret Harte,* edited by Geoffrey Bret Harte (Boston, 1926). Most of the material in the account of Mark Twain is drawn from Albert Bigelow Paine's *Mark Twain: A Biography* (New York, 1912). I have also consulted Mark Twain's *Autobiography* (New York, 1924), William Dean Howells' *My Mark Twain* (New York, 1910) and Clara Clemens' *My Father: Mark Twain* (New York, 1931). My interpretation has obviously been influenced by Van Wyck Brooks's *The Ordeal of Mark Twain* (New York, 1920), though I am by no means in complete agreement with Brooks. To Bernard DeVoto's *Mark Twain's America* (Boston, 1932) I am indebted for information about the frontier. Among the few books available on the regional writers are: George Cary Eggleston's *The First of the Hoosiers* (Philadelphia, 1903), Lucy L. Cable Bikle's *George W. Cable, His Life and Letters* (New York, 1928), and Grace King's *Memories of a Southern Woman of Letters* (New York, 1932). Pattee's *A History of American Literature Since 1870* contains the best bibliographies of the regionalists.

CHAPTER III

In this chapter I have used several volumes of the *Chronicles of America*: Volume 39, *The Age of Big Business,* by Burton J. Hendrick (New Haven, 1919); Volume 40, *The Armies of Labor,* by S. F. Orth (1919); Volume 41, *Masters of Capital,* by John Moody (1919). Other works I have consulted are: *A History of Labor in the United States,* by John R. Commons *et al.* (New York, 1918), *A Documentary History of American Industrial Society,* Volumes IX and X, edited by John R. Commons *et al.* (Cleveland, 1910), *Dynamite,* by Louis Adamic (New York, 1931), *The House of Morgan,* by Lewis Corey (New York, 1930), and *God's Gold,* by John T. Flynn (New York, 1932). William Roscoe Thayer's *The Life of John Hay* (Boston, 1915) is the standard biography. Mildred Howells' *Life in Letters of William Dean Howells* (New York, 1928) contains the essential biographical data and is an invaluable document. It is usefully supplemented by Oscar W. Firkins' *William Dean Howells: A Study* (Cambridge, 1924) and by Howells' autobiographical books: *Literary Friends and Acquaintances* (New York, 1900) and *Years of My Youth* (New York, 1916).

CHAPTER IV

F. O. Matthiessen's *Sarah Orne Jewett* (Boston, 1929) is the only detailed study; I have also used *Letters of Sarah Orne Jewett,* edited by Annie Fields (Boston, 1911). *The Letters of Henry James,* edited by Percy Lubbock (New York, 1920) and James's autobiographical *A Small Boy and Others* (New York, 1913) and *Notes of a Son and Brother* (New York, 1914) are the principal sources. *The Letters of William James,* edited by his son Henry James (Boston, 1920) and C. Hartley Grattan's *The Three Jameses* (New York, 1932) are also useful. To Van Wyck Brooks's *The Pilgrimage of Henry James* (New York, 1925) I am indebted for many suggestions, though I am not in agreement with his central thesis. *The Life and Letters of Emily Dickinson,* by Martha Dickinson Bianchi (Boston, 1924) and *Letters of Emily Dickinson,* edited by Mabel Loomis Todd (New York, 1931) contain the known biographical facts.

CHAPTER V

For the background of the farmers' struggles I have consulted *The Agrarian Crusade,* by Solon J. Buck (New Haven, 1920) and *The Populist Revolt,* by John D. Hicks (Minneapolis, 1931). Thomas Beer describes other aspects of the nineties in *The Mauve Decade* (New York, 1926). Adams' life is abundantly documented in *The Education of Henry Adams* (Boston, 1918) and *Letters of Henry Adams,* edited by Worthington C. Ford (Boston, 1930). I have also consulted James T. Adams' *The Adams Family* (Boston, 1930) and Brooks Adams' *The Degradation of the Democratic Dogma* (New York, 1919). Of Hamlin Garland's several autobiographical works I have drawn particularly on *A Son of the Middle Border* (New York, 1917), *Roadside Meetings* (New York, 1930), and *Companions on the Trail* (New York, 1931). The two latter volumes contain much valuable material on other authors of the period. Elizabeth Bisland's *The Life and Letters of Lafcadio Hearn* (Boston, 1906) is informative and uncommonly interesting. The best biography of Bierce is Carey McWilliams' *Ambrose Bierce* (New York, 1929), and the best of Crane is Thomas Beer's *Stephen Crane* (New York, 1923).

CHAPTER VI

C. C. Regier's *The Era of the Muckrakers* (Chapel Hill, 1932) gives the background of the muckraking movement. I have also drawn upon a number of autobiographies: *The Autobiography of Lincoln Steffens* (New York, 1931), Frederic C. Howe's *Confessions of a Reformer* (New York, 1925), *Living My Life,* by Emma Goldman, and *Bill Haywood's Book* (New York, 1929). Franklin Walker's *Frank Norris* (New York, 1932) contains some new information, but its critical sections are weak. Isaac Marcosson's *David Graham Phillips and His Times* (New York, 1932) is less than adequate. I have drawn freely on Charmian London's *The Book of Jack London* (New York, 1921), and I have read in manuscript Fulmer Mood's excellent critical biography of London. Upton Sinclair's *American Outpost* (New York, 1932) and Floyd Dell's *Upton Sinclair* (New York, 1927) are both valuable.

CHAPTER VII

Though there is a wealth of material in periodicals about contemporary writers, there are, naturally, few books devoted to them. Dorothy Dudley's *Forgotten Frontiers: Theodore Dreiser and the Land of the Free* (New York, 1932) is less revealing than Dreiser's *A Book About Myself* (New York, 1922) and *Dawn* (New York, 1931). Anderson also has written about himself, in *A Story Teller's Story* (New York, 1924) and *Tar* (New York, 1926). Some of the brief critical biographies of contemporary authors published by McBride are useful, especially R. M. Lovett's *Edith Wharton* (New York, 1925) and Barrett H. Clark's *Eugene O'Neill* (New York, 1926). The poets of the period are discussed in such books as Louis Untermeyer's *American Poetry Since 1900* (New York, 1923) and Conrad Aiken's *Scepticisms* (New York, 1919).

CHAPTER VIII

For some of the material on the younger generation I am indebted to articles and reviews by Malcolm Cowley: his five articles, "Exile's Return," etc., in the *New Republic* for Sept. 23, Sept. 30, Oct. 21, Nov. 11, and Nov. 18, 1931; his review of E. E. Cummings' *VV* (*Viva*) in the *New Republic* for January 27, 1932; his review of Dos Passos' *1919* in the *New Republic* for Apr. 27, 1932. This material will presumably be incorporated in his forthcoming book, tentatively titled *The Lost Generation*. Edmund Wilson's *The American Jitters* (New York, 1932) is a record of the depression years.

INDEX OF NAMES

313